Sabine Bröck

White Amnesia – Black Memory?

American Women's Writing and History

PETER LANG

Europäischer Verlag der Wissenschaften

Die Deutsche Bibliothek - CIP-Einheitsaufnahme

Bröck, Sabine:

White amnesia – black memory? : American women's writing
and history / Sabine Bröck. - Frankfurt am Main ; Berlin ;
Bern ; New York ; Paris ; Wien : Lang, 1999
  (Bremer Beiträge zur Literatur- und Ideengeschichte ;
  Bd. 25)
  ISBN 3-631-33545-8

ISSN 0941-1488
ISBN 3-631-33545-8
US-ISBN 0-8204-3605-4

© Peter Lang GmbH
Europäischer Verlag der Wissenschaften
Frankfurt am Main 1999
All rights reserved.

Printed in Germany 1 2   4 5 6 7

To Cheikh
jere-jef

Before Page One

My Habilitation has been accompanied over the years by the well-meaning anticipation of many people; my sincerest gratitude goes to all of them.

I am grateful to my parents for their support and occasional pestering and to my sister for taking for granted what I do. Günter Lenz taught me and nudged me on – gently but firmly. Renate Hof's insistence helped to find structure and tenacity. Gesa Mackenthun, Klaus Milich, Anne Koenen, Vera Kutzinski, Gabriele Semrau, Mark Stein, Rondha Cobham, Christine Noll-Brinkmann, Berndt and Jutta Ostendorf, Ingrid Wendt, Teresa Toulouse, Gisela Ecker, Gisela Engel, Brigitte Rathert, Gabriele Bauer, Sabine Brinkmann and Ingrid Apel – all asked and answered nagging questions and bore occasional bouts of self-pity. Verena Lueken, Brigitte Bosing, Susanne Schlüter-Müller and Charlotte Schaeder offered the patience of intimate friendship. Barbara and Cornelius Noack provided affinity and creature comforts; Susanna Noack helped me to trust my final draft. Raimund Schieß diligently scanned the entire manuscript, and Rainer Rebuschat assisted in the final word-processing.

I thank the American Council of Learned Societies for providing me with time and money for uninterrupted concentration, and Steven Wheatley for his friendly interest in my work. Everybody who helped making my time out in Amherst productive: thank you for a trimming year. Margo Hennessy made the connection between Foucault and our intimate voices. Anne Halley and Jules Chametzky regaled me with the most delicious hospitality and introduced me to the breaking of bread; I feel gifted by their wisdom and the generosity with which it was given. A special Thank You goes to John Bracey for sending extra push and invaluable source material. My gratitude also goes out to Werner Sollors who in the thickest of it took the time to read the entire manuscript and made emphatic suggestions, not all of which I could incorporate.

Sara Lennox is a model intellectual mom; also, she was the first person to scribble in the margins of my drafts. Jane Marcus shared her intellectual curiosity, her passion for remembering, her anger and exuberance across generations; I thank her, also, for reading and criticizing the entire manuscript. Without Heike Paul this text would not exist in the present form: she heard me into writing and urged me to the keyboard unfailingly.

I thank my son Youssoupha Sarr for his ready acceptance of mama's work, for not messing up the paper piles on my desk and for keeping me afloat every day with shared laughter. I am deeply grateful to Aida Sow for prayers, and to our family in Joloffe for welcoming Youssou. I give this book to Malick Sarr, who did not waver in his loving conviction that this thing would be finished, even if it meant for him to father and mother our son for a time.

Contents

Preface

Picture this. In 1874, two formerly abolitionist ladies – one white and one black American – have the opportunity to view the famous William Turner painting *Slavers Throwing Overboard the Dead and Dying, Typhoon Coming on* (1840) which holds the viewers' attention, respectively, by a symbolically readable glaring white light, and by black bodies and severed black limbs floating in the Atlantic sea.[1] An argument ensues. The black lady writes to her white acquaintance:

> August 6, 1874, 9 A.M.
> Dear Miss Hooper,
> I hold nothing against you. I wish for you all the best. I think the difference between us may be reduced to the fact that while you focus on the background of the Turner painting, I cannot tear my eyes from the foreground. It is who we are.
> Yours sincerely
> Mary Ellen Pleasant
> (Michelle Cliff, *Free Enterprise*)

The use of "background" and "foreground" in Cliff's passage is a black voice's supreme irony: focusing on the background really means, in the context of the Turner painting, focusing on the visible center of the impressionist's picture. It dominates its surrounding scene with a brilliantly fantastic Atlantic light that has led other (white) viewers, like John Ruskin, to ignore all but its fascination and relegate the slaves thrown overboard to a literal footnote.[2] To create a "foreground" also amounts to a re-reading of the Turner painting, in the sense that the slaves' bodies are visible only rather marginalized in its lower right-hand corner.

---

1 It is not by mere personal interest that the Turner picture appears in this privileged position of my text: it has by now iconic status in the various contributions involved in the 'reconstruction' of the Middle Passage; see Cliff 1993, Dabydeen.

2 Dabydeen writes: "Ruskin thought that Slave Ship represented 'the noblest sea that Turner ever painted (...) the noblest certainly ever painted by man.' He wrote a detailed account of the composition of the painting, dwelling on the genius with which Turner illuminated sea and sky in an intense and lurid splendour of colours" (IX). Ruskin does not devote a single sentence of his enthralled description to the picture's subject (Ruskin 158-160); the footnote to his celebration reads: "She is a slaver, throwing her slaves overboard. The near sea is encumbered with corpses." (160)

This division of attention is paradigmatically valid throughout US-American culture – and should be taken up urgently – but with a twist. White women should re-concern themselves with the white light in American history, not in order to ignore the picture's foreground but rather to critically understand their own participation in its glare.

What I am quite aware of: this is a gesture of self-authorization. I take Michelle Cliff's text to guarantee my 'meaning,' to safeguard my self-positioning, and to signal my engagement as a white speaker who is striving to be knowledgeable of (my own) racialization and black work against it. As do, in their recent essays on whiteness, Shelley Fisher Fishkin (quoting Ralph Ellison), Michael North (drawing on Michael Harper) or Henry Wonham (following Toni Morrison). The cultural context has changed: 19th century black writers had to find white authorities to vouch for their slave narratives' authenticity; white intellectuals at the end of the 20th century find themselves compelled to make visible their connectedness to black thinking, if in some cases only as so much as a token gesture. And, of course, that does not mean the hierarchies are reversed, so 'our' (as white Americanists) quoting Ellison, Morrison, Harper, and Cliff always borders on gestures of appropriation bound into pressing exigencies of the academic marketplace.

The question to what extent my own position as a German Americanist of a third post-Holocaust academic generation is at the same time identical with and different from American women's whiteness would be complex enough to merit its own exploration. Suffice it to say that it produces a tension towards my particular Americanist subject, a certain friction of reading from a position of involved distance that may and should be felt.

Introduction

1. Reading White Women Writers

In the spirit of my preface, this book will not be a rounded out evaluation of American women writers in terms of all possible depths of their work; it will function as a rather particular questioning. I am reading a series of very diverse works by 20th century white American women writers that are each significant for a specific take on American culture by their respective authors, for a particular subject position framed in and by the literary text, located at a willed distance from dominant American cultural tenets.

The theoretical assumption of a binarily fixed opposition between one dominant (and, by implication male, Anglo-Saxon, Protestant) culture and its marginalized and suppressed subcultures has been of course deconstructed in the wake of poststructuralism and a proliferation of multicultural discourses. Those approaches have rather focussed on the complex, interweaving processes among and within subject positions partaking in different, at times even antagonistic cultural interpellations.[3] A number of critics have taken on the idea of fluid, more transgressible "boundaries," "contact zones," or "borderlands" within American culture, where cultural differences meet and get to be negotiated, or have to be radically confronted. The image of a clearly hierarchical opposition between "dominant culture" and "minority" has given way to an assessment of more microcosmic examinations of the multiple contradictions among various subcultures; of the ambivalent role of popular culture as facet of the capitalist market's economic power and as possible repository of resistance; of the intricate social and cultural complications of what Henry Louis Gates has called Bennetonisation of America.

However, I would like to insist on retaining the notion of a dominant culture as a somewhat requalified category. Though its deconstruction has been productive, its reappropriation becomes necessary in the face of an ultimately unchallenged and unbroken continuity of white patriarchal political and economic power structures throughout the 20th century, and the recent public emergence and growth of a

---

3 I am drawing on the contributions of Bammer; Braidotti 1991, 1995; Brooks Higginbotham; de Lauretis 1987, 1990; Fuss; Gates, Jr. 1985; S. Hall; Hutcheon 1988; E. Jameson, F. Jameson; Meese and Parker; Mohanty, Russo and Torres; Omi and Winant; Radhakrishnan 1990, 1993; Shohat and Stam, Trinh; West 1990; Wynter 1984, R. Young 1995.

militant political Right, within and outside established political institutions and cultural channels.

In this context, I treat literary texts as a kind of cultural practice, as textual agency participating in the making and unmaking of cultural, epistemological as well as ethical repertories. I will deal, then, with the following primary texts:

* Gertrude Stein's *The Making of Americans*
* Josephine Herbst's trilogy *Rope of Gold*
* Joan Didion's "The White Album," "Slouching Towards Bethlehem," and "Sentimental Journeys"
* Lillian Smith's *Killers of the Dream* and *Strange Fruit*
* Flannery O'Connor's *The Artificial Nigger*, and *A Late Encounter with the Enemy*
* Rosellen Brown's *Civil Wars*.

Gertrude Stein's avantgarde claims, Josephine Herbst's quasi-marxist approach, Lillian Smith's anti-racist ethics, Flannery O'Connor's grotesque, Joan Didion's moralistic rigor, or Rosellen Brown's feminist consciousness – all these texts are positioned in some form of critical opposition to "America" and engage constitutive American myths.

On the other hand, all these texts share a blind spot in their respective memory of American history. My concept of history here is not based on an idealistic approach of transparent, immediate, quasi mimetic access to the historical past of any given society. Following Hayden White, I am looking at history as narrativized so that what a nation, or any group of people, assumes to be its history would be a complex, self-conflicting, competitively articulated, perpetually supplemented sum of representations figuring in a society's cultural memory.[4]

None of the primary texts I am discussing, however much they engage in revisionist projects, confronts the Middle Passage or its consequences as crucially necessary for an American white consciousness of historical and cultural genealogy.[5] By analogy then, I want to employ insights of Cultural Studies research to a thinking about American history and how its blackness does or does not get to be remembered in the literary imagination.[6] How do literary texts by white women writers engage or evade the blackness of American history; how are they able to imag-

---

4 Hannah Möckel-Rieke lucidly discusses the concept of "cultural memory" in a recent article in *Amerikastudien/American Studies*. See Benjamin, Halbwachs, Felman and Laub, Friedlander, Le Goff, Koselleck, Morrison 1987, Ricoeur, White 1987, 1989, 1992; R. Young 1990.

5 See Binder, Davis, Davis and Gates, Inikori and Engerman, Morgan 1972, 1975; Patterson, Sánchez-Eppler 1991, 1993; Spillers 1987, Roediger 1991, 1994.

6 See Fisher Fishkin, Holloway, Morrison 1992, Pieterse, Reising, Sollors and Diedrich, Ross 1989.

ine or compelled to ignore a negotiation of the American "Africanist presence" (Morrison 1992,6) at the core of a national memory – which in turn is at once impulse and effect of American culture? How do they acknowledge or obscure the whiteness of their historical imagination?

In employing "whiteness" as critical category, my work owes primarily to the poignant analyses of whiteness in its multifold cultural and social implications that African-American literary writing and Black Studies have provided over many decades.[7] It is secondarily aligned with the more recent, self-reflective considerations of Abel, Childers and Hooks, Dyer, Frankenberg, Stanford Friedman, Homans, Wonham and to some extent also de Lauretis (1990). I should stress at this point that "white" (and for that matter, "black") here will not be taken for and treated as an identical essence of being, but rather as a constituted, and constitutive, performative entity, a socially, culturally and historically contingent representation of self and self-location.

My readings are begging the question why white women writers, who have located their texts at an angle of a distinctly radical difference to dominant American culture, have all but ignored the racialized constructedness of the myths they set out to dissect or to counterwrite and have actually partaken in the American national consensus's foundational fiction of racially innocent origins. Women writers' own marginalized location has enabled their "disloyalty to civilization" in many respects; how, then, have they proceeded to evade a serious examination of the intricate connection between a patriarchal, bourgeois and ethically cynical American cultural memory **and** its "wholly racialized" character (Morrison 1992, 12)? How do the texts themselves signify on that refusal to own one of the excruciating American historical nightmares and on its relegation to the exclusive memory and cultural agency of African-Americans who have been forced to be victims and cure of a malady in one and the same move? What does it mean with regard to literary texts that memory – as one crucial facet of the making of a national culture – is segregated along strongly racialized lines, and how does that racialization work in literary writing? Following Morrison in *Playing In the Dark: Whiteness and the Literary Imagination* I want to show that this process does by no means work as a hermetically sealed act of suppression or ignorance of a certain historical reality but as an ambivalent process leaving traces, marks and aggressive lacunae on every text. To push the paraphrase of Morrison a little further, I want to examine how the texts are being haunted by a ghost in the literary machine, as it were.

I will read texts into an intertextuality that classically belong to (and have been read within) entirely different and even contradictory literary canons, cultural tra-

---

7 Baldwin, W.E.B. Du Bois, Ellison 1964, DuCille "Occult", Gilroy, Goldberg, Huggins, Hooks 1990, 1992; Jordan 1968, 1974; S. Kaplan, Murray, Walker 1983.

ditions, and various periods. That intertextuality, consequently, makes readable a markedly common field of signification related to the texts' whiteness of memory. The structural separation into two sets of literary readings, then, mirrors a cultural difference. O'Connor's, Smith's and Brown's texts – all motivated by a sense of willed or inherited passion for the South – are characterized by inscriptions of the presence of black history more pronounced than the texts discussed under the organizing heading of "displacement" which partake in a particularly Northern, post Civil War evasion of the 'blackness' of United States history.

I am aware of the most recent proliferation of criticism and research on the topics of whiteness, and racialization across the fields of Black Studies, American Studies and Feminist and or Gender Studies. However, there has not been all too frequent purposeful overlapping and interdependent articulation of these fields. Also, I see a danger for the recent work by white scholars to mythologize itself as white discovery all over again, thus unwittingly repeating the ethics of appropriative suppression Morrison has so deftly criticized; my work, of course, cannot claim to signify beyond that problematic tension – what I am able to do is to rather self-consciously locate my own text within the tension between my authorial and the object's whiteness and a heritage of Black Studies critique without which it would not have been possible.

My approach will work against a distinction so common in US humanities – be it literary criticism, or historical research – between studies of a priori black affairs (that is basically everything that has to do with slavery and any consequences thereof, as for example the history of institutionalized racism) and studies of American historical phenomena, as for example Settlement, Revolution, Independence, the Gilded Age, the Frontier, World War I and II, the Depression, McCarthy, Vietnam, that are, by silent agreement, a priori white, unless otherwise noted. (The Civil War is, for obvious reasons, an exception.) Why are memory and historical consciousness segregated, why does black memory stand in as a national reservoir of historical shame and responsibility? Why can whites afford nostalgia instead, and hold on to universality and innocence masking for ignorance and naiveté? By way of which filtering process is a perception of racialization of American history bypassed? I situate this approach within the postcolonially inflected range of the New Americanists' project to study the "multiple histories of continental and overseas expansion, conquest, conflict and resistance which have shaped the cultures of the United States" (Kaplan and Pease 1993, 4). My aim is to connect the critical examination of the national project with an exploration of the historical whiteness of American women's writing, an aspect that white feminist criticism has as yet not tackled thoroughly.

16

2. Tracing the Project

My original intention was to work out the question of women's narrative interventions onto the – to borrow from Derrida – scene of (theoretical) writing. It was based on the assumption, mirroring a lack or suppression in feminist theory itself, that one could speak of women as representative subject of collective agency – not self-identical, but coherently figuring as a kind of interest group, at least as a figure of thought – that could be and would have to be pitted against patriarchal thought. I wanted to situate my readings of women's writing in contrast to, in dialogue with, and as supplement to theorizing within the 'proper' genre, that is critical theory. What I have arrived at presently, however, as the following chapters will demonstrate, is a critical reading of American *white* women's literature in terms of its historical amnesia, denial or nostalgic displacement of historical address.

In my discussion of American 20th century women's writing, I wanted to hold a balance between two different, in a certain way even antagonistic moves: to continue speaking of women writers as a category, and in the very act of doing so, fracturing the very term and its options, and engaging the 'contrariness' of the category, its resistance to categorical value. Rachel Blau DuPlessis in *The Pink Guitar* (1990) provided a useful approach to hold on to the concept of woman writer:

A woman writer is a "marked marker." She is marked by the cultural attributes of Woman, gender sexuality, the feminine... She is marked by being variously distinguished – defined, singled out – by her gender. Others may note it even if she does not, or claims not to. She is marked by some unevenly effective traditions of both "unspeaking" and "unspeakable" female self, and by some also uneven set of incentives to cultural production, although she makes many, many things. She – any woman – is culturally represented and interpreted (in all forms of representation from pop song to prayer, from B-movies to modern paintings). The works and the workings of these representations, in picture and text, ideologies and discourses, mark or inflect precise configurations of her personal markings. Her own marks on a page; and what she can, or may, mark (or notice) will bear some marks of this matted circumstance of gender. (161)

My aim, starting from DuPlessis' point, was to analyze how these "marked markings" would become more complicated and contradictory as soon as one factored in the aesthetical interests of diverse women writers, as mediations of their respective class/race subject positions and political affiliations.

The differences within poststructuralist theories notwithstanding, scholars have seemed to agree on the observation that the 20th century has seen the fragmentation, devaluation and demise of the two "grand récits" inherited from the 19th century: Humanism and Marxism. (Psychoanalysis, for reasons widely debated, seems to have had a tougher life, and survives strongly, if with far reaching modifications.) Poststructuralist French critics – as the heirs of the linguistic turn – performed their work mainly as reading/s of various philosophical and literary texts (distinctions that Derrida has sought to transcend as mere genre variations) of the master narrative tradition, or concerned themselves with authors within their own male, Western genealogies that could function as examples of newly valorized modes of writing, privileging fragmentation, decentering, and a-totality over telos, fixity, plot and closure (Hoffmann).

In its early stages, this critique could be judged as Robert Young does in *White Mythologies* as self-criticism, as indictment of a Western tradition of thinking that, in its insistence on mastery and its creation of hierarchical dichotomies between self and other, between man and nature, subject and object, has literally and metaphorically subjected the rest of the world to its paradigms. I would like to make a distinction, however, between those early critiques and the ensuing reception and dissemination of poststructuralist thinking which, helped by political/ historical factors like the final collapse of the Communist countries and neo-colonial take overs in the so-called Third World, by a rapid development in media technology, a proliferation of computer languages/virtual reality techniques and by a disenchantment with modernity in almost all cultural areas, mutated into the postmodern Zeitgeist, an encompassing cultural phenomenon ranging from Madonna to the Yale Critics, from the Buonaventura Hotel to Fukuyama's "end of history," from mushrooming marketable multicultures in Western centers to the international public triumph of capitalism. A Zeitgeist that is, that demands indifference and uninterested pluralism, a delight in word games without much consequence, a contempt – in the final analysis – of historical memory and a surrender of human agency; it speaks to me not so much of Derrida's radical play than of ethical, political fatigue.

In the 1970s and 1980s an ethical lack, a disinvestment, dominated poststructuralist theories which may at least partly explain why the radical potential of the critique has been so swiftly diffused and has become submerged in/under what I call the Zeitgeist. Only at the end of the 1980s and in the early 1990s, long overdue connections were established between the camps of theoretical philosophical critiques (of reading, language, culture) and the camps of various groups of cultural producers who could speak as the "other," the victims/objects of the discourses that poststructuralist critics so ardently fracture; thus, notions of agency, subjectivity and history emerged other than those dominated by the Western Platonic and Enlightenment tradition. Without that connection, theory had been performed as a series of mind exercises allowing itself to be appropriated for unethical and repressive, indeed again masterful gestures of power; even if that power sometimes seems, for all its lack of humanist telos, diffuse enough to be invisible. My notion of ethics here is based on a respect for collective memories of displacement and destruction: Middle Passage and slavery (as underside of imperial Euro-American master narratives), not as mythical telos, but in the sense of African-American culture's witnessing.

I wanted to concern myself with women's narrative writing read as intrusions of feminisms into those late 20th century controversies, as signification on critical theory. At my actual scene of writing, however, it became obvious that the very intervention of women writers and intellectuals on philosophical, theoretical grounds has produced another master (or mistress, for that matter) narrative that again has become increasingly embattled among women. Actually, that is not a new historical phenomenon: Black women intellectuals have, for decades, sharply criticized white women's claims to universal representation that excluded them from acknowledged authorship.

This particular strand in feminism, theorizing from a location that could in a categorizing manner be called white, Western, middle-class, academic, rather young to early middle-aged parochialism, has come under serious deconstruction itself in the 1980s. It is interesting to note, however, that this interruption of white theorizing itself has become theorized as new, as a product of poststructuralist theory almost as much as of nonwhite interventions – which makes it appear at least partially as a history-less white birth, all over again, even in the acknowledging nods to Black women's intellectual labor. American (and to even lesser extent European) feminist theory has had little theoretical grasp of its having been racialized since its early beginnings. Black and Third World critics or those who have dis-aligned themselves[8] from an exclusively white middle class Western feminism have re-raised that question in the late 1980s and early 1990s.

That is to say, originally I wanted to have my text gesture in two directions, have two layers of argument: to criticize phallogocentric theory through women's writing – to perform, as it were, a gender and genre transgression in one move, and also to criticize white women's writing for its own hegemonial suppressions.[9] I wanted to position my own writing as a double gesture of position and negation. However, my own protracted engagement with and investments in Black (Women) Studies that had produced my dissertation, resurfaced in the form of nagging scepticism of the meaningfulness of that project. I could not continue working as if my

---

8 However, feminist critics, including myself, should be aware of the danger of appropriating the black critique and of subsuming its edge under relativistic and pluralist assemblages, of using Black women as rejuvenation, stimulus, and reservoir of ethical energy, see DuCille "Occult," Homans.

9 Another question that I did not have the space to explore is the ambivalent relationship between Jewishness and whiteness within the American context, even though I am aware of the danger, thus, of reducing the potentially "off-white" complexity of Jewish writing by way of subsuming it strategically.

subject position white and the cultural and literary tradition entailed by this position within American Studies needed no thorough re-examination. As has probably happened with other white scholars in the field of Black Studies, Morrison's *Playing In the Dark* opened up a field of questions that should have been ours in the first place – for reasons Morrison herself dissects in such challenging manner: the look had to be redirected from "the server to the served" (Morrison 1992, 90). I finally had to acknowledge a deep racialized split segregating white American and black American women's writing of historical memory. The space that *Beloved* allegorically opens for white feminism with its surprising gesture of having a poor white woman midwife the black protagonist's child "appropriately and well" (*Beloved 85*) – is that earned? That became my driving question. No matter what kind of rebellious, anti-patriarchal, anti-capitalist or avantgarde subject positions white women's writing was able to imagine, silence has been kept about America's racist genesis and its aftermaths: the conflict in recent feminist theory about Eurocentrism and unacknowledged whiteness/privilege holds up but a mirror image to a tradition of white denial. It became clear that the kind of integrated, complex ethical memory that could effectively function as countermemory has been evaded time and again by white women writers of different prominence. Its literarization in the century after *Uncle Tom's Cabin* has been left to black writers (male and female) for whom writing, in most cases, has been a matter of spiritual survival so that they have not seen much choice to elide or forget. A radical shift in my attention entailed: the balance tipping towards considerations of the 'real' of American history, and its amnesia in narrative constructions by white women writers who had otherwise undertaken ambitious projects of indirect historical critique.

3. Acknowledgement – Beloved' s American Memory*

> We live in a land where the past is always erased and America is the innocent future in which immigrants can come and start over, where the slate is clean. The past is absent, or it is romanticized. This culture does not encourage dwelling on, let alone coming to terms with, the truth about the past. That memory is much more in danger now than it was thirty years ago. (Morrison)
> History is the subject of a structure whose site is not homogeneous, empty time, but time filled by the presence of the now (Jetztzeit). (Benjamin)

---

* A slightly different version of this chapter under the title "Postmodern Mediations and *Beloved's* Testimony" was published in *Amerikastudien/American studies*. See Möckel-Rieke.

In the ambivalent tension between two poles, exhibited by poststructuralist historiography and moral analytic engagement I situated my own work. These two approaches do not necessarily clash, and they converge in fictional narratives, as in *Beloved*. The questions I was struggling with (and that still function as subtext to my readings) ran in the following direction: Do we necessarily have to construe a contradiction between history as real and textuality? Women's memories constitute, in textuality, particular histories; they assert meaning, not "the truth," or a mimetic picture of "reality," but they do not have to be "true" to say that we need them to question the Western myth of history as a "metahistorical category" (Robert Young 1990, 22). Does an insistence on materiality of experiences automatically, unavoidably lead to totalization, claim a transcendent role for history, since "the real is itself a category constructed as an ontology through discourse," and "even the evocation of a category beyond discourse must nevertheless itself be a discursive strategy" (Young 1990, 109)? Has poststructuralism developed a concept of historical materiality? Are there ways to deal with material conditions and events that can escape "historizing"? How do we deal with history as "epistemic violence" (Spivak 130) when it can only be engaged in counter-narratives, which in turn, historize? How does communal memory (or the lack of it) structure subject positions? How do subject positions, in turn, constitute/afford memory? What kind of memory? Nostalgia unequals memory. Are certain kinds of memory – of the Middle Passage, for example – damned to be outside narrative, but then again, can they enter consciousness without narrativization? What works for, what against it? Did slavery allow figuration, and by whom?

Beloved became, for me, paradigmatic as a cultural intervention in pushing towards a more justly complex memory and revision of American history. It criticizes and/or rewrites a host of black and white texts functioning before in different genres, like slave narratives as documents, the 'female' tradition of sentimental novels, the black literary tradition, the American white philosophical tradition and historiography, as well as key literary texts, but also feminist and poststructuralist theories, by going inside a historical event in the Foucauldian sense. Morrison's text demonstrates, indeed, ways to 'integrate' or reconcile our sophistication about history as constructed, written, textual, with an approach like Rich's in *Blood, Bread and Poetry*, which speaks for acts of "re-memory" of experiences in the real world that we cannot afford to forget. It shows that the ethical concerns of memory are not necessarily a contradiction to sophisticated postmodern textuality, that a cultural memory's investments can be put into writing to keep social track of the actual horror of slavery. *Beloved* opts for a materialist approach that is not caught up in traditional Marxism or Humanism, that criticizes Western historiography's tendency to bring Third World people, Western women and other groups "without history" into the "evolutionary narrative of Western history,"[10] but that recognizes the material force of conditions like the Middle Passage. It confronts the notion of Fredric Jameson's (and Elaine Scarry's, for that matter) hurt of history in resistance to a certain coldness, a lack of compassion in poststructuralism, which made it easier for the political right and all sorts of interested factions to make "the end of history" out of a critique of particular concepts of history (Jameson, Scarry, Kunow). *Beloved* is writing, but it insists on an excess, on a moral decision to acknowledge a referent, a materiality independent of particularly interested textualizations, of specific and diverse "language games," and thus is able to keep an ethical stance, a judgement that enables one to distinguish the slaveholders' versions of the "benevolent institution" from a slave narrative's truth. *Beloved* answers a question that DuPlessis has asked, among others:

> Because of the suspicion of the center in avantgarde practice, the desire to displace the distinction between margin and center, because of the invention of a cultural practice that would allow us constructively to question privileged explanations, drawing on avantgarde practice seems more fruitful for me. Its idea of power and language seem more interesting: the resolute lack of synthesis, the non-organic poetics, the secular lens. But while the 'postmodern' dispensation of centerless heterogeneity of discourses seems more plausible as a position, one is thereafter shocked by the quietism and asocial turns of its dual poetics of immanence and textuality, at odds with historical responsibility to the political and functional contexts of language. If one could retain a passionate, feeling ethics without the uniformities of telos ... is it possible? (DuPlessis 1990, 153)

The acknowledgment that 6.000.000 Jews were murdered by an abominable regime, or that innumerable African people were captured into slavery with, again, millions of them dying in the Middle Passage is only possible from the point of view of an ethical commitment which itself is directly connected to the memory of those individuals and communities who have had to live with traumatic loss and destruction of lives. The angle from which to deal with history's textuality, then, the hold we can get on a swirl of signifiers, is not the magical referent in some supposedly extra-discursive real but the ethical impulse of memory/testimony/witnessing:

> Disremembered and unaccounted for, she cannot be lost, because no one is looking for her, and even if they were, how can they call her, if they don't know her name? Although she has claim, she is not claimed.[11]

---

10 Karl Marx, "The Future Results of the British Rule in India," quoted in R. Young 1990, 2.

11 Toni Morrison, *Beloved* 274. All subsequent references to the novel are given in parenthetical page numbers in the text.

In recent debates about memory two intellectual approaches have developed relatively independently of each other. One of these approaches is to discuss memory in descriptive, formalist terms: as a human faculty, as a mnemonic technique, as a culturally stabilizing repertoire combined of brain capacities, psychic abilities, scientific knowledges, and social rituals. That kind of quasi disinterested, disengaged focus on memory has occupied Western European intellectuals fascinated with the phenomenon as such, leading to questions like: how does the mnemonic faculty work within the individual, how does memory become collectivized, e.g. on a national level, which techniques have human societies in history used to remember, to not fall prey to forgetting over time?

The second tendency, in its textual practice and its theoretical inscriptions, can be directly related to the recent moment of postcolonial writing that has concerned itself, on a specifically local as well as on a transnational level, with a recuperation of lost history, with representing the undersides of modernity's imperial discourses. I am thinking here of writers and critics as diverse as, for example, Wilson Harris, Caryl Phillips, Charles Johnson, Sherley Anne Williams, Michelle Cliff and Toni Morrison. They share a focus on a decidedly ethical and political need for a far reaching restoration of Western cultural memory to the effect of re-inscribing, foregrounding a crucial cultural lack by way of what Bhabha has called the "supplement" of memory of oppressed cultures[12]. The effect of an 'unthinking' of hundreds of years of dismemberment in the 'official' records, then, would be a challenge to what Morrison has called a "national amnesia."[13] Morrison and other authors writing from the perspective of dominated and marginalized cultures or subcultures have invested considerable urgency in this making of memory that seems to have become so very compelling at the end of the 20th century. For those writers (and their critics), cultural memory in our historical moment finds itself in a state of "referential debt" to the victims of history. (Felman 115).

For them, memory in some factual unproblematic fullness, as a mnemonic faculty, as a transparent option to recollect the past cannot be assumed to be in-

---

12 Homi K. Bhabha introduces his application of the Derridean supplement, that is always more than and different from a simple addition, as follows: "It is from the liminal movement of the culture of the nation (...) that minority discourse emerges. Its strategy of intervention is similar to what parliamentary procedure recognizes as a supplementary question. (...) being 'after' the original, or in 'addition' to it, gives it the advantage of introducing a sense of 'secondariness' or belatedness into the structure of the original. The supplementary strategy suggests that adding to need not 'add up' but may disturb the calculation." Bhabha 1990, 305.

13 Toni Morrison 1989, 120. I thank Heike Paul for bringing the interview to my attention.

nocently present in a given culture; hierarchies of empowerment or struggles between various social factions institutionalize procedures of selection and exclusion. Precisely because memory can only find representation in medial form, one has to deal with the question of power: since all of a society's past is not equally accessible to memory and selective decisions do not come to pass via free-market competition, one cannot eclipse the problem of agency, individual and collective. Since memory needs mediation (meaning it is not automatically there, as an abstract, prestructured phenomenon), it may be subject to repression, culturally and individually. Indeed it may be a general human brain faculty to not be able to forget (Eco 254), but historical experiences, as Toni Morrison's novel *Beloved* so clearly enacts for us, can be disremembered. To ignore the terms of motive, intention, interest, or particularly invested perspectives and subject positions in any discussion of memory amounts to irresponsible omission.

Toni Morrison's work stresses how interested, how invested cultural memory actually is precisely because it is an act of mediation. Her project is part of a wider effort to politically own memory and not to discuss it in merely formal terms. Different camps of writers on the so-called margin have dealt with that paradoxical cultural need. As Haitian writers Bernabe, Chamoiseau, and Confiant have argued recently:

And the history of colonization (...) favored exteriority and fed the estrangement of the present. Within this false memory we had but a pile of obscurities as our memory. A feeling of flesh discontinued. (...) Our chronicle is behind the dates, behind the known facts: we are words behind writing. Only (...) artistic knowledge can (...) bring us (...) back to the resuscitation of consciousness. (Bernabe, Chamoiseau and Confiant, 896)

The cultural memory inscribed in the hegemonial "writing" of Western documents, imperial monuments, colonial rituals, trade records, and individual – fictional or autobiographical – recollections have as a general rule not contained the "words" of colonial or enslaved subjects; their visceral experiences, their memories of oppression and resistances have become left "behind" by Western historiography, prose, and poetry. Those "obscurities" now, in keeping with a continuing history of social and economic decolonisation and cultural reorientation, need to be displaced by way of artistic recuperation of the colonial and imperial past from the point of view of those previously muted subjects. This recuperation is by necessity an artistic act and challenge, since in most cases, "chronicles" of the dates and facts of colonization – coherently figured from that subaltern perspective – do not exist. The pervasive ellipses of Western historiography will only be pointed out and filled in by way of the (literary) imagination. Contemporary artistic, literary consciousness thus will have to *assume* a possibility of protocol, to *invent* a position of witness. What Paul Sharrad claims in a recent article in *Callaloo* (about Guyanaen writer Wilson Harris), speaking of a double task that post-colonial writers have to work out, aptly fits Morrison's novel *Beloved*:

(O)n the one hand, imaginative liberation from the tyranny of a history which denies them a past (and thus a presence), and, on the other, immersion in a history to recover/recreate a past. Writers grapple with the paradox of shaping narrative to affirm an evolving recovery of identity while resisting the totalizing hold of a single linear flow of time (especially as represented and controlled by hegemonic power). Their historical witness is at once a confession and a denial of the selective effacements of the recorded past. We can play on the notion of "witness:" firstly, there is the writer as witnessing observer of historical events; secondly, the writer as witness for some court of historical review; thirdly, witnessing may be taken in the religious sense of giving testimony of grace and vision. At the root level, there is also the old English "wit" – "to know" – which for the oral "counter-histories" of the enslaved and the colonized also means to remember. (Sharrad 94)

Witnessing

At this point, the postcolonial challenge to witnessing meets another tradition of counter-writing: there is a productive, if difficult point of overlapping and closeness between Jewish Holocaust memory work and Black and Third World diasporic texts in their shared engagement for cultural processes to transcend amnesia. Most directly, Shoshona Felman and Dori Laub have addressed that problematic task of testimony in their recent work. (1992) Rooted in Laub's experience in therapeutical work with members of families who survived the Shoah, and in Felman's investigations of the options and limits of narrative beyond the utter destruction of social and individual voice by the fascist "Final Solution," their provocative text – if analogically extended to other historical configurations of eliminatory and genocidal character, like the Middle Passage – challenges us to rethink the politics of narrative mediation altogether. Drawing on Celan's much acclaimed *Bremen Speech* and on Claude Lanzmann's film *Shoah*, their text struggles to retain a notion of narrative that would enable us to hear history's "victims" instead of smoothly producing social forgetfulness or the hegemonial selectivity of cultural memory. Witnessing, literarily and therapeutically, in that context becomes the key trope for their recuperation of narrative, in that it would ensure and inscribe acts of remembering, and thus re-membering (in the sense of bringing back to a society's cultural memory) a representation of the lost or suppressed experience of destruction. As Karen Remmler writes in an article about survivors' Holocaust writing that very much parallels Felman's and Laub's approach:

Yet, the remembering of the tortured body reinstates an agency that does not deny the experience of victimization, but recognizes the possibility of resistance against becoming a victim only. (Remmler 224)

The connection here between witnessing and resistance is crucial: writing as witness is supposed to have a healing, redemptive effect, on the one who remembers (and/or her fictional protagonists), and on her potential readership. So far, a closeness of the literary discourse about post-Holocaust writing and the postcolonial (black) discourse about literature addressing Colonialism, the Middle Passage, and Slavery may be usefully established if as a somewhat daring gesture. It seems to me that Felman's and Laub's pertinent explorations of the very grounds of narrative mediation under and within the conditions of a Western modernity that has revealed its destructive capacity to the utmost extreme in the Shoah, may and should be made productive. Approached with all appropriate humane respect due to the Shoah's uniqueness in history, this analogy could enable a crucial re-reading and resituating of Western cultural memory in face of its own imperial suppressions of historical constellations like the Middle Passage which preceded 20th century's German destructive finality.[14]

One striking difference remains, however: in case of black writing the redemptive act of witnessing must be delivered as a retroactive gesture.[15] The words of contemporary Black American or postcolonial authors cannot lay claim to personal, visceral authenticity in the same sense that Shoah survivors may be able to speak in the first person of their own experiences. Morrison herself, for example, writing about the Middle Passage, was not there and then where and when it happened; instead, she necessarily figures – in the same way that writers like Phillips, Harris, or Cliff engage that role – as a self-appointed witness of her own invention. A second difference may problematize the conjunction: the notion of an authentic witness is based on the assumption of subjectivity, voice, and access – even if only partially and in limited ways – to a society's symbolic order. However brutally and perfidiously German Fascism tried to dehumanize the Shoah's victims, it was a socially and intellectually owned fact in Western

---

14 I hope not to have my work implicated in the somewhat popular public game of regressive point-scoring for victimization, nor do I intend to "make hay with the Holocaust," in Letty Progrebin's words. Rather, I understand my approach here as shared by work like Paul Gilroy's in his *The Black Atlantic* where he argues along similar lines for a necessity of the comparative and conjunctive approach. See Progrebin, as cited in Tania Modleski, "Doing Justice to the Subjects: Mimetic Art in a Multicultural Society: The Work of Anna Devere Smith," in Abel, Christian and Moglen 63. Or see Gilroy 205-212.

15 Anne Koenen's "Toni Morrison's *Beloved* and the Ghost of Slavery" in Fabre and Raynaud 53-66, stresses the aspects of "ritualistic healing" in *Beloved*.

societies that Jewish people had a powerfully resonant religion, a written language of reference and a cultural memory particularly theirs. To quote Remmler again:

> The blow to the head (*of KZ torture*, my italics) destroys the world represented by the knowledge stored in the mind. It is destroyed as the violated body loses access to the symbolic realm and its voice is reduced to a physical scream of pain. (Remmler 24)

The words "reduce" and "loses" are crucial here because they bespeak an acknowledgement of a previous partaking in the Symbolic that was not granted to African 'chattel' on board of the Middle Passage vessels[16] and on Southern auction blocks. By contrast, Western (mis)constructions of African peoples, which, dating back through Hegel's and Kant's ruminations about the mindlessness of Africans to the very far reaches of Western cultures[17], have been rather persistent in their attempt to *a priori* exclude African/Black cultures, philosophies, religions, and histories from their range of perception and theorizing.[18] Black writing in the diaspora had to inscribe the cultural memory of human beings of African origins against a Western canonized consciousness that denied any human capacity to its colonial victims while at the same time blaming those very victims for its alleged absence. As Henry Louis Gates observed:

> Accused of lacking a formal and collective history, blacks published individual histories which, taken together, were intended to narrate in segments the larger yet fragmented history of Blacks in Africa, now dispersed throughout a cold New World. (...) The recording of an authentic black voice – a voice of deliverance from the deafening discursive silence which an enlightened Europe cited to prove the absence of the African's humanity – was the millennial instrument of transformation through which the African would become the European, the slave become the ex-slave, brute animal become the human being. (Gates 1985, 11)

Black slave narratives, thus, in witnessing to the Middle Passage and slavery, had to speak from a non-existent social, historical and cultural position, in acts of purposefully willed and quite scandalous self-authorizing that was, however,

---

16 One of the most intimate and chilling observations on the Atlantic Slave Trade and its flesh traffic is Hortense Spillers's 1987 essay "Mama's Baby, Papa's Maybe: An American Grammar Book."
17 See Bernal and Chukwudi Eze.
18 Robert Young (1990 and 1995) places Hegel's infamous remarks about Africa in the context of white mythologies that precisely denied cultural faculties like the "art of memory" to the very peoples subjected to their claims; in his more recent project he traces Western conceptions of culture more specifically in their colonial and racist articulations. Jan Pieterse has impressively documented those workings of white representation in his monumental documentary history.

subject to severe tactical and strategic restrictions of their outspokenness. Their testimony, accordingly, may be judged to contain as many occlusions, ellipses and rhetorical displacements as it revealed factual information, in spite of the authors' ethically impeccable impetus. As if herself signifying on that early tradition of inscribed black memory, Morrison in *Beloved* takes up and challenges the literary form and content of slave memoirs. She describes her project as follows:

> (Yet) no slave society in the world wrote more – or more thoughtfully – about its own enslavement. The milieu, however, dictated the purpose and style. (...) Over and over, the writers pull the narrative up short with a phrase such as, "But let us drop a veil over these proceedings too terrible to relate." In shaping the experience to make it palatable to those who were in a position to alleviate it, they were silent about many things and they 'forgot' many other things. (...) But most importantly – at least for me – there was no mention of their interior life. (...) my job becomes to rip that veil (...) Moving that veil aside requires, therefore, certain things. First of all, I must try my own recollections. I must also depend on the recollections of others. Thus memory weighs heavily in what I write. But memories and recollections won't give me total access to the unwritten interior life of these people. Only the act of imagination can help me. (Morrison 1987, 110)

Of course, every literary representation of experience is an act of the writer's imagination, even in cases of direct and authentic witnessing. However, the claim to an immediacy that will reach the potential reader in the very legitimacy of a first-person narrative of a 'true' witness cannot be made by a writer like Morrison. She has to ask her readership for a particular and double suspension of scepticism: not only – as with all other acts of encounter with testimony in the face of its necessary literariness and thus constructedness – but also because the 20th-century author's voice may only invent the articulation of the slave 'lost' in the Middle Passage. Writing more than a hundred years 'after the fact' of slavery Morrison does not literally remember her own violation in *Beloved*, yet she does insist on a relentlessly subjective voice of memory inscribed in its most intimate place: a person's body. The question arises if a writer (and, in turn, her reader) may at all be able to remember another person's "body in pain"[19]? Karen Remmler, in her above mentioned article about Holocaust survivors' writing, has argued:

> Aware that pain defies language, they nevertheless depend on metaphor to remember the dismemberment of their bodies and psyches through physical and psychological deprivation. It is the contextualisation of the metaphor in their texts, however, that remem-

---

19 Elaine Scarry's work came to be crucial for my own thinking about *Beloved*, and seems to have figured large for Karen Remmler, as well.

bers the presence of the body through the word instead of detaching it from material referentiality. (Remmler 217)

How does this metaphorization apply, if the memory is created by someone who is not, like the authors Remmler discusses, a survivor herself? If Remmler speaks of the

disjuncture between the apparent ineffability of the pain and suffering experienced by Holocaust survivors and the moral imperative to give testimony to an audience temporally removed from the event (Remmler 221)

what needs to be added is another project, another dilemma: one that could be termed 'as-if-testimony.' Provocatively, her protagonists' very bodies in *Beloved* become the locus of her literary strategy to invent witnessing. Morrison directs her readers to violated black flesh and blood as the site of black people's most painful memories, as if to dare us to accept the authenticity of their claims by way of exposing us to their arguably most interior, most private pain. A writing of the body's pain, the literary focus on the body's vulnerable materiality, then, becomes Morrison's strategy to mediate a slave's experience, to allow her readers fictional contact with a human being who historically was not entitled to claim any acknowledged access to the Symbolic. By way of drawing the reader into an emphatic relationship with those pained 'speaking bodies' of black slaves, Morrison creates an intimacy that results in powerful effects of verisimilitude. This literary strategy entails considerable danger: it always borders on "pornotroping" (Spillers 1987, 67) – a parading of the black body as stimulans and satisfaction for a (white) readerly voyeuristic gaze. It does work in *Beloved,* however, because Morrison safeguards her writing against that possible kitsch of suffering by way of the cutting precision of her very imagery and by way of disrupting all-too-easy readerly identification with estranging anti-narrative fissures and lacunae in her text.

With this strategy of working through pain, Morrison symbolically extends an offer to overcome trauma backwards in time, literally giving it to her protagonists, but addressing the "60 million and more" of *Beloved*'s epigraph, the human loss in the Atlantic slave trade. She assumes for her narrative voice the stance of a belated "narrator-as-eyewitness," whom Felman characterizes as follows:

[she] is the testimonial bridge which, mediating between narrative and history, guarantees their correspondence and adherence to each other. (...) Once endowed with language through the medium of the witness, history speaks for itself. (Felman 101)

29

The "speaking for itself" of historically lost memory is what I think *Beloved* is aiming at, succeeding and purposefully failing at the same time, as I hope to show.

The fictional production of bearing witness to destruction crucially changes the "very modes of the relationship between narrative and history" in that "re-memory[20]," to paraphrase Felman, not merely records, but rethinks, "and in the act of its rethinking, in effect transform(s) history"(Felman 95). Morrison's project of memory accordingly implies a necessary reconfiguration of historiography and of Western mediations of history. It also indirectly addresses another contemporary discursive domain: I read Morrison's project as a critical response to those poststructuralist theories that have figured the realm of dissemination and signification as one of playful surplus, of proliferating meanings shored up in and by excessive amounts of linguistic information which leaves social subjects but with vexing decisions of selection and evaluation. Whereas I do not entirely disagree with that claim, I see literary productions such as Morrison's marking an omission in those theories: Certain historical experiences, for example, have not (or only as of very recently) enjoyed linguistic circulation, and accordingly, social mediation; it seems to me that critical theory should address that very absence which upsets its own notions of unrestricted semantic abundance. The invention of witnessing on Morrison's part thus fills a gap, points to a suppression enacted by the Symbolic, to a lack, or rupture of signification, as opposed to what poststructuralism has seen as the free-floating and "constant polysemy" (Friedlander 4) of the signifier.

Testimony and Gender

The particular testimony of female survivors of the Middle Passage and of female slaves[21] was hardly ever speakable in its full complexity even within the black community, and completely lacked an appropriate medial audience outside the African-American community's oral channels of communication along female generational lines of transmission. Morrison's act of emphatic invention may thus be seen as an ultimate effort to secure wider public availability of those

---

20 In *Beloved*, "rememory" appears as noun and verb interchangeably, the vernacular stressing the aspect of the ex-slaves' self-conscious psychic work of rememberance.

21 Female slave narratives are rather rare documents and, as the controversial debates accompanying the publication history of Harriet Jacobs's *Incidents in the Life of a Slave Girl* (1861) have shown, they enjoyed a rather embattled status. See Yellin 1981.

moments of African-American maternal and daughterly testimony[22] that have been kept within the family as it were: circulating[23] across the rather more private spaces of kitchen gatherings, nightly story telling sessions, neighbourly exchanges, inter-generational advice giving and beauty parlor gossip. African-American women's literary texts have been marked for generations – from the publication of Harriet E. Wilson's sentimental novel *Our Nig* in 1859 up until the 1970s' surge of outspokenly womanist black female writing – by the pressure to mask, evade, or omit from consideration those parts of African-American female experience that were related to sexual abuse, as physical violation, and as psychic degradation and humiliation.[24]

James Olney describes the general aesthetic and political expectations that came to bear on writers of slave narratives as follows:

> The writer of a slave narrative finds himself in an irresolvably tight bind as a result of the very intention and premise of his narrative, which is to give a picture of slavery *as it is*. Thus it is the writer's claim (...) that he is not performing any act of poiesis. To give a true picture of slavery as it really is, he must maintain that he exercises a clearglass neutral memory that is neither creative nor faulty – indeed, (...) 'creative' would be understood by sceptical readers as a synonym for 'lying.' Thus the ex-slave narrator is debarred from use of a memory that would make anything of his narrative beyond or other than the purely (...) episodic, and he is denied access (...) to the configurational dimension of narrative. (Olney 150)

I take exception to this argument, because to focus on the slave narratives' restrictions as a lack of the "configurational dimension" reduces a complex terrain: certain experiences, as for example the sexual torture or rape of African-American women, as felt by victims, seem to have been less permissible than others, for example the prototypically cast scene of militantly enraged confrontation of a heroic male slave with his master. Morrison has alluded to a special responsibility she sees for the 20th-century writer, to create a public space for, or even to liberate the "unspeakable" and "unspoken"[25] testimony of African-American slaves' experience inasmuch as crucial aspects of their oppression –

---

22 See Bröck 1990, 225-237, for an examination of the relation between the work of African-American women writers like Margaret Walker, Toni Morrison, and Alice Walker and the oral heritage handed down to them along the lines of female ancestry and family. Also Bröck 1988 for a discussion of the particular meaning of oral cultural transmission for black women writers.

23 I am indebted to Hannah Möckel-Rieke's suggestion of the phrasing here.

24 See again Bröck 1988. From the wealth of critical production after the 1970s – directly related to the "explosion" of literary creativity – I want to single out the two collections by McDowell and Wall.

25 See Toni Morrison "Unspeakable," 9.

namely the sexual violence enacted on slave women and against the black community as a whole, and their emotional and visceral reactions to it – have almost never been confronted directly. *Beloved* thus struggles to find a voice with which to inscribe her protagonists' subjectivity: not only what happened to them on the outside, but how it felt on the inside. This interiority of textual characters, specifically female slave characters, in narratives got to be negated by the selective procedures of social mediation because of moralist and ultimately sexist biases of writers, readers and publishers. The scandalous exteriority of slave life (that is, their legal existence as cattle and how that status took shape in everyday-detail, the brutality of measures taken against slaves, the very structures of their oppression, the risk of resistance taken or not taken) already made for a dangerous truth to tell, particularly for a 19th-century audience. To address issues of traumatisation, shame, guilt, fear, of often futile rage at sexual denigration and abuse would have been an impermissible transgression. Mae Henderson's approach to this conflictuous terrain that extended well into the African-American community itself, appears pertinent:

> Rather than measuring a division between the races, however, Morrison (..) measures a division within the race (...) Her task as a writer, therefore, is to transgress these discursive boundaries by setting up a complementary and dialogic relationship between the 'interiority' of her own work and the 'exteriority' of the slave narrative. (Henderson 1991,63)

Morrison's novel, then, faces the far-reaching challenge of creating female testimony that would incorporate the rudimentary and always already too reticent memory of authentic slave narratives and supplement them, in Bhabha's sense of supplement as addition which changes the composition of the whole, with its author's compassionate imagination *without* forsaking the integrity of the 19th-century slaves' memories she wants to recuperate. The novel does address the genderedness of cultural memory's selectivity, but for all its insistence on giving voice to African-Americans' publicly muted female "ancestors[26]," it does not regard gendered oppression as a challenge for its black female characters exclusively. Rather, in foregrounding its male protagonist's hyper-sexualisation as well as his utter sexual humiliation, or desexualisation by white racism, in achieving male testimony, that is, on the human costs of retaining or creating black male (sexual) dignity, the novel bears witness to the profoundly gendered implications of a suppression of interiority for both, black women and men.[27]

---

26 See Nellie Mc Kay's interview with Toni Morrison in Gates and Appiah, 396-411, 398, 399.

27 See Barnett, one of the very first authors to have taken on Morrison's novelistic reconfiguration of black masculinity in the novel.

"To rip the veil drawn over proceedings 'too terrible to relate'" is what Morrison has set as the goal of her particular mode of testimony. Her work intends to redress the loss of African-American experience in/for the larger American cultural memory as well as it works to uncover hidden aspects within the black community's literary accounts that have fallen prey to the exigencies of gendered oppression.

Black Memory and Realism

In that Morrison's text calls for a patient readerly concentration on Black memory it also, in a particular move of what Bhabha called "timelagging" (Bhabha 1991, 207), redirects attentiveness to a claim of referentiality that post-modernity has registered as naive, illusory, metaphysical, and dispensable. I am using postmodernity here in a double sense: as a critically productive moment of deconstruction of master narratives, of logocentric thinking, and of Western teleologies; but also, in paradoxical connection with it, in Cornel West's sense, who speaks of "a world of fragments bereft of human will – a world of flashing images, quick information and consumer activities that promotes historical amnesia and fosters political apathy." (West 1988, 27)

Beloved calls upon readers to resist what German cultural critic Klaus Scherpe distinguished as the "aesthetic fascination" of the postmodern project: "a pointedly ecstatic surrender of the subject to indifference." (Scherpe 274, my translation). It seems to me the significant, cross-genre impact novels like *Beloved* (and a host of other cultural interventions by African-American and postcolonial writers) have had on Western cultural discourses over the last fifteen years to challenge and maybe help reverse that tendency. For all its fragmentation of form, *Beloved* tells a 'real story' that it wants its readers to believe. Decidedly, Morrison wants to create the "revelation of a kind of truth." (Morrison 1987, 113) This will to truth takes up realism's ethical gesture, if not its discredited appearance. Morrison herself puts it that way:

> The work that I do frequently falls, in the minds of most people, into that realm of fiction called fantastic, or mythic, or magical, or unbelievable. I'm not comfortable with these labels. I consider that my single gravest responsibility (in spite of that magic) is not to lie. (Morrison 1987, 115)

Beloved works on two levels: against a homolinear white American narrative of exclusionary historical progress it puts the ghost back in the machine, as it were, by all surrealist means necessary; on the other hand, it insists – against white postmodernity's tendency to dispose of morality – on moral "responsibility," as Morrison herself has called it.[28] *Beloved* as testimonial text thus inserts itself crucially into the postmodern crisis of "realism and representation,"[29] a crisis imminently pertinent to a discussion of cultural memory.

In a discussion of postmodern narrative 'versus' humanism's historical thinking, Elisabeth Ermarth, for example, characterizes the latter's "weakness" as follows:

> The perpetual mediation of historical thinking – between aspect and depth, primary and secondary characteristics, inside and outside, public and private – requires a kind of estrangement from the present that entails dematerialization, abstraction, disembodiment. The rationalization of consciousness that supports historical thinking always seeks to transcend the present, concrete, arbitrarily and absolutely limited moment by linking it with past and future, cause and project. The present requires a future to complete or at least improve it, and consequently a dialectical method for getting there from here or, in a word, for achieving transcendence of this inadequate present. By emphasizing what is linear, developmental, and mediate, historical thinking by definition trivializes the concrete, specific detail and trivializes the finite and present moment. (Ermarth 218)

Beloved, by contrast, suggests a different kind of historical thinking, one that does not deny or evade the mediation but that strives to overcome disembodiment and dematerialization in its very move. Morrison prompts a collaboration between readers and her writing in bodying forth as it were, a certain memory. That memory is at once relational to historical thinking as its suppressed underside, and also seeks to be concretely present in the readerly moment in its effort to make tangible a certain mental, physical pain, and spiritual responsibility. In other words, the effort is not to transcend the moment – the moment of a child dying in the Middle Passage, or the moment of Sethe killing her child as they are re-felt by readers; but to make readers *bear* its impact, at the same time that the question of its linkage to past and future is addressed. That seems to me to contradict a logic by which "to live in historical time is to live with one's immediate present effectively neutralized," (Ermarth 221) and raises the question if the entry of previously "non-historicized" subjects like the dead Africans of the Middle Passage into history would not change its composition.

In *Beloved* history (and humanism, I take it) accommodates Denver as the one who will take a self-conscious and self-confident (if not without reservations) step into living in and with white American society. However, she will also in turn – and this is what *Beloved* enacts for a forgetful 20th-century readership – modify history and historical thinking by her very agency. She foreshadows a

---

28 Interview with Morrison, Darling 5.
29 So the title of a 1993 collection by George Levine, of contributions to a conference about realism.

present that is by necessity constituted as an act of urgent recovery materialized with and in her memory. That is to say, *Beloved* does take part in the project of "an alternative temporality:"

> Breaking down the convention of historical time reveals the arbitrariness of its "neutrality," and this opening permits us to focus on precisely those questions of value and proportion that history defers. (Ermarth 221)

But the novel does not work this effect by foregrounding its own narrativity and making the questioning of representation in the abstract the very impulse of its textual drive. One could tentatively say that it rather does so by pushing realism to its very limits, expanding realism's range to the point of burst. History is unspeakable, not primarily because of the inherent slippage of signification but because of an ethical impasse of the human capacity to *speak* torture. For this project of stretching realism, *Beloved* as a narrative construction of duree, flexibility and "want"[30] within closure, functions as the appropriate medium.

Closure appears as one option of the novel which becomes most manifest in Denver's development. After having saved her mother from being eaten up by her trauma, the ghost of her baby child, Denver goes on to become an active member of late 19th-century Black society, and thus to be in history, which the novel opposes to the "no-time" of a traumatized Sethe (191). Denver successfully contacts the abolitionist Bodwins for work, to support Sethe and herself; she has the prospect to attend Oberlin College. Baby Sugg's admonition that there is "no defense" (245) against (white) evil or failure, but to know it and "go on out the yard" (245), that is, to live in worldliness in spite of its threat, is just as important a textual reservation vis-a-vis Denver's self-uplift as is Paul D's held back objection to Mrs. Bodwin's college plans for the girl: "Watch out. Watch out. Nothing in the world more dangerous than a white schoolteacher." (266) But Morrison brackets this objection off to us, the readers, and refuses to have the girl be impeded by the knowledge of it. Denver, after spending the longest time of her life in virtual isolation, cut off from the Symbolic and from any real life outside 124, as it were, will at the end participate in her own community's making of meaning and of cultural memory, however much ambivalent and conflicted that process might turn out. Having re-entered social life, Denver becomes part of a cultural repertoire that may (and will) be claimed as black history. To inscribe, with the sign "Oberlin" an entire history of African-American (women's) intellectualism and academic productivity into her novel, is indeed an acknowledgement on Morrison's part of black people's success within the Symbolic of American society – as opposed to Beloved's ghostly stories that threaten-

---

30 Interview with Morrison, in Mc Kay 411.

ingly diffuse into "just weather" (257) only to be reclaimed by surrealistic work.

Memory, Narration and Crisis

Certain kinds of cultural memory need artistic invention to be present to our historical moment when oral, collectively produced means of preserving culture have been relegated to a status of the quaint – for example to oral history collections in prestigious university libraries – by more profitable and powerful media. In this context, the novel as genre seems appropriate, given narrativity's specific, intrinsic insistence on making sense, to answer that particular end-of-the-20th-century political necessity of restoring suppressed history to cultural memory, and of symbolically entering the survivors into history, at long last.

As a text, *Beloved*, even in its extremes of absence of narrative sequence and syntax, gestures towards sense by making palpable the lack, the gap in signification. Thus the novel seems particularly able to constitute cultural memory in a way that I see negated by our absorption in a postmodern media environment characterized by an overall insistence on "presentness," a rapidly changing time frame of virtual realities, and non-referential modes of representation. The point that needs to be made is that there is a psychological correspondence between the work of cultural memory on the one hand, and a necessary willingness to concentration, to attentiveness on the other hand that requires integrative thought in time, versus endless fragmentation and self-referentiality. *Beloved* openly struggles with the referential effects and affects of mediation; it reminds us of narration as a medial translation of an urgency, be it ethical, social, political, or personal. Morrison's use of the novel as medium interrupts the postmodern media scene in a gesture of "contra modernity" (Bhabha 1991,198) in strategic retrospect, to irritate us, as it were, with pastness. It is in emplotted narrative[31], with its inherent desire of wholeness and its inbuilt drive for closure, that we register absence, and the impossibility of expression – in opposition to the cut up, flashing and two-second-bit structures of so many contemporary medial forms. In narrative, it is possible to enact the sometimes torturous passing through to memory, to go from *Beloved*'s: "And then no words. Humming. No words at all. (...) No. No. Nono. Nonono,"(163) the verbal degree zero that signifies Sethe's killing of her child, to Morrison's redemptive story that ends in a survivor's being

---

31 I take the concept of emplotment from Hayden White; especially pertinent in my context here is Hayden White, "Historical Emplotment and the Problem of Truth," Friedlander 37-53. See also Brooks.

"her own best thing." (273) Celan's commentary seems particularly poignant here:

> Within reach, close and not lost, there remained, in the midst of the losses, this one thing: language. (...) But it had to pass through its own answerlessness (...) it (...) yielded no words for what was happening – but it went through those happenings. Went through and could come into the light of day again, "enriched" by all that.[32]

Beloved enacts the answerlessness, which I take to mean the impossibility to respond to a traumatic event with words, in the ultimate collapse of signification into the mono-syllable "no," strengthening its effect of denial by repetition, "nonono." Ultimately, the act of killing the child cannot be *said* by Sethe, that is, not even Morrison can make her say what she actually did. We as readers, however, are being put through what happened by an excessive visceral richness of words circling obsessively to get a syntactic and semantic hold of memories that enabled child murder; by an effort to figure, in words, an answer to the trauma of a black mother killing her own child. This process necessarily requires of the reader a giving of great patience and empathy; it becomes a challenge to the fast consumption media culture that most contemporary readers have become accustomed to in our everyday lives: soundbites, clips of imagery, and fragments of text as all-pervasive medial flashes on our brains cannot elicit from us the work of cultural memory. The law of genre demands fast forgetting; the mind's capacities must be freed for constant and instant processing of information in a simulated state of limitless, immediate presence and a present tense that has become irresponsible to history. Answering history requires a kind of mediation that claims and takes time, requires a medium that may enact time, as it were.

A novel struggling with the task of inventing lost or suppressed cultural memory inevitably reaches the limits of narration, at least in any transparently mimetic sense. Morrison's production of interiority, intimate testimony in and of the flesh, contains its own negation in that any authorial narration is an act of generative control. Within the text, memory has to appear as im-mediate, to suspend our disbelief at a novel that claims to speak historical truth as effectively as possible. However, this effort of mediating the immediate leads to a crisis in and of the text. "This is not a story to pass on" (275) seems to be Morrison's self-reflective comment on that crisis; the rememory does not complacently evolve into story. It remains outside, in excess of the survivors' story that is at the novel's end safely beyond trauma. By nuance, my reading here differs from other critical commentary that has mostly focused on the ambiguity of the phrase "to

---

32 Paul Celan, "Bremen Speech 1958," quoted in Felman, "Education and Crisis, or the Vicissitudes of Teaching," Felman and Laub 1-56, 50.

pass on," as meaning to transmit, to forget and to forgo, stressing the "unspeakability of the subject" (Valerie Smith 353) and the "complexities of transmitting an account that reflects, and indeed comments upon, its own incommunicability."(Freeman 145) My point is rather to acknowledge the impossibility of "story." Morrison has indeed found words to communicate the subject, the most painfully telling words that have been tried on a 'topic' like this in decades – her verdict in the novel's coda signifies to me, however, that her most important communication to us has not been emplottable as story.

Morrison's text, but not, as she maintains, a community in the real world, may linger on Beloved's trace that becomes "just weather,"(275) not the "breath of the disremembered"(275) – something so demanding and inconceivable at the same time, not even Morrison's verbal creation can contain it within the story proper. Is she saying that whereas African-Americans have been able to enter 'history' and have become the agents of their own cultural memory, there is a certain memory in the flesh, a pain so visceral it cannot enter consciousness, and a history so absent, it cannot enter the mediation of cultural memory? So that a writer can surrealistically gesture at it as Morrison does in Beloved's monologues, but story, in the sense of emplotted cultural memory, cannot reach it? Writing on somebody's back – as schoolteacher does on Sethe's – defies any syntactic medium of human communication. Torture deconstructs language, its grammar and its emplotment capacity which means that a representation of torture cannot adequately find a form, since all mediation in Western cultures is directly or indirectly contingent on a functioning language. That de(con)struction also throws into sharp relief 20th-century's medial optimism; no matter how much poststructuralist intellectuals have struggled with the instability and unreliability of signification, there has in the wider society remained a deep-seated cultural belief, a human(e) desire – that everything is sayable, communicable, knowable, and may thus find an expressive narrative form. Paradoxically, there is only language – witnessing to the unspeakable – to put up against this optimism, only language to remind us that not everything can be narrated.

The story meets its disruption after Sethe's and Denver's "unspeakable thoughts" in Part Two, at a point where one could rightfully expect a narrative climax, since the novel up to this point has prepared readers for a revelation of the characters' innermost motivations that would propel the plot to satisfying closure. Instead, two monologues accumulate disintegration: characters (Sethe's grandmother, Sethe's mother, Sethe, Beloved) are blurred and merged, one voice is speaking in various registers of personal memory at once, any time frame is abandoned.

now she is going to her face comes through the water a hot thing her face is mine she is not smiling she is chewing and swallowing I have to have my face I go in the grass opens she opens it I am in the water and she is coming there is no round basket no iron circle around her neck she goes up where the diamonds are I follow her we are in the diamonds which are her earrings now my face is coming I have to have it I am looking for the join (...) now I am her face my own face has left me I see me swim away a hot thing I see the bottoms of my feet I am alone I want to be the two of us I want the join (...) her smiling face is the place for me... it is the face I lost (...) she is my face smiling at me doing it at last a hot thing now we can join a hot thing. (213)

The historical reality of Middle Passage and slavery that the novel tried so painstakingly to establish as its referent becomes utterly elusive in Beloved's incantatory language at the same time that its excess of pain overwhelms memory. The text oscillates on two levels: the memory of the monologue's "voice" having lost its coherence in pain, as well as conceivably the author's memory, who cannot/refuses to respond in narrative form: "How can I say things that are pictures?" (210)

Between the question "How can I say things that are pictures" and the repeated invocation of "a hot thing" (slavery's branding iron) Morrison has jammed – in the jazz sense of the word – piles of words in a stunningly inconspicuous language register that makes their meaning ever more deadly:

All of it is now it is always now there will never be a time when I am not crouching and watching others who are crouching too I am always crouching the man on my face is dead his face is not mine his mouth smells sweet but his eyes are locked some who eat nasty themselves I do not eat the men without skin bring us their morning water to drink we have none at night I cannot see the dead man on my face daylight comes through the cracks and I can see his locked eyes I am not big small rats do not wait for us to sleep someone is thrashing but there is no room to do it in if we had more to drink we could make tears we cannot make sweat or morning water so the men without skin bring us theirs one time they bring us sweet rocks to suck we are all trying to leave our bodies behind the man on my face has done it it is hard to make yourself die forever you sleep short and then return (210)

Those passages figure a radical break-up of narrative sequence in the very core of the text and a strategic reduction of syntactical structure that seem to bare a narrative act to its bones, as it were. Calling into question the very possibility of emplotment, this text within the story seems to resist what it at the same time frantically tries to represent, and it refuses to match the novel's restorative thrust.

The rhythmical passages circling back on themselves, leading nowhere, function in the novel like the outer limit of its crisis. From there, it is as if the text is retracing its way into story to be on safer mediating ground, firmly setting the plot to end on a hopeful tone of self-ownership and a projective future agency for her protagonists. One of *Beloved*'s most stunning achievements, and the one most pertinent to a discussion about cultural memory, is thus to pull two antagonistic cultural impulses together in one text: the necessity and option to make and narrate memory to get beyond the haunting ghosts of history on the one hand, and on the other hand, a strategically failing attempt at mediating historical trauma. The novel's ultimate gift to its readers is – to quote Felman one last time

to make the referent come back, paradoxically, as something heretofore unseen in history; to reveal the real as the impact of a literality that history cannot assimilate or integrate as knowledge, but that it keeps encountering in the return of the song.[33]

---

33 Quoted from Felman's discussion of Lanzmann's film in "The Return of the Voice: Claude Lanzmann's Shoah," Felman and Laub 204-283, 276.

1. Making and Unmaking Whiteness

1.1 The Politics of Remapping

> Racial reasons for persecution are convenient because in Western civilization today so many different breeds live in close contact with one another. The racist cries are raised not because those who raise them have any claim to belong to pure races, but because they do not; in other words, because today several ethnic groups occupy one city or one state, or states that share in one civilization are engaged in nationalistic wars. Hence comes the paradox that has been so often pointed out: that it is the most mongrel peoples of the world who raise the war-cry of racial purity. (Benedict)
> That white Americans must be allowed to remain white was precisely the point. The people of a new nation had at all cost to prevent loss of nationality. (Jordan)
> Arguing that 'pride in their African heritage is something that white children should be taught along with blacks,' Philips presses for 'a more complex paradigm to explain African cultural retentions than has hitherto been advanced,' one that recognizes the constant process of cultural exchange that has continued throughout American history. (Fisher Fishkin)

The discourses on race and racism (R. Young, Gilroy, Goldberg, DuBois, Omi and Winant) and on the special impact racialization has had on and within American society [34] have, over the last few years, gotten another spin: whiteness has been discovered to be a (skin)color, too, by white scholars. As David Stowe in a recent article in *Lingua Franca* has phrased it:

Behold the race traitors of the Nineties. Back in the Jim Crow South, the label was used to revile whites thought to be too cozy with blacks. Now, activists are embracing the bigot's epiteth in the same ways gays and lesbians have appropriated the word 'queer' – as part of a small but growing vanguard resolved to battle racism in America by renouncing the privilege of whiteness. While their perspectives and actions may seem distant from the academy, the race traitors are in fact the political wing of a movement that has spawned a journal and a proliferation of scholarly books. It may not be premature to speak of a new humanities subfield: whiteness studies. (...) Why is white the default setting of so much of our scholarship about America, ranging from literary studies to labor history? (...) [I]t is always 'the black' who needs to be explained in reference to whites.

---

34 See for example Brion Davis, Gossett, Gregory and Sanjek, eds.; Benedict, Myrdal, Baldwin, Jordan, West 1990, Gates 1985, 1993)

But, as the activist and writer Coco Fusco claims, 'racial identities are not only Black, Latino, Asian, Native American and so on; they are also white. To ignore white ethnicity is to redouble its hegemony by naturalizing it.' (Stowe 68)

Stowe's extensively bibliographical narrative is one of a series of essays trying to come to terms with the new field, differing slightly according to range and temperament in their genealogical listings.[35]

In a 1988 article in *Screen* Richard Dyer articulated this insight into the unnaturalness of whiteness in the context of a discussion of white American Hollywood films; a particularly apt move considering the aplomb with which the Hollywood film industry has played up visual whiteness and in the reverse, how the industry and the film genre itself have been propelled by investments in whiteness within the aggressively racialized cultural setting of the public gaze. Ever since *Birth of the Nation,* that white gaze has haunted the movie screen, and thus mass audiences' visual fields, by imagery and other filmic codes that reveal the interdependency of white subject positions, racism and the act of seeing an/other. Dyer's formulations bear lengthy quoting here because they not only frame a conception of white and whiteness; they also, at a very early moment, point to the difficulties of "doing whiteness":

Trying to think about the representation of whiteness as an ethnic category in mainstream film is difficult, partly because white power secures its dominance by seeming not to be anything in particular, but also because, when whiteness qua whiteness does come into focus, it is often revealed as emptiness, absence, denial or even a kind of death. (...) [W]hite domination is reproduced by the way that white people colonise the definition of normal. [I]f the invisibility of whiteness colonises the definitions of other norms – class, gender, heterosexuality, nationality and so on – it also masks whiteness as itself a category. White domination is then hard to grasp in the characteristics and practices of white people. No one would deny that, at the very least, there are advantages to being white in Western societies, but it is only avowed racists who have a theory which attributes this to inherent qualities of white people. Otherwise, whiteness is presented more as a case of historical accident, rather than a characteristic cultural/historical construction, achieved through white domination. (...) The colourless multi-colouredness of whiteness secures white power by making it hard, especially for white people and their media, to 'see' whiteness. (...) Yet the strength of white representation (...) is the sense that being white is coterminous with the endless plenitude of human diversity. (...) Let me state that, while writing here as a white person about whiteness, I do not mean either to display the expiation of my guilt about being white, nor to hint that it is also awful to be white. (...) Studies of dominance by the dominant should not deny the place of the writer in relation to what s/he is writing about it, but nor should they be the green light for self-recrimination or trying to get in on the act. (Dyer 232-235)

---

35 Some names re-occur: Ellison, Baldwin, Murray, Morgan, Roediger, for example; other contributions, for example Sylvia Wynter's 1979 essay seem lost except for one mention I found in DuPlessis 1995.

Quite strikingly, as usual in American academic publishing, only a very small number of articles get to be imbued with the power of immediate canonization. There appears to be a general agreement, judging by the recurrence of reference, to credit Toni Morrison's *playing in the dark* with a midwifely role – a phenomenon that in and by itself belies one of the properties of American whiteness that Morrison and others have criticized, namely white culture's need to be electrified, as it were, by black stimulation. That this may sound sexy to some people, is no happenstance; in fact, most of the euphemistic metaphorics of older (like Ellison and Murray) and more recent proponents of the study of racialization and its impact on white America swerve around notions of "mixing," "synergy," "homage," "intimate contact," "fertilization," "hybridity," "mulatto" and "jazzing it up."[36] As Harryette Mullen has observed succinctly, if bitterly, "black soul may be a more lucrative commodity than black bodies ever were" (Mullen 88). Accordingly, signifying terms like "appropriation" or "theft" which at least allude to oppressive and unequal cultural/social power relations between the mixing groups, have comparatively less academic market value than the attraction of codes however idealistically calling on partnership and eroticism.

To work against the self-perpetuating neutralization of whiteness has created an academic surge that discusses its research confidently in terms of a paradigm shift not unlike that which produced black studies or feminist/gender studies. What tends to get lost in this enthusiasm is the historical debt the whiteness discourse owes to bygone generations of white and black Americanists, and to Black Studies research inside and beyond university departments. To leave traces within the Humanities beyond the mere faddish, whiteness and/or racialization studies will have to own the history of, and the history of the study of white racism – a connection easily obscured by the neo-conservative reflexes of an anti-moralism often bolstered conveniently with an abhorrence of trivial and immature political correctness' pressure.

Shelley Fisher Fishkin's essay in *American Quarterly* (1995) rather forwardly claims the 1990s as a turning point for American Studies. Appropriately titled "Interrogating 'Whiteness,' Complicating 'Blackness': Remapping American Culture" it indeed stakes a new field. An erudite bibliographical essay encompassing the academic production of discursive whiteness over the last ten years, it is a service to Americanists who have so far not engaged in the question. However, there are objections to make against glaring gaps in Fisher Fishkin's genealogy and against the essay's very claim of remapping:

---

36 It would be a promising project to trace the development of racialized discursivity along the evolving tropes of contact, from negatively connotated "miscegenation" to quite positively judged politically correct "creolization." See R. Young 1995.

In this essay I will provide a brief overview of over a hundred books and articles from fields including literary criticism, history, cultural studies, anthropology, popular culture, communication studies, music history, art history, dance history, humor studies, philosophy, linguistics and folklore, all published between 1990 and 1995 or forthcoming shortly. Taken together, I believe, they mark the early 1990s as a defining moment in the study of American culture. For in the early 1990s our ideas of "whiteness" were interrogated, our ideas of blackness were complicated, and the terrain we call 'American culture' began to be remapped. (Fisher Fishkin 429)

Fisher Fishkin constructs a color-indifferent "we" – subject of American Studies, enlisting a number of respected black scholars and spokespeople like Henry Louis Gates and David Bradley for her project. This construction ignores the historical fact that white scholars, as Donna Haraway has said it for white feminists "were forced kicking and screaming to notice" (Haraway 199): it has been Black Studies' oftentimes scornful and anti-harmonizing energies that pushed white America, and white scholars, into the direction of finally taking into account the racism at worst, color blindness at best, of the American academy. Capitalizing on a correct insight into the problematics of separate Black Studies to leave the mainstream canon basically undisturbed, Fisher Fishkin's narrative myth of genesis reflects the recent white scholars' coming to awareness of the racialized field of American culture but may by no means entitle a representative claim for the collective (black and white, one would have to assume) "we" she assumes:

While the idea of the social construction of "blackness" was increasingly discussed in the 1980s, the idea of "whiteness" as a construct did not receive widespread attention until the 1990s. (...) The 'whiteness' that had previously been largely invisible in the stories we told about who we were suddenly took center stage as the site where power and privilege converge and conspired to sabotage ideals of justice, equality and democracy. (Fisher Fishkin 430)

Whereas the latter has been the focus of interest for generations of black scholars, particularly and intensely so within the post Civil Rights Movement Black Studies departments, it is a new phenomenon that white academics study whiteness' construction, which, as Richard Dyer has argued, might have its own drawbacks. While he rejoices in the fact that a study of whiteness by white scholars will help to leave behind a specific 1980s chic of (white) looking at the ethnic 'other,' and in the process actually othering the objects of this gaze without acknowledging white particularity he also cautions his readers against the solipsistic narcissism involved in that project.

That solipsism might be one reason not to credit certain earlier black work in the project of remapping. Absent from Fisher Fishkin's essay is for example Sylvia Wynter's investigation of "blanchitude" and American culture from 1979, owing its ethics and rhetorics to a historical moment of black struggle that seems to be readily negligible for Fisher Fishkin:

The West was now [at the time of Négritude] to become conscious of the cultural death it had inflicted on itself by channeling all libidinal energy to a productive finality. As the self-confidence of the axiomatic culture weakened, the stigmatized cultures began to counter-define themselves, in terms of the larger world, moving out from the underlife into the mainstream to extend the work of cultural transformation. (...) Négritude drew attention to that implicit cultural blanchitude which had been central to the social machine of the world system. Blanchitude had been nothing else than the constituted NORM of culture in relation to which all other cultures had been made subservient. It was that normative culture of blanchitude that inscribed the globe, coding value and non-value, binding the structures of production under the hegemony of its imaginary social significations. (Wynter 1979, 150)

Studies investigating the congruity and mutual contingency of US-American whiteness and white racism which were not surprisingly written in the decade after the politically and culturally militant 1960s, are entirely missing.[37] Characterized by a striking amnesia, Fisher Fishkin's frame of reference are the multiculturalist attacks on WASP hegemony of the 1980s: the essay remaps American culture as an answer to those most recent "canon wars" (429):

It is by understanding and celebrating the hybridity of mainstream American culture, and acknowledging the multicultural tributaries that have fed that mainstream, that we can collectively forge what Gates refers to as 'new, and vital, common American culture in the twenty-first century.' (...) We must learn to reclaim our complex roots while not ignoring the history of racism that allowed us, for over two hundred years, to ignore and deny who and what we really were all along. (Fisher Fishkin 455)

Granted its positively enabling energy, mapping in this instance becomes a decisive power gesture in the Foucauldian sense of making knowledge, demarcating it, and possessing the title to it. The essay's very title creates "remapping" not only as a domain of American academia, but as a national challenge:

We are now and have always been a culture in which a vast range of voices have constantly shaped each other in profound ways. (...) the new vision of our culture will be truer than any that we have had before – and more interesting. It will also be a healthier base on which to build our society's future. Forging such a vision may not be easy, but it is a challenge we should be eager to embrace. (Fisher Fishkin 456)

Fisher Fishkin's expediency to project this color line syncretism immediately as a national enterprise that will have always already integrated ethical and material conflict in its exuberant "common" subjectivity of forging a vision strongly recalls

---

37 See for example Brion Davis, Kovel, Fredrickson, or Jordan 1968, and 1974.

the tradition of Jeremiadism from which no progressive American movement or issue seems to have been able to escape.

This tendency gets echoed most audibly in Henry B. Wonham's collection *Criticism and the Color Line. Desegregating American Literary Studies* (1996). The editor signs himself as heavily indebted, in turn, to Ellison, to Morrison, and to Fisher Fishkin, whose essay is reprinted in the collection. Wonham, too, wants to contribute to a "new vision" of American identity and culture; he is rather outspoken in his claim to a unifying middleground against African-Americanists' "racial essentialism," the "selfdefeating obstacles [they] threaten to erect" and against "their nativist counterparts" (Wonham "Introduction," 4,5) even though he may concede that "a space of 'difference' was essential to the emergence of black voices" and "its constant articulation remains a necessity"(4). Again, in his scenario, the anti-racist work of the 1960s and 1970s is buried in the rather neutralizing mention of "Baker, Stephen Henderson, Amiri Baraka and other pioneering African-Americanists" who "painstakingly marked out (...) a space of cultural difference"(5).[38] By contrast, Wonham suggests, the "task of criticism" should be

to document the "embarrassing" presence of this Other in cultural places where one least expects to find it, to historicize rather than to deny the cultural exchanges that produce American identity. (Wonham 6)

The authors in his collection depict

the color line as a site of cultural mutation, and they share the desire to read much of American literature with Sundquist as the product of "two traditions that are always dynamically defining each other." (Wonham 6)

With surprising speed, the new debate about whiteness, blackness, and the color line has evolved into a national project of reconciliation. As if indeed American culture – even within academia – could not bear negativity, every moment of contention or even resistance becomes immediately subsumed. There may be no local moments of critique: within a time span of not even three years, the academic industry has made the jump from particular observations to nationalizing and "dynamically" narrativizing projects like Wonham's collection. Metaphors signifying other than mutual empowerment and enrichment, because they might "concur in treating racial difference (...) as a problem to be solved by essentialist critical practices" (Wonham 6) have become consequently alien to those projects; questions of racist oppression, power, resistance and agency have nonchalantly disappeared along with "essentialism."

---

38 For Wonham, black women intellectuals do not exist, judging by the absence of any reference to black women scholars or thinkers except for Toni Morrison.

Wonham anticipates this rebuke. His aggressively positive rhetorics, however, betray a marginalization of a more contrary concern:

[D]aring to celebrate transgressions of the color line, (...) arguments about canons and 'sacred texts' inevitably raise related questions about institutional legitimacy, questions that are politically and emotionally charged. (...) It might fairly be asked if, in highlighting the sometimes fluid, sometimes turbulent, sometimes illusory exchange of cultural practices along the color line, the critical perspective in these essays works to cancel or neutralize black difference (...) [O]nly the most cynical reader would accuse either Morrison or the contributors to this collection of wishing to erode the institutional integrity of African-American studies by blurring the frontiers of black/white cultural difference. In calling for an end to the segregation of American literary studies, the scholars assembled here do not invite a return to the assimilationist ideal of a "race-blind" American literature. Rather, they dispense with essentialist conceptions of race in order to chart the literary historical effects of dynamic cultural difference. The point, in other words, is not to erase the color line, but to historize a mutually constitutive relationship between African and European cultures in America. (Wonham 14)

The cynicism, it seems to me, is on his side: to eclipse generations of scholarship on race and racism in the United States that has time and again focused as much on the social construction of race as on its material effects and on the complicated tension between those poles, under the marker "essentialism" calls for an integration of American culture on rather lopsided terms.[39] Both, Fisher Fishkin and Wonham, draw for a legitimation of their project on Ralph Ellison who called on the unacknowledged "synthesis of our diverse elements of cultural style" and on a "true interrelatedness of blackness and whiteness" as the basis of "the nation's heritage" (Ellison 1964, 55,24). The unspoken subplot of the new national narrative might indeed be prefigured by Ellison: the authors of those remappings of the color line do share with Ellison's narrator in *Invisible Man* a love for the American "principle" that might explain a reverberation of the 1950s in the 1990s – sounding out the more internationalist 1960s and 1970s in its articulations:

Could he have meant – hell, he must have meant that we were to affirm the principle on which the country was built and not the men, or at least not the men who did the violence. (...)Did he mean to affirm the principle, which they themselves had dreamed into being out of the chaos and darkness of the feudal past, and which they had violated and compromised to the point of absurdity even in their own corrupt minds? Or did he mean that we had to take responsibility for all of it, for the men as well as the principle, because we were the heirs who must use the principle because no other fitted our needs? (...) Or

---

39 Of course, one part of Wonham's signifying environment is Afrocentrism (DuCille "Postcolonialism") against which some of his contempt might be understandable, given its melanin politics. This must remain speculation, and as such, the invisible ground of polemics that will hurt other African-American scholars more than it will benefit his argument.

was it, did he mean that we should affirm the principle because we, through no fault of our own, were linked to all the others in the loud, clamoring, semi-visible world, that world seen only as a fertile field for exploitation by Jack and his kind, and with condescension by Norton and his, who were tired of being the mere pawns in the futile game of "making history"? Had he seen that for these too we had to say 'yes' to the principle, lest they turn upon us to destroy both it and us? (...)America is woven of many strands; I would recognize them and let it so remain. (...) I denounce because though implicated and partially responsible, I have been hurt to the point of abysmal pain, hurt to the point of invisibility. And I defend because in spite of all I find that I love. In order to get some of it down I have to love. (...)[My grandfather] accepted his humanity just as he accepted the principle. It was his, and the principle lives on in all its human and absurd diversity. (Ellison 1952, 574,575,580)

However, whereas Ellison's narrator is able to hold an ambiguous sarcasm – as in *Invisible Man*'s episode of "optic white" (Ellison 1952, 196-230)[40] – such subtlety is lost in Wonham's introduction. In his "celebration" of America's mixed heritage, Ellison's self-deprecative, self-deconstructive irony – he lets his narrator signify precisely on whiteness as appropriation and thus characterizes any fantasy of "common" heritage as always already compromised by white power schemes and black tricksterhood – is overwritten with an unproblematized self-identical sense of nationhood shared by black and white.

Thus, this particular academic project reinvigorizes America by drawing on its alleged creolization. Post-racialized intellectuals engage to re-write the nation by way of attesting to mutually fertilizing cultural "creative exchanges" that have "produced" (Wonham 3) American culture; the speculation must be allowed here whether at the core of these approaches is a need for positive national identification of (mostly white) intellectuals, which – as a strategy against the contempt heaped on the proponents of multiculturalism – might seem attractive to destabilize a marginalization within the academy. This newly found American power: a culture integrated, a possessive national(ist) white sentiment of pride in a "shared" heritage, however, becomes disseminated at a time of severest legal and political onslaught on the lives of African-Americans; white intellectuals discover their 'blackened' origins at a time of governmental abandonment of social justice for African-American people.

To be aware of this particular historical irony seems a rather more necessary challenge for white discursivity on racialization than to construct a defense line of a creolized national heritage against black essentialism. As Berndt Ostendorf has argued, there is a danger of

translating political conflict into cultural difference. It can be read in two ways: 1) as a multilateralization of a binary structural racism (nobody really wants to tackle the eco-

---

40 See also Mullen 74.

nomic base of it). For multiculturalism "culturalizes" the problem of the color line. 2) Multiculturalism displaces the problems of race from political economy into problems of text or representation. (Ostendorf 722)

To my mind, scholars should admit to the inevitable ambiguity of whites studying whiteness, to an inevitable narcissism inherent in that very gesture. Probably the best we can do, then, is to continually bracket our self-consciousness without dispensing with it. Academic work on whiteness does not make – as such – good "race treason"; the question, however, of why and how that should be useful, necessary, and effective is crucial even if it exceeds the limits of the present text. I do submit, though, that even within the realm of academic discourse, scholars face ideological, not only scientific or aesthetical challenges: a swallowing up of (our) discursive power within nationalistic frameworks is counterproductive to working through the problem of racism and the color line. More than ever before this seems to have become a global issue that does neither require nor bear national sublimes or limitations. The very development of a racialization discourse owes its existence to the postcolonial moment (McClintock, DuCille "Postcolonialism") of a weakening of white Western (and among those prominently US-American) national narratives' (assumed) omnipotence to represent the course of world histor/ies (Shohat and Stam). To retrieve, then, a discourse on the color line – recasting it as a binding tie rather than a splitting boundary – for projects of national narrativization strengthens an (US)American exceptionalism critical intellectuals had better be wary of.

1.2. Signifying on Slavery: From Uncle Tom's Cabin to The Women's Room

> I had intended, that is, to tell a happier story about the insight and strength to be found in strategies of coalition, both political and rhetorical. Instead, as I worked, the relation between feminism and abolition increasingly seemed to be characterized by patterns of exploitation, appropriation, and displacement; similarly the potential for aesthetic erasure and absorptions marred any simply positive reading between poetry and politics. (Sánchez-Eppler)
> The abolitionist discourse encoded in the antislavery emblems structured the free antislavery feminists' discourse and dramatized their oppression as women in a patriarchal society. But by conflating the oppression of women who were enslaved and the oppression of women who were free, by collapsing the literal enslavement of (...) black women into the figurative enslavement that they felt they suffered, white free antislavery feminists obscured the crucial difference between the experience of women who were held as chattel and their own experience. (...) On one hand, the free women misinterpreted the situation of slave women, and on the other,

49

they misinterpreted their own: they were not, after all, literally in irons. (Yellin)

The one founding moment of headlong confrontation between women's writing and the 'black' trauma of American history is *Uncle Tom's Cabin*[41]. A literary call that reverberated through the entire black literary tradition (Spillers "Changing") it received a belated but direct answer by a white woman writer in the 20th century who countered its abolitionist message with the ultimate plantation legend, *Gone With the Wind.* (Fiedler 1979) Beecher Stowe's novel could well be regarded as one of the constitutive texts of American culture, as Leslie Fiedler and Jane Tompkins have convincingly argued (Fiedler 1966, Tompkins). Critical interest has not abated; almost every generation of critics has cast the novel anew within its respective mold, either rejecting it as trivial, racist, tear-jerking trash, as a speculative bestseller that does not deserve literary scrutiny; or proposing it as early feminist, far-reaching commentary on a necessary "domestic" transformation of American culture and society, as a sincere pamphlet against American slavery that stands the test of time, and as germinal text for a revalued Sentimental Tradition. (Spillers "Changing," Sundquist) I read *UTC*[42] here as a site of white female engagement against slavery that prefigured and encoded American white feminist investments, its controlling metaphorics overshadowing the history and theory of the American women's movement (Wiegman 1992).

As Moira Ferguson (1992, 1993) and Vron Ware have demonstrated, a practice of signification on slavery has a longstanding and international tradition in Western feminist history partly because of the direct convergence of women's emancipatory activities with abolition struggles, partly because a general tradition of political iconography to operate with the metaphor of slavery for debasing and oppressive conditions (Patterson), has provided a firm platform for feminist allegories. In the US particularly, however, this allegory has had a very specific historical resonance that is passively evoked every time the sign gets to be activized, at the same time that its referent gets to be suppressed as routinely. The major distinction of an American discursive, rhetorical use of the topos of slavery was the system's very factualness within the boundaries of every American's existence, no matter at what remove.

From the early women's movement's beginnings in the ante-bellum years of the 19th to the post-Civil Rights Movement white feminism of the 20th century, militant signification on slavery has punctuated white American women's rhetorics;

---

41 Cited hereafter in the text as UTC.
42 I am taking the liberty to benefit of the canonicity of *Uncle Tom's Cabin*; in the same way, I assume Marilyn French's *The Women's Room* to be disseminated thoroughly enough to allow my metaphorical usage.

what will concern me presently is the shift from a white female gaze on the black (male)[43] slave's location controlled by an electrifying, politically astute mixture of outrage, empathy, maternalism, religious fervor and sensational eroticism, to an insistence on looking at one's female white self, on locating a 'room of one's own' as the grounds of politics. This substitution of collective female altruism: articulating the black slave's right to freedom with collective egoism: articulating one's own (white, middle class, female) emancipatory interests, was facilitated precisely by a white female racism that not only erupted in the historical separation between former abolitionists and the women's movement over the suffrage cause[44] but that had been contained germinally in the attitudes of white middle class women towards the black slaves metaphorized so perfectly by Beecher Stowe's interest in *UTC*.

To find Hortense Spillers' polemical notion of "pornotroping" appropriate to name both a driving motivation and mode of expression of white abolitionist rhetorics (Spillers 1987, 67) does not appear too far fetched, if we situate Beecher Stowe's repeated fictional "peep"(ings) at the "poor" slaves in the context of non-fictional political rhetoric of her times.[45] As an example she herself calls "necroscopic," Sánchez-Eppler cites a passage from Angelina Grimke's *Appeal to the Christian Women of the South*. Both of those terms struggle to signify the strange, subconscious melange of (white) feelings that went into the pitying gaze on the (black) slave: abhorrence at the slave's degradation, shame, an illicit voyeuristic interest in the abject, a sexual gaze on the (often male!) body reduced to body, even if in forbidden fantasy; identification and the will to forever be spared such humiliation, to be a subject different from the "wretched thing" regarded – all merged in the Victorian psyche; and found but coded representation. In its very excess the gaze of white (female) abolition effects disintegration, undermining its own desire to reconstruct the slave's humanity:

---

43 The problematics of gender and race crossover eroticism in this white female altruism would be necessary to trace; again this would require another project to exceed the space and focus of this study.

44 The focus of my study does not permit nor does it necessitate elaboration on this point; for the historical presentation see DuBois, Karen Sánchez-Eppler 1993, Yellin 1989. To my knowledge, there is as yet no study, however, to work through the intricacies of Republican politics of the post-bellum years and research their elaborate and intriguing schemes to separate the two movements. Successful bilateral efforts at getting an Equal Rights Association off ground which would have been able to resist that divide et impera could have had unforeseen consequences for the course of American history. Studies I have seen seem to take the clash of interest between women's and black men's suffrage for granted, for which there is no natural reason at all.

45 In 1853, a children's version appeared under the actual title "A Peep Into Uncle Toms Cabin," see Spillers "Changing," 30.

Our business is to take away the stone which has covered up the dead body of our brother, to expose the putrid carcass, to show how that body has been bound within the grave-clothes of heathen ignorance, and his face with the napkin of prejudice, and having done all it was our duty to do, to stand by the negro's grave in humble faith and holy hope, waiting to hear the life giving command of 'Lazarus, come forth.'This is just what Anti-Slavery societies are doing; they are taking away the stone from the mouth of the tomb of slavery, where lies the putrid carcass of our brother. (Grimke in Eppler 1993, 2)

Beecher Stowe employs rather similar textual strategies to capitalize on the willingness of her would-be abolitionist readership to be 'thrilled' into empathy. This is but one of the scenes that capture the slave's humiliation in terms of a humane excitement:

Tom had a remarkable smooth, soft voice, and a habitually respectful manner, that had given Legree an idea that he would be cowardly, and easily subdued. When he spoke those last words, a thrill of amazement went through everyone, the poor woman clasped her hands, and said,'Oh, Lord!' and every one involuntarily looked at each other and drew in their breath, as if to prepare for the storm that was about to burst. (...)'An't you mine, now, body and soul?' he said, giving Tom a violent kick with his heavy boot, 'tell me!' In the very depth of physical suffering, bowed by brutal oppression, this question shot a gleam of joy and triumph through Tom's soul. He suddenly stretched himself up, and, looking earnestly to heaven, while the tears and blood that flowed down his face mingled, he exclaimed, 'No!No!No! (...)The two gigantic negroes that now laid hold of Tom, with fiendish exultation in their faces, might have formed no unapt personification of powers of darkness. The poor woman screamed with apprehension, and all rose, as by a general impulse, while they dragged him unresisting from the place. (*UTC* 507-509)

Sánchez-Eppler's "Bodily Bonds: The Intersecting Rhetorics of Feminism and Abolition" (1988) demonstrates how the rhetorics of white women comparing themselves to those powerless slaves had a certain limited usefulness and justification in the 19th century, under legal, social and cultural conditions which did not grant white middle class women the right to vote, nor the legal right to own property; and which dominated white women's lives as well as their bodies with absolute patriarchal possession and control:

Feminists and abolitionists were acutely aware of the dependence of personhood on the condition of the human body since the political and legal subordination of both women and slaves was predicated upon biology. (...) Thus, the bodies of women and slaves were read against them, so that for both the human body was seen to function as the foundation not only of as general subjection but also of a specific exclusion from political discourse. For women and slaves the ability to speak was predicated upon the reinterpretation of their flesh. Feminists and abolitionists share a strategy: to invert patriarchal readings and so reclaim the body. Transformed from a silent site of oppression into a symbol of that oppression, the body becomes within both feminist and abolitionist discourses a means of gaining rhetorical force. (Sánchez-Eppler 1988, 229,230)

However, the very usefulness of the metaphor constitutes it also as a gesture of dominance and asymmetry:

The bound and silent figure of the slave metaphorically represents the woman's oppression and so grants the white woman excess to political discourse denied the slave, exemplifying the way in which slave labor produces – both literally and metaphorically – even the most basic of freedom's privileges. (...) At stake in the feminists' likening of women to slaves is the recognition that personhood can be annihilated and a person owned, absorbed and un-named. The irony inherent in such comparisons is that the enlightening and empowering notions of identification that connect feminism to abolitionism come inextricably bound to a process of absorption not unlike the one that they expose. Though the metaphoric linking of women and slaves uses their shared position as bodies to be bought, owned and designated as a grounds of resistance, it nevertheless obliterates the particularity of black and female experience, making their distinct exploitations appear as one. The difficulty of preventing moments of identification from becoming acts of appropriation constitutes the essential dilemma of feminist-abolitionist rhetoric. (Sánchez-Eppler 1988, 231)

Even Sánchez-Eppler's own very careful phrasing reveals that one inadvertent result of this metaphorical procedure is the eclipse of black women: the black woman in this metaphorical equation appears but as a sign of extreme gendered vulnerability. A potential alliance was always already threatened by white women's denial of their own sexualization within a Victorian public discourse that they did not want to or could not afford to refute:

[F]eminist-abolitionists emphasize the similarities in the condition of women and slaves; nevertheless, their treatment of the figure of the sexually exploited female slaves betrays an opposing desire to deny any share in this vulnerability. (...) Thus in the writings of antislavery women the frequent emphasis on the specifically feminine trial of sexual abuses serves to project the white woman's sexual anxieties onto the sexualized body of the female slave. (...) The figure of the slave woman, whose inability to keep her body and its uses under her own control is widely and openly recognized, becomes a perfect conduit for the unarticulated and unacknowledged failure of the free woman to own her own body in marriage. (Sánchez-Eppler 1988, 233, 234)

UTC also inscribes this latent erasure of black women as subjects of women's emancipation, and consequently as potentially powerful allies: the two characters who could most readily embody that alliance, Eliza and Cassy, who both exhibit daring endurance, ingenuity and model-like domesticity as slave mothers, as much as they embody (sexual) victimization, are denied any agency as free women in the realm of American women's political activities by the novel's closure, safely dispatching them, with husband and family, to Liberia. This closure certainly, however unwittingly, fostered the pervasive reception of the novel focussing exclusively on the black man (slave or free) as object/subject of political considerations and options. In setting up the relation between women's rights activists (like Beecher Stowe herself) and abolition as a complementary, but latently competitive binary of white women vis-à-vis black men, the novel's deep structure prefigures a breakup of a possible solidarity between black and white women that could have been an effective historical means to counter the sexist **and** racist influences tearing the two reform movements apart after the Civil War.[46]

As it happened, white women began leaving "Uncle Tom," whom they considered no longer "poor" and dejected, to himself and took up their own lot. The assumption to speak as woman for woman, however, by logic of the controversy, would necessarily banish black women from the argument's purview: as black people, black women were not addressed by a plea that insisted on having "antagonistic interests" vis-à-vis "negro suffrage" (Stanton 1869, epigraph in DuBois). This schism, sharpened by an insurmountable sexism within the abolitionist movement and a growing racism within the women suffrage movement would eventually swallow up any possible public space in which black women might have sought to labor alongside white women as women:[47]

American women of wealth, education, virtue and refinement, if you do not wish the lower orders of Chinese, Africans, German and Irish, with their low ideas of womanhood to make laws for you and your daughters (...) to dictate not only the civil but moral codes by which you shall be governed, awake to the danger of your present position and demand that woman, too, shall be represented in the government! (Stanton 1869 in DuBois 178)

This changing rhetoric that would win out over contemporary efforts of other movements' voices calling for an insistence on indivisible equal rights for all men and all women[48], indicates a transition of politically valid, respectable, accessible and marketable subject positions; from the white woman acting on the slave's behalf (accessing thereby her own entry into the public sphere) to representing herself: a white female middle class empowered agent. This shift could only function – given the pressures of patriarchy, racism and capitalism – at the cost of negation of the black male, and erasure of the black female as historical agents of emancipation:

---

46 Again, for fleshing this out by way of historical fact, see DuBois; and Hine, King and Reed.

47 The controversy surrounding black women's (non)representation at the 1893 Chicago World Columbian Exposition provides a lugubrious instance of the separation between American women, see Kuppler.

48 See the history of the Equal Rights Association and its erosion in the Reconstruction years in DuBois 79-104.

[I]n this triangulated schema whereby one either calls for bringing white women into the space of the universal (male) subject or the black man into the space of the universal (white) subject, the missing subject of both arguments is the black woman (...). (S. Smith 34)

As has become obvious by now, I am not interested here in factual historical reconstruction by detail; the focus is on a signifying scenario of crucial importance for American civil society: how 20th century white feminist disinvestment in the 'race question' was prefigured by the dispensation with "Uncle Tom" (and, hidden from sight, in the same move: the effacement of black female agency) in the post-bellum years. The post-abolitionist feminist discovery of politics in the first person, based on the displacement of an already problematical identification with black ersatz embodiment by the white subject embodying herself, provided, that is my point, the rhetorical environment for the historical amnesia in women's literary imagination of the 20th century.

Thus, only by way of ironic echo, not only in its very title, the 1970s bestseller *The Women's Room* takes up and immediately dismisses the legacy of *UTC*: it uses the term of slavery to make a feminist argument in the interest of white middle class women's liberation. Marilyn French, the author, and the novel itself will figure for my purposes here as rhetorical metaphors for the dominant strand of American feminism in the 1970s. French even re-establishes this signification in her own introduction to the 1994 reprint with a colorful replay of the 19th century parallelism[49]:

Morally, the conventional happy ending of women's novels alleviates male guilt. If one is a big massa down on the plantation, one prefers to believe that one's slaves are happy. This one does not have to consider one's ethical relation to them. Aristotle believed that only those with slavish natures would submit to slavery. Those who are enslaved therefore must have slavish natures and therefore are happy in slavery because... Women live happily ever after: one need never question whether she really enjoys bending over the washboard doing laundry for ten, or working the switchboard all day, and then coming home to cook and clean. She is happy because it is in her nature to be so. (French XVII)

Marilyn French – and generations of young white consciousness-raising feminists for whom her novel was as immediate as a bible – voice a radicality that capitalizes on but erases black history in the same move. Says one of the novel's protagonists:

---

49 Faludis' self-congratulatory comparison between *The Women's Room* and *Uncle Tom's Cabin* in the Afterword to the 1994 paperback reprint has the same effect.

For forty-odd years I've been a member of an oppressed people consorting with the enemy, advancing the enemy's cause. In some places that's called slavery. I'm through with it. (French 633)[50]

The novel's two controlling metaphors for (white) women's oppression are slavery and rape; however, French feels entitled to make ample use of both[51] while altogether evading a historical subtext of lynching, white male rape of black women as well as actual slavery. Given the author's proposal that her novel aims at keeping (American) women's memory alive to ward off patriarchal silencing and forgetfulness (French 679), *The Women's Room* becomes a telling instance of segregated (white) memory. Only the 'blackened' signs – in cooperation with the notorious political slogan "women are the niggers of the world," used to connote white female suffering – are ubiquitous in the novel.

A fictional genealogy of American feminism that could indeed realize the novel's excessively mimetic claims to historical verisimilitude would have to trace black and white women's investments in the two grand reform movements of the 19th century – both predecessors of American feminisms at large. French decidedly ignores that history as much as she eschews an investigation of the 1970s women's movement's roots in the Civil Rights Movement. The progressive emptying out of the sign of its referent, after the abolition of slavery, became the hallmark of a white feminist movement that cast itself as representative of women as category, but to whom black women as subjects, indeed their history of slavery and their agency deriving from that experience, were mute. Finally, the white middle class women's movement of the 1970s, so truthfully apprehended in *The Women's Room*, appropriated the sign from its referent altogether.

French's novel is able to raise the ante of 19th century thinkers by openly extending the allegory of slavery into the realm of sexuality, reproduction and marital rape, thus constituting white women as slaves themselves.[52] If Sánchez-Eppler in the context of white female abolitionist rhetorics can speak of "the presentation of slavery as a sexual, marital and domestic abuse" (1988, 246), French, a century after the Civil War, turns the metaphor on its head and describes patriarchal abuse **as** slavery. Catherine Stimpson criticized this development as early as 1971:

---

50 The allusions are ubiquitous, see, for example, French 217, 229, 230, 326.
51 Including a rather reckless take on the myth of the 'black rapist'.
52 She evacuates black women from her picture except for portraying one as a victim, also, of sexual abuse, who gets sentenced for murder of her rapist. A group of white women sets up an armed rescue mission to free the black woman, without success. As a result one of the novel's white protagonists dies gunned down by a police squad.

I believe that women's liberation would be much stronger, much more honest, and ultimately more secure if it stopped comparing white women to black so freely. The analogy exploits the passion, ambition and vigor of the black movement. It perpetuates the depressing habit white people have of first defining the black experience and then of making it their own. Intellectually sloppy, it implies that both blacks and white women can be seriously discussed as amorphous, classless, blobby masses. It permits women to avoid doing what the black movement did at great cost and over a long period of time: making its protest clear and and irrefutable, its ideology self-sufficient and momentous, its organization taut. (Stimpson 34)

Catherine Stimpson's essay; Frances Beal's contribution to Robin Morgan's collection *Sisterhood is Powerful* (1970): "Double Jeopardy: To Be Black and Female"; Sara Evan's book *Personal Politics: The Roots of Women's Liberation in the Civil Rights Movement and the New Left* (1980), Alice Walker's novel *Meridian* (1977) and her short story "Advancing Luna – and Ida B. Wells" (1981) all tried to come to terms with racism, with the tangled relationship between white (feminist) women and the Civil Rights Movement, and within it, the difficult ambivalences between black and white women. The vantage point of a 1990s academic (white) feminism seems to have eclipsed this second political moment of white women's involvement in, and profiting of, the cause of civil rights, by a very thorough saturation with discursive exigencies of theoretical study;[53] a text like Ruth Frankenberg's critique of feminism's unacknowledged whiteness, *White Women, Race Matters* (1993) meets a generation of younger women's studies scholars with a radical flourish promising historically new insight:

For when white people – and I was especially concerned about white feminists, since the project has its origins in the feminist movement – look at racism, we tend to view it as an issue that people of color face and have to struggle with, but not as an issue that generally involves or implicates us. (...) Thus, as white feminists participate alongside women of color in developing new theoretical articulations of 'difference' and the 'multiplicity' of women's experiences, there is, I fear, a danger that while increasingly theorists of color speak from concrete conceptualizations of what that multiplicity means to them, for white women visions of 'difference' and 'multiplicity' may remain abstract. (...) To speak of whiteness is, I think, to assign everyone a place in the relations of racism. It is to emphasize that dealing with racism is not merely an option for white people – that, rather, racism shapes white people's lives and identities in a way that is inseparable from other facets of daily life. (Frankenberg 6, 10)

---

53 Furthered by the ineffectualness or disappearance of an older feminist generation's personal memories.

Her argument in fact but reiterates the charges and arguments of the post Civil Rights Movement generation, whose legacy remains understudied.[54]

After more than two decades of feminist movement/s and gender(ed) theorizing (Hof 1995), of course, feminisms have had their momentous impact on American culture and academia, and have by far surpassed the propagandistic analogizing of the 1970s; the parallelism between 'blacks' and 'women' as oppressed groups has been replaced, however, by an ethnocentrically biased auto-focus of white women's theory and practice, as Chela Sandoval has pointed out in 1991:

> [W]hat I hope to have demonstrated is a commonly cited four-phase feminist history of consciousness (...) which I schematize as 'women are the same as men,' 'women are different from men," women are superior,' and the fourth catchall category, 'women are a racially divided class.' I contend that this comprehension of feminist consciousness is hegemonically unified, framed, and buttressed with the result that the expression of a unique form of U.S. third world feminism, active over the last thirty years, has become invisible outside its all-knowing logic. Jaggar states this position quite clearly in her dictionary of hegemonic feminist consciousness when she writes that the contributions of feminists of color (such as Paula Gunn Allen, Audre Lorde, Nellie Wong, Gloria Anzaldúa, Cherrie Moraga, Toni Morrison, Mitsuye Yamada, bell hooks, the third world contributors to *Sisterhood Is Powerful*, or the contributors to *This Bridge Called My Back*, for example) operate 'mainly on the level of description,' while those that *are* theoretical have yet to contribute to any 'unique or distinctive and comprehensive theory of women's liberation.'(Sandoval 9)[55]

Adrienne Rich's call on white women to acknowledge their own privileged location within history (Rich 1986) – by way of response to Third World Women's interventions against white women's ethnocentric 'noblesse oblige' (Mc Dowell, Hooks and Childers) – tried to open a debate within white academic feminism about differences within the category "women"; that debate would consequently be supported and theorized but also be removed from its historical grounds, by poststructuralist demands. (De Lauretis 1990, Abel, Haraway, Homans, Friedman) Between the unproblematical allegory of (white) women as slaves, and the imagery of feminist theorist Jane Gallop's guilt-tripping (of white feminist academics in face of black feminist political and theoretical pressure) lies a complicated and unbalanced history of white denial, retreat, and hesitant acknowledgement:

> I realize that the set of feelings that I used to have about French men I now have about African-American women. Those are the people I find inadequate in relation to and try to please in my writing. It strikes me that this is not just idiosyncratic. (Gallop 169)

---

54 It remains to be seen whether the most recent return of academic interest in the 1960s as a historical period will fill this gap.

55 Exemplary texts for the appropriateness of Sandoval's criticism are Moi, and Braidotti 1991 and 1994.

Susan Stanford Friedman vividly narrates the phases of this black/white conflict in a recent article in Signs,[56] summing up her own argument as follows:

These three cultural narratives of denial, accusation, and confession – emerging as they do from different locations in the societal distribution of power along racial lines – can be interpreted provisionally as parts of a single story about race and ethnicity in the feminist movement, a metanarrative that can be reconstructed in its simplest structural form as follows: 'I'm not a racist, we are all women,' says a white feminist. 'You are a racist, you are different from me,' says a woman-of-color feminist. 'You're right, I am a racist,' says a white woman. I do not propose this metanarrative as a fixed structure that drives all feminist discourses on race. To do so would be reductionistic, blind to the nuanced heterogeneity of many manifestations of these cultural narratives. Moreover, each script has made and continues to make important contributions to feminist discourse. But what this strategically constituted metanarrative discloses is the underlying binary of white/other that operates within a victim paradigm of race relations. (...) By itself, it represents a dead end. It is hindering the development of a more broadly defined multicultural feminism whose agenda centrally includes the eradication of racism and the globalization of feminist theory and practice. (Friedman 11,12)

My objection to Friedman consists of a somewhat cautionary observation: it seems to me that rallying calls to a mutual multicultural goodwill of acknowledging differences beyond a white/black binary too easily negate not only the particularly oppressive character of that cultural, political and social relation, they also too nonchalantly step around the necessity of theorizing of precisely white women's/ and feminists' theoretical and historical investments in this relation. White feminist theory that owns up to its historical gaps, suppressions and misjudgements – beyond personalized moralistic declarations – may provide a theoretical and political platform for alliances beyond the binary opposition Susan Stanford Friedman criticizes.

Jane Gallop's guilt is treated too peripherally in Friedman's estimation – even though I agree with her rejection of latent "fetishization" – when she writes:

At still other times, this guilt has resulted in an embrace of 'other' women (...) At its most extreme, this embrace tends towards a fetishization of women of color that once again reconstitutes them as other caught in the gaze of white feminist desire. (S. Friedman 11)

I suggest that to read Gallop against herself, to take the "guilt" seriously, in order to proceed from it to responsibility,[57] may enable a willingness to concede that American history has left white women, and white feminism, something to make

---

56 This article provides also the best bibliography on the subject to date to my knowledge.

57 Which would necessitate to read past Gallop's narcissism.

up, something to re-member. Concluding with Robyn Wiegman's provocative observations then, serves the function of keeping the debate open:

The significance of the erasure of race cannot be underestimated, for while the socio-symbolic articulation of bonds among women makes possible a transcendence of male-dominated ideologies (...) this politics of identification (...) can only work to further deny the violent materiality of 'race' as a determinant of power relations among women. (...) The counter to this asymmetrical reading of cultural relations necessitates an expansion of feminist theory's gaze to include questions not only of masculine differences but also of disparities that traverse the sacrosanct division of gender, those in which women maintain power over various groups of men. (...) Any coherent notion of 'woman' is so thoroughly saturated by racial marking that incalculations of 'woman/women' become quite inadequate as the foundation for a feminist politics that seeks to escape the historical privilege of its white and Western formulations. (Wiegman 1992, 61,63)

2. Haunting Absences, Willful Displacements

2.1. Gertrude Stein's America: History as Repetition, Repetition as History

> The outstanding fact of late twentieth century European culture is its ongoing reconciliation with black culture. The mystery may be that it took so long to discern the elements of black culture already there in latent form, and to realize that the separation between the cultures was perhaps all along not one of nature, but one of force. (Snead)
>
> Listening up to completed understanding of the repeating that sometime is a completed history of each one is all my life and always I live it I love it and I live it. (Stein)
>
> Gertrude Stein did not like hearing him (Paul Robeson) sing spirituals. They do not belong to you any more than anything else, so why claim them, she said. (...) Gertrude Stein concluded that negroes were not suffering from persecution they were suffering from nothingness. She always contends that the african is not primitive, he has a very ancient but a very narrow culture and there it remains. Consequently nothing does or can happen. (Stein)

Gertrude Stein's texts have been receiving pronounced critical attention over recent years as avantgarde modernist subversions of the 'grand recits.' Mostly, critics have dealt with the formally innovative aspects of her writing:

> While some readers have successfully tried to decode Stein's "enigmatic" writings, others have maintained that the search for consistent patterns of meaning would violate the anarchic and migratory character of Stein's anti-patriarchal polysemy or have labeled her attempts at displaying 'a self-contained movement' as failures of communication. (Schiller, 511)

Lately, a tendency may be registered to situate Stein's work in historical, social and cultural contexts, to point out the importance of her textual debunking of patriarchal epistemology for feminist theory, to study her early work within the genre of immigrant writing, or to pay attention to Stein's subject position as a lesbian and as a Jewish woman writer.[58] Whereas I am aware of the particularly American conflictedness of Jewish people's whiteness that has offered by no means a socially se-

---

58 Schmitz, Ruddick, Walker, DeKoven 1983, 1988; Chessman, North, Saldivar Hull, Doane, Steiner, Bröck 1992, Hornung, C. Peterson. For extensive bibliographical references, see Kellner.

cure positionality, and whereas I am also aware of the potential attraction American blackness held for Stein as a late Victorian Baltimore 'outcast' herself,[59] I will treat the object of my inquiry here, *The Making of Americans*, as a white modernist avantgarde text.

In keeping with my introductory epigraph, I want to read *The Making of Americans*[60] as a literary artifact speaking to the interpenetration of white and black cultures. My stress, however, will not be placed on a reconciliatory aspect of this intercultural contact; I will read the novel as an ambivalent undertaking to appropriate or partake in black culture while at the same time negating its agency and history altogether.

MA starts out innocently enough, in a narrative mode, with the shortest possible allegory to evoke an oedipal mystery of family history, with a questioning of tradition and how to confront it:

> Once an angry man dragged his father along the ground through his own orchard. "Stop!" cried the groaning old man at last, "Stop! I did not drag my father beyond this tree." (*MA* 3)[61]

The text, however, abandons this beginning immediately – it is left behind only to haunt the reader as a beckoning of Stein's ambiguous position: will her text rupture the tradition of filial rebellion?

The first chapter, "The Dehnings and the Herslands," though it surprises us with a highly idiosyncratic style, actually narrates the immigrant and early Western American origins of the Hersland clan – if it says very little about the Dehning family – and its solid middle class American "family living" tradition.[62] *MA* then proceeds to decompose, to **un-make** any possible narrative of the "Hersland family" aggressively, in favor of an assortment of haphazard stories of people in and around the family, of quasi- philosophical musings of a narrative voice about the "bottom nature of human beings," about repetition as driving force in life and human history; of elliptic speculations about the nature of perception and writing, of making a descriptive list of "all kinds of men and women," of stylistic exercises as to how to capture the rhythms of speech and the mechanics of an exchange of words, of sheer loads of repetitive verbiage. It reads like a sometimes very funny, sometimes extremely tiring "stop and go" pattern of starting up one of the stories,

---

59 See C. Peterson on "Melanctha," Rogin, and Wynter 1979.

60 I am using, if not otherwise noted, the abridged Bernhard Fay edition. Hereafter as *MA*.

61 Significantly, Stein took this anecdote from Aristotle, see Doane 92,3.

62 Stein seems to have taken it as a given that all the "Americans" surrounding the family of her autobiographical remembering were white, or that is what we are lead to believe due to Stein's neutralizing: no color marking is white.

pretending to keep the narrative going, interrupting itself, abandoning the thread, digressing, making another effort at taking it up, renouncing it again, beginning again – until the narrator reaches a point of disillusionment, only to keep on "beginning."

Sometimes then very often there is to me not any kind of a whole one really in any-one and anything and now I am not really caring anymore anyway about this thing, about being a whole one in any one in any way. I am altogether a discouraged one. I am now altogether a discouraged one. I am going on describing men and women. (...) I know very well I am not knowing all the ways men and women are feeling living. (...) Do not crowd on me so all the other ones. *(MA 308, 323)*

Ruddick, and Doane see in these passages a transition to a third narrative voice, an "autobiographically projected" one (Doane 103). As Doane phrases it, "[t]he narrative is turned inside out and becomes the story of its speaker in the attempt to speak" (Doane 103).

The voice of the good son, the chronicler of middle-class life, gives way to two other voices: that of a psychologist, whose uses the characters to illustrate a theory of human nature with serious pretensions to truth, and the intimate voice of a hypnotized producer of sentences, with moods of her own and bodily rhythms that affect her way of putting words together. (...) [T]he intimate voice, once located, keeps slipping back into dialogue with the other two, which in fact are retained long after the third voice has joined them. Stein expresses "herself" as much through the conversation among the three as through her passages of seemingly unmediated self-revelation. (Ruddick 67)

Ruddick claims however, correctly to me, that the voices do not follow one another in isolated succession/progression. Which entails for me to hold the entire text in its intra-polylogue, as it were, accountable, and not to focus on Stein's tex-tual progress in favor of disregarding the 'politics' of her narrative.

In the course of the novel (...) Stein's disguised lesbianism emerges as a force that transcends conventional subjectivity and displaces her originally unconcealed masculine yearning (...)

writes Alfred Hornung (Hornung 106). In a similar vein, Ruddick and de Koven see *MA* as Stein's argument with and final critique of her philosophical fa-thers, like William James, and of her real father, connected to her textual coming out. To quote Ruddick:

Just as she was privately affirming her own sexual identity (in her lesbian relationship with Toklas in Paris), and in the process freeing up her rage at her own prohibiting father, her novel unleashes erotic processes in language that deal a blow to the ideological uni-verse of the nineteenth-century "fathers." (Ruddick, 57)

MA gradually inverts its narrative into a satirical, radically scornful[63] germinally lesbian reading of patriarchal power, in its scattering and paralyzing of the alleged family's story of progress. This is how Stein finally orchestrates the "unleashing":

> Everywhere something is done. (...) Everywhere where the thing that is done by some one comes to be done it is done it is done and done by some one. (...)There are almost quite enough doing that thing, every one doing that thing, any one doing that thing is doing that thing in the way that one, the one doing that thing is naturally doing that thing(...) The way of doing what is done and done in a family living is a way that a family living is needing being one in way existing(...) Any one in a family living is not knowing that another one in the family living is doing something and doing it again and again. Any one in a family living is doing something and doing it again and not any other one in the family living is knowing that thing is knowing that that one is doing something and is doing it again and again and again. (*MA* 409,412)

The orgasmic "someone doing something, again and again" that the text obsesses with, no matter how concealed under anyones and everyones and their family living, is resonant of the address to the "brothers singular" in the beginning of the text that critics have unanimously read as its coding of Stein's "singularity" as a lesbian writer:

> Now singularity that is neither crazy, sporty, faddish, or a fashion, or low class with distinction, such a singularity, I say, we have not made enough of yet so that any other one can really know it, it is as yet an unknown product with us. It takes time to make queer people, and to have others who can know it, time and a certainty of place and means. (...) Brother Singulars, we are misplaced (...). We flee before the disapproval of our cousins, the courageous condescension of our friends who gallantly sometimes agree to walk the streets with us. (*MA* 20)

"Someone has been standing up and is then doing something," becoming visibly queer, because "any one can go on not doing this thing not living in any family living." And, in the last pages of *MA*, there "are many of them, that is a natural thing." (*MA* 406, 407)

In that last chapter, a coda to the text, Stein gives up any narrative or even descriptive claim, any kind of recognizable voice. The "History of a Family's Progress" contains no further interest in, or information about the Herslands or Dehnings family development. It is instead an extended meditation – at once static and musical – on writing oneself out of the oppressive structures of "family living," which at that point has become a metaphor for the patriarchal dominance of American culture *MA* tries to vanquish.

---

63 Ruddick spends much attention on examining the allusions to incest in one episode of MA (Ruddick 110) which, curiously, has been cut from Fay's abridged version.

Those last pages of *MA* essay the final rupture with remembering "family," life and death, and thus continuing under its influence, which is for Stein equated, and thus discredited, with historizing: "It is the element of remembering that makes novels so soothing."[64] The last sentence, however, casts typical Steinese doubt – she leaves the choice of "writing" or "history" to her readers: "Any family living can be one being existing and some can remember something of some such thing" (*MA* 416). Stein herself, as Doane remarks,

> did not go on remembering "family living," or borrowing from it in her writing as a paradigm of explanation. She later claimed that she wanted to do what she was doing so completely that she would lose it – lose, in other words, both the scientific and literary practices of the nineteenth century which relied upon a belief in reason, progress and patriarchy. (...) Having lost the 19th century, she never expressed any regret or nostalgia for it. Instead, she became an ardent advocate of the 20th century. (Doane 142)

Making America: Stein and Caliban

The point of my reading will be to bracket this aesthetic optimism and investigate *MA*'s complex ambivalence about American 19th and 20th century mythologies. Stein does move away from 19th century aesthetics, away from a humanist portrayal of bourgeois, male-controlled family growth as allegorical for history's progress, but she is not able, or not willing to step out of her own complicities with its suppressions. For all her breaches with bourgeois morality, patriarchal sexual politics and law-enforcing linearity in the realm of the Symbolic, her uncritical acceptance of American history as white middle class life and its ethnocentric noblesse oblige is stunning.

MA directly addresses its readers to establish both a political interest for and a clear commitment to a subject that will later be eroded, but whose confines the text ultimately does not renounce:

> Bear it in your mind my reader (...) [this is not a] kind of novel with a plot and conversations to amuse you, but a record of a decent family progress respectably lived by us and our fathers and our mothers, and our grandfathers and grandmothers (...) And so listen while I tell you all about us, and wait while I hasten slowly forwards, and love, please, this history of this decent family's progress. (...) I have it, this interest in ordinary middle class existence, in simple firm ordinary middle class tradition. Middle-class, middle-class, I know no one of my friends who will admit it, one can find no one among you all to belong to it, I know that here we are to be democratic and aristocratic and not have it, for middle class is sordid material unillusioned unaspiring and always monotonous for it is always there and to be always repeated (...) and I say it to you and you are to listen to

---

64 I take this quote from Doane (151) who is citing from Stein's "Portraits and Repetition."

it, yes, here in the heart of a people who despise it, that a material middle class who know they are it, with their straightened bond of family to control it, is the one thing always human, vital, and worthy it – worthy that all monotonously shall repeat it – and from which has always sprung (...) the very best world we can ever know, and everywhere we always need it. (*MA* 31)

History, in any sense of transcending "family existence," is actually the one thing most absent in Stein's myopic eulogy to the white American middle class, which stands in sharp contrast to Stein's claim to "believe in reality like Caliban." At its beginning, *MA*'s "history" of the Dehnings is spaced with episodes of washing routines signaling in its metaphoricity a white (cultural/ historical) spotlessness; the idealized cleanliness functioning as a screen for historical American "dirt" (blackness) that white immigrants could not afford to be tainted by.[65]

He was not foreign in his washing. Oh, no, he was really an American. It's a great question this question of washing. One can never find any one who can be satisfied with anybody else's washing. (...)
It was good solid riches in the Dehning house (...) And always there were complicated ways to wash, and dressing tables filled full of brushes, sponges, instruments and ways to make one clean (...)
In ways to wash, to help out all the special doctors in their work, in sponges, brushes, running water everywhere, in hygienic ways to air things and keep one's self and everything all clean, this house that Julia was to make fit for her new life which was to come, in this it was very like the old one she had lived in, but always here there were more plunges, douches, showers, ways to get cold water, luxury in freezing, in hardening, than her mother's house had ever afforded them. In her mother's house there were many ways to get clean but they mostly suggested warm water and a certain comfort, here in the new house was a sterner feeling, it must be a cold world, that one could keep one's soul high and clean in. (*MA* 14, 27, 30)

As Roediger suggests:

[B]lackness came to symbolize that which the accumulating capitalist had given up, but still longed for. Increasingly adopting an ethos that attacked holidays, spurned contact with nature, saved time, bridled sexuality, separated work from the rest of life and postponed gratification, profitminded Englishmen and Americans casts Blacks as their former selves. (...) Blackness and whiteness were thus created together. (Roediger 1991, 95)

MA's purview does not present any awareness of the acutely racialized inflection of American history, even though the narrative voice's insistence on the use of cleanliness contains undertones of a carefully measured and checked irony. "Clean" (white), of course, is also the color of an innocent racial consciousness. The puritan

---

65 And, it should be stressed again, that was a particularly close to home contaminative influence for Jewish immigrants. See Rogin.

litany of "Wash me and I will be whiter than snow" seems to have reached far beyond Anglo-Saxon subjectivity. It functioned for otherwise rather diverse immigrant populations as a unifying barrier against being contaminated with insight into an American history that was not predicated on immigrant (upward) mobility, freedom of feudal servitude, destitute poverty and religious persecution and capitalist promise. Morrison has extracted this acculturation:

The new setting would provide new raiments of self. (...)In the New World there was the vision of a limitless future, made more gleaming by the constraint, dissatisfaction, and turmoil left behind. It was a promise genuinely promising. (...) One could move from disclipline and punishment to disciplining and punishing; from social ostracism to social rank. One could be released from a useless, binding, repulsive past into a kind of history-lessness, a blank page waiting to be inscribed. (...) As a metaphor for transacting the whole process of Americanization, (the) Africanist presence may be something the United States cannot do without. (...) American means white, and Africanist people struggle to make the term applicable to themselves with ethnicity and hyphen after hyphen after hyphen. Americans did not have a profligate, predatory nobility from which to wrest an identity of national virtue while continuing to covet aristocratic license and luxury. (...) Africanism is the vehicle by which the American self knows itself as not enslaved, but free; not repulsive, but desirable; not helpless, but licensed and powerful; not history-less, but historical; not damned, but innocent; not a blind accident of evolution, but a progressive fulfillment of destiny. (Morrison 1992, 34, 35, 47, 52)

MA emphatically – by way of a textual insistence not warranted by any narrative need – integrates immigrant success with American (white-) washing:

Nay how can he [Henry Dehning] ever have it in him to feel it now as really present to him, such things as meekness, or poor ways or self attendance or no comforts, it is only a fear that could make such things be now as present to him, and he has no such a fear ever inside him, not for himself ever or even for his children, for he is strong in a sense of always winning. (*MA*, 12)

Following Priscilla Wald's[66] discussion of a possible connection between the actual turn-of-the-century history of immigration legislation, and *MA* as a novel, Alfred Hornung reads the text as a largely autobiographical immigrant narrative:

The generic evolution from the realistic Victorian novel to the birth of an experimental modernist fiction can be seen as corresponding to the process of of cultural transformation of Europeans into Americans. (...) A modernist experimental version of the realistic immigrant novel seems to have provided the necessary frame to incorporate all of

---

66 Priscilla Wald is credited by Hornung with "drawing analogies between the passage of laws and stages of the composition of *MA*. The comprehensive naturalization legislation of 1906, Wald maintains, coincides with Stein's resuming composition of her novel" (115).

Stein's latent and manifest concerns, particularly at a time when American naturalization politics became very exclusive. (...) As the title of the novel suggests, the goal seems to be the creation of a collective subject, that of the making of Americans. (...) While the "foreign" and "foreign American" generations underwent the sea voyage and difficulties of getting settled in the new land, the "American" generation gains its identity through the powers of the recollective and reconstructive mind. (Hornung 1995, 104,105)

Hornung takes *MA*, or at least its narrative part, in terms of its content seriously and more literally minded than recent poststructuralist criticism has been willing to; his reading however, shares *MA*'s assumptions with regard to American genealogy and thus by ignoring white ethnicity, "[redoubles] its hegemony by naturalizing it."[67] Hornung quotes Stein's famous passage:

It has always seemed to me a rare privilege, this, of being an American, a real American, one whose tradition it has taken scarcely sixty years to create. We need only realize our parents, remember our grandparents and know ourselves and our history is complete. The old people in a new world, the new people made out of the old, that is the story that I mean to tell, for that is what really is and what I really know. (*MA*, 3)

and then goes on to abstract from there the gist of his argument:

The process of the making of Americans takes place in the story of three generations (...). Self-knowledge is apparently the result of relating family relationships and narrative accounts. (Hornung 105)

MA's white immigrant optimism is entirely ignorant of, or negates the role of the Middle Passage in the making of America and claims an access to the New World that can by no means be considered representative of all Americans. White third generation young Americans' attempts at recuperation of the processes of their Americanization, like Stein's, include a sharing in the project of national forgetting; slave narratives and early black American autobiography after the Civil War would have rather different stories to tell about American origins (Davis and Gates). No general American acquisition of generationally connected self-knowledge can be filtered from Stein's particular narrative: for Americans of African descent both, the possibility to know their ancestors and the option to narrativize their generations, were severely restricted if not completely destroyed by Middle Passage and slavery. Hortense Spillers phrases it compellingly:

The symbolic order that I wish to trace in this writing, calling it an "American grammar" begins at the "beginning," which is really a rupture and a radically different kind of cultural continuation. The massive demographic shifts, the violent formation of a modern African consciousness, that take place on the subsaharan continent during the initiative

---

67 Coco Fusco, in Hooks 1990, 171.

strikes which open the Atlantic slave trade in the fifteenth century of our Christ, interrupted hundreds of years of black African culture. We write and think, then, about an outcome of aspects of African-American life in the United States under the pressure of those events. (...) The human cargo of a slave vessel – in the fundamental **effacement and remission of African families and proper names** – offers a counter-narrative to notions of the domestic. (...) Even though the captive flesh/body has been "liberated," and no one need pretend that even the quotation marks do not matter, dominant symbolic activity, the ruling episteme that releases the dynamics of naming and valuation, remains grounded in the originating metaphors of captivity and mutilation so that it is as if neither time, nor history, nor historiography and its topics, shows movement, as the human subject is "murdered" over and over again by the passions of a bloodless and anonymous archaism, showing itself in endless disguise. (Spillers 1987, 68,72; emphasis added)

I want to place *MA*'s evolving project of producing **one** "orderly history of everyone" in the context of "rupture" and historical "effacement." Seen from this angle, the envisioning of a "universal, anthropological self" (Hornung 108) which critics have located as textual drive in *MA*, appears as a rather obsessive aim: a totalizing gesture predicated on Stein's belief in a "bottom nature" of all "kinds of people"[68] with only "variations" to disturb the "resemblance" (*Gradual* 245). Even if indirectly, those observatory musings share in contemporaneous pseudo-scientific discourses of human development that particularly within the American context were insistently punctuated by racialized and racist considerations.[69]

Critics have seen *MA*'s dramatic abandonment of "history" in favor of a textualized desire to produce "lists" and "descriptions" as a democratic inspiration implying in its very universalization that "potentially all people can become Americans" (Hornung 109). Others read it – post Barthes – sharing Stein's "contempt for ordinary mimesis" (Schiller 521) as progress on an aesthetical scale: "Gertrude Stein did not only attempt to reform the conventional role of reference but increasingly worked to **abolish** it completely" (Schiller 517). Realism, to Stein, was melodrama: an assortment of fictions about their lives people hold on to for sentimental reasons.

A gradual dissolution of Stein's 'imperial' project is – as *MA* cannot fail to demonstrate – inevitable, since the infinite information gathered becomes too excessive to retain. The possibility of absolute knowledge about "all kinds of men and

---

68 Gertrude Stein, "The Gradual Making of Making the Americans," 253. Hereafter as Gradual.

69 For a pertinent discussion of the conflicting but also intermingling theories of monogenesis (which might be heard in the allusive "bottom nature of human beings") versus polygenesis ("all **kinds** of men and women"), see Fredrickson. *MA* 's abandonment of the listing project marks the point at which the theories cancel each other out, while in *Gradual* Stein describes a manageable project of encompassing description.

women" is not negated, however, it only does not hold anymore aesthetic promise for *MA*; the coda passages abandon it laconically:

> There are kinds of men and women. Many of each kind of them have been living. Many of each kind of them are living. Very many of each kind of them have come to be dead ones. Many of each kind of them are living. There will be lists of kinds of men and women. There will be many lists of them. There is coming to be a list of kinds in men and women. There will be a list of them. There has been some decsription of a piece of a list of them. There will be a list of them. (*MA*, 398)

MA's disillusioned consequence is the retreat into the self-referential and immanent textual "bliss"[70] of its final chapter. Behind *MA*'s optimistic will to truth about everything and anyone in terms of quasi scientific classifications lies not so much a democratic impulse as a pronounced disinterest in particular human beings' historical agency of their own making of (and being made into) Americans (that is, melodrama) – a dynamic category that no activity of typological listing will cover.

(Incon)sequence and sentence

Stein creates the "American language," as Maxine Hong Kingston has it, "sentence by sentence" (Hong Kingston 182), resulting in an inspirational break of narrative sequence. With respect to "American language" – a phrasing that claims a stark amount of representativity and cultural democracy – a hesitation should be allowed, however: It seems to me to be a subject position bespeaking cultural affluence and entitlement to be able to break sequence. The postmodern exultation in Kingston's praise has become extensively controversial, as is audible in Homi Bhabha's phrase about the "fragmented, displaced agency of those of who have suffered the sentence of history" (Bhabha 1992, 56), and whose artistic struggle might be therefore with the problematic options for re-narrativization and critical, yet effective self-inscription into language's sequentialness.

MA's preoccupation with sentences marginalizes their "Americanness," in favor of a relentless, almost didactically orchestrated tripping over (and into) the maze of

---

70 The term is Roland Barthes': "Repetition itself creates bliss." Barthes, too, works with allusion to 'blackness' in trying to establish a relation between certain kinds of repetition, and the feeling of bliss: "[T]o repeat excessively, is to enter into loss, into the zero of the signified. But: in order for repetition to be erotic, it must be formal, literal, and in our culture this flaunted (excessive) repetition reverts to eccentricity, thrust toward marginal regions of music. The bastard form of mass culture is humiliated repetition (...) the word can be erotic on two opposing conditions, both excessive: if its is extravagantly repeated, or on the contrary, if its is unexpected (...) In both cases, the same physics of bliss, the **groove**, the inscription, the **syncope** (...) (Barthes, 41,42, emphasis added).

narratological conventions beyond national languages, forcing readers to unlearn how to read. The excessive authorial struggle to free a novelistic text of 19th century conventions seems to overwrite any project of writing Americans' history promised at the outset of *MA*. Particular "American families" have finally turned into "someones living," curiously disembodied, disnamed; the text piles up blank abstracted activity, as it were, reveling in an extended series of predicates continuously present: being in living, doing, remembering, hearing, saying something, knowing something, standing and doing something, existing; the signification drowned out by its own sound.

For Stein, Americanness has become language – paced by antirealist abstractions. Both of the commanding tropes of *Gradual*, beginning and moving in spaces of time, share in American mythology via their metaphoricity, transferring what Stein considered prototypical American (cultural/historical) activity into the very mechanics of language: the American ancestor "always making for himself a new beginning" (*MA*, 54) is transformed into the motor impulse of her writing: "and then, to begin again" and into its factual pulsing shape.

> I will try to tell it in every way I can as I have in all the writing that I have ever done. I am always trying to tell this thing that a space of time is a natural thing for an American to have inside them as something in which they are continuously moving. Think of anything, of cowboys, of movies, of detective stories, of anybody who goes anywhere or stay at home and is an American and you will realize that it is something strictly American to conceive a space that is filled always filled with moving and my first real effort to express this thing which is an American thing began in writing The Making of Americans. (*Gradual* 258)

Again, a quintessential American location: "a space filled with moving"[71] translates brilliantly into a textual operation, into Stein's notorious (and gender/raceless) continuous present.

The novel (a)voids history of Americans, since any representation/construction of it would necessarily take a site of compromised negotiation of the realism Stein wants to leave behind. Her making of Americans becomes mired in textual stasis and authorial disavowal; it is ultimately not the text's interest to invest in a **particular** reality of American patriarchy. Consequently, the 'last' abstract narrative voice in *MA* retreats into isolated circularity, its critique of the liaison between patriarchy and realism pointing back on itself as the sole sign of that critique:

---

71 To write "American" here is almost an act of erasure: the connotations of both "space" and "moving" having been so starkly different for Americans depending on their individual axes of race, class and gender.

Thus to both write as a genius and to love as as a lesbian, Stein negotiated the cultural position of man, effectively identifying against herself as woman. (...) As she pursued her singular genius against the norm, she pursued an autobiographical practice against the norm, resisting (...) the evolutionary story, the self-conscious narrator, the identification between autobiographical narrator and autobiographical subject, the unitary voice, all the rhetorical and narrative components of a patriarchally inscribed identity. From the writing position of the 'man/woman' she could critique the narrative of the paternal origins and the identities those origins secured. (S. Smith 73,4)

Repetition Pounding Louder: Displacing Blackness

My point is that we as critics should not partake in that projection: the lonely genius is (quite a masculine) fiction Stein styled for herself as maybe the only space she could envision to make and name her writerly self. Obviously she felt able to abandon the "I" narratologically, as she did in favor of the "someones" in the last chapter of *MA*, and even more obviously, in *Tender Buttons*. A strategy of forsaking individual ego would not be effective, however, in an early 20th century's cultural/literary marketplace characterized by aggressive hostility against female authorial subjectivity (Bröck 1992, B. Scott).

I will argue in the following that in her endeavor to counterwrite Victorianism, Stein indeed found artistic inspiration: in the black culture having surrounded her before her self-exilation to Paris. Even though she decided not to acknowledge its influence publicly, a connection might have been visible to some of her contemporaries – as we hear echoed in Richard Wright's otherwise so opaque applause to "Melanctha;" it has certainly been a lost cultural fact for decades up until the very recent surge of (white) critical interest in modernism's articulations with blackness, Africanness and "savagery" (Du Plessis, North, Marcus, Bröck 1992). Western modernity, as Matthew Brown phrases it, has "learned to 'cover up' this global and political point of rupture – African culture – through 'progressive' assimilation" (Brown 492).

How can woman write with authority? Few other women writers struggled as recklessly with the question as did Gertrude Stein. In that sense of subversion par excellence, she figured prominently on my list of authors whom I wanted to read as crossover texts of an engagement with patriarchal knowledge. When I was working on "Melanctha," however, I began to grope for an explanation of its strange vernacular quality that could not be anchored in postmodernist celebrations of her textual ruptures:

The text transforms hysteria into a desire that it speaks and embodies. As my close examination of the text tries to demonstrate, Stein is thus able to free female desire from the bounds of sentimental and melodramatic genres. However, she achieves this by using racist stereotypes of the "tragic mulatta" for her literary camouflage. (Bröck 1992, 505)

72

"Camouflage" is the key term here that Michael North pushes a step further in his 1994 reading of "Melanctha" as Stein's strategy of "donning the African mask" (North 66), of literalizing Baltimore black vernacular speech patterns[72] "to make a break with (her) own cultural past" (North 66). Other critics have responded to the same strangeness without perceiving or acknowledging its actual connection to blackness. According to Lisa Ruddick "Melanctha" envision(s) the possibility of a near-mystical participation in a sort of life-force whose sound is repetition. In "Melanctha," something called "real being" was associated with feelings bordering on "religion"; the character about whom those feelings circulated was the heroine, "whose structural signpost in the story was **repetition**, and whose thematic sign-posts were an intimacy with the cycles of birth and death and a (similarly nonlinear, if not repetitive) wandering [sexual drive and desire]." (Ruddick 100, emphasis added).

Without taking into account any white/black inter-cultural contact Ruddick reads Stein's "hymn of repetition" in terms of an early psychoanalytical orientation, predating Freud (Ruddick 99) and

from a more spiritual perspective, [as] an expression of Stein's reverential sense of participation in the mysterious workings of the natural world. (...) Matter – what in *The Making of Americans* is called 'the solid dirt' – is where repeating happens. To feel 'recurrence' is to know 'the dirt.' (Ruddick 101)[73]

In a similar gesture, Georg Schiller senses blackness in Stein's writing without establishing a black creative context for it, however. He observes with reference to *Tender Buttons*:

This repetitive **rap** emphasizes the phonic properties of words and empties them out of their semantic content, an impression that is underscored by the hectic and driven quality of the **repetition**. (Schiller 519, emphasis added)

One reason for this critical 'miss' is the strategy Stein adopted in her writing – if one looks at the 'progression' from "Melantha" to *MA* – to accumulatively erase any embodied blackness in favor of inscribing "black style"[74] in its purest, most writerly abstraction.

---

72 She absorbed black speech mainly when working as a medical student with black patients and workers in a hospital. Most critics mention her apprenticeship there without following up on its consequences for Stein's aesthetics, except North, and C. Peterson.

73 The swirl of connotations in the cluster of "repetition," "rhythmic matter," and "dirt" becomes dizzying at this point if one cares to read beyond Ruddick's completely de-racialised reading where "race" is only a matter when black people occur.

74 I am using James Snead's term advisedly in the following passages.

Even if allowing for some ambiguity, Stein opposed masculine cultural properties on the one hand; on the other, she faced what Victorian ideology offered as a natural binary alternative she wanted at all cost to destruct. An oedipal narrative of origins, cleanliness, hardness, patriarchal linear articulation, teleological contours, and bourgeois identification of the legitimate artistic heir are, in this scheme of things, pitted against illegitimacy, dirt, sloppiness, (female) simplicity, shapelessness (not incidentally, all signifiers for blackness in a racist dictionary) – a series of oppositions vexing *MA* before their eventual ecstatic release in self-referential "beginning again" and "repetition." To find her textual production crammed between these two compromised interpellations necessitated a creative search, a "listening," indeed, for artistic options.

I always listen. I always have listened. I always have **listened to the way** everybody has to tell what they have to say. (...) I had left the medical school and I had for the moment nothing to do but talk and look and listen, and I did this tremendously (*Gradual*, 241, 243, emphasis added).

Critics have commented on Stein's intellectual and visceral loneliness before meeting Toklas – a biographical 'fact' that is written into *MA* most expressly by the now notorious "I am writing for myself and strangers," which only eventually, after years of singular production, gives way to her content with having found somebody "to hear her into speech" (Rich 1984, 185).

MA resolutely solves the dilemma by **enjoying** that which "leaps out of the frame"[75]. For white culture of Stein's time, that prototypical transgression – one which was nevertheless all around and intimately close to home – was black culture, but a black culture deprived of its own agency.[76] In a special issue of *Cultural Studies,* white cultural critic Ewan Allison poignantly characterizes the ways in which "black music" (which I use as a metaphor for and an instance of black style) has been "the inspiration in forging creative white ways of being admirable for their **presence to the times**" (Allinson 439, emphasis added) – a condensation which fits Stein's impetus and effect as neatly as his critical point: "white appraisals flowed unreflectively over the ideologies of black suppression" (Allinson, 439).

So what her text aggressively ignores – any racialized 'inflection' of American history – returns in it as aesthetic seduction: the jouissance of the "pounding"[77]. Repetition moves her, and "slowly it sounds louder and louder and louder inside me through my ears and eyes and feelings." (*MA* 302). Black style provides her

---

75 Hirsch comments on this similarity between Stein's and Barthes' antirealism (Hirsch 521), quoting Barthes 57.

76 See Lott, Roediger 1991, or Wynter 1979 on the pervasiveness of black cultural/ musical attractions available for white consumption at the turn of the century.

77 A term that soundingly conjures up (African/black) drum beat.

authorial imagination with a "space filled with moving" beyond the frame of tradition and helps to accept "queerness," to lovingly acknowledge "singularity," to make modernism.[78] Metaphorically speaking, she jazzed or ragged herself out of the 19th century.[79]

[L]istening up to completed understanding of the **repeating** that sometime **is** a completed history of each one is all my life and always I live it, I love it and I live it. (...) Sometime there is a history of each one, of every one who ever has living in them and repeating in them and has their being coming out from them in the repeating that is always in all being. Sometime there is a history of every one. Sometime there will be a history of every kind of men and women. Sometime there is a history of each one. There must be such a history of each one **for the repeating in them makes a history of them.** The repeating of the kinds of them makes a history of the kinds of them, the repeating of the different parts and ways of being makes a history in many ways of every one. (...) Repeating is **the whole of living** and by repeating comes understanding, and understanding is to some the most important part of living. (*MA* 219, 131 160, emphasis added)

Stein works repetition to create language as matter: as sound, like syncopated drumming, instrumental riffs, or improvisations. Rhythm drives her writing, the "organizing force of black style" that Leopold Senghor called "the most perceptible and least material thing" (Snead 68). To read the coda passages of *MA* to oneself aloud might be necessary to catch the beat of a "non-progressing temporal movement" (Snead 66):

There is no time to begin being in any family living for some being in family living. There is being in family living for some being in family living. There is no time for beginning being in any family living for some being in any family living. There is no time of beginning doing anything again for some being living in a family living. There is no time for being in any family living for some being in any family living. There is no time for not being in any family living for some being in any family living. When some one has done something, that one might then do that thing again. When some one has done something and some other one has done something and both of them have not then been doing some other thing, both of them might do something and one of them might do that thing and tell the other one and the other one might then be going on doing the same thing. When some one has done something that one might then do that thing again. When some one has done something and has then not done something that one might then do that thing again might then do something and then not do something. When some one has done something and some other one has then done something and it is a similar thing and they both then have not been doing something, they have similarly not been doing something then, they might be doing something and not doing something together. They might

---

78 The debate as to where exactly to place Stein's work on the continuum of modernism/postmodernism has occupied a number of critics, see DeKoven's essay in Kellner; it is decidedly not a focus of my argument here.

79 Carla Peterson's article focuses mostly on the influence of blues 'mentality' and vernacular idioms on "Melanctha," not on Stein's 'musical' writing.

and some one may think that they will and they may and then they may not, they may and then they may not, and they may not at all do something and not do something together. (*MA*, 404, 405)[80]

The two consecutive passages are taken quite at random; they only qualify as audiovisual demonstration for *MA*'s elective proximity to African-American music which "(exemplifies) the principles of repetition and montage in black culture" (Brown, 492). If one suspends critical fixation on genre, in this case literary narrative, Matthew Brown's discussion of black music properties[81] reveals parallels between the characteristics of music and literary writing in a Western tradition "concentra(ting) on harmonic, tonal or melodic development. (...) With harmony and melody predominant, shifts in a Western piece of music are experienced as motivated." (Brown 493).

In his carefully phrased exposition this

> trajectory is de-emphasized in the African-American tradition. Interplay between rhythmic patterns are predominant, and a shift occurs at the point when those patterns are rearranged. The montage form is heard (...) in traded phrases (...) in the abrupt shifts of meter and tone in African drumming. Bot reflect a montage technique that avows rupture. Western styles, however, are goal-oriented, **seeking resolution** through structured deviation; their shifts are covered over by harmonic progression. (...) The call-and response character of gospel and go-go, the **repetition** within the blues form, the **cuts to improvisation** within jazz performances – all exploit **circularity** and announce **disruptions** as fundamental expressive tools. (Brown 493, emphasis added)

Trying to hear again Stein's hymnic, circular word (over)flow compels one almost in visceral terms to feel the attractiveness of black music for her project of writing off / sounding out Victorian narrative.

Ruddick connects this formal daring as much with Stein's incipient knowledge of Freud's work and an anticipation of later psychoanalytical insight as with a "uniquely self-analytical way" of body-writing, as it were (Ruddick 99, 103). There are two arguments to be made in answer to that. One is contained in James Snead's discussion of tensions within Western culture's post-Renaissance suppressions of repetition and rhythmic returns. A "cycle of desire and repression" (Snead 68) came to haunt Western consciousness in modernity's philosophical suspicions, artistic configurations and early psychoanalytical explorations, after and through

---

80 Another suggestive idea comes to mind upon so much "doing that thing": Stein's very good ear might not have been beyond catching black sexual innuendos to inscribe them into these last passages of her text which have been read by most critics as rather celebratory significations of her coming-out, as early manifestations of the erotic voice of *Tender Buttons*.

81 Brown bases his observations on Middleton, Chernoff and Murray.

contact with African cultures figuring – in homogenized compression – as "radical alterity" (Brown 492). Snead reminds us that repetition and cyclical views of life and history are neither 'African' nor 'oriental' sui generis (and thus always already connotated as "primitive"); in European (cultural) history, those motions of cultural "coverage" (Snead 61) have rather been either subterranean, "observing periodic regeneration of biological and agricultural systems," and surviving in everyday life's ritualistic habits, or have been absorbed into a rhetoric of accumulation and growth versus decline and loss. Snead argues that

[b]latant repetitions of the folkloric, traditional or mnemonic sort that had character-ized Euopean oral poetry, medieval sagas and other form of narrative right into late six-teenth-century baroque literature began to be transformed into the pretense of an external reality being depicted, culminating in **literary realism** in the late nineteenth century. (...) In a sense, all representational conventions such as literary realism suppress repetition and verbal rhythm in the telling in favor of the illusion of narrative verisimilitude. (Snead, 73, emphasis added)

Thus, to propose – however emphatically – that Stein uncovered an "aggressive and primitive fantasy beneath an initially civilized narrative," as Ruddick (85) does, encapsulates Stein's choice of an artistic form within the binary regime of an ulti-mately racist culture/nature opposition. It serves to obscure any possible relation to American black art forms which are a priori subsumed under the primitivizing connotations of "natural expressivity." A borrowing on Stein's part of Freud par-takes in a larger modern project of borrowing that 'discovered' its own (cultural) "unconscious" as sayable/writable in its gaze at, and its listening to "primitivity" – a "dark continent" its own culture had constructed in the first place:

Only after Freud, Nietzsche, comparative and structural anthropology and the study of comparative religion could the frantic but ultimately futile coverings of repetition by European culture be seen as dispensable, albeit in limited instance of "uncovering." Moreover, the very aspects of black culture which had seemed to define its non-existence for the phenomenologist Hegel may now be valued in positive terms, gived a revised metaphysics of rupture and opening. (Snead, 64)

My second point is: the mention of Caliban next to Cézanne as model, in Stein's own declaration of her love for the "hymn of repetition," suggest to me black style as artistical and intellectual challenge:

In black culture, repetition means that the thing circulates there in an equilibrium. (...) (T)he thing (the ritual, the dance, the beat) is there for you to pick it up when you come back to get it. If there is a goal (Zweck) in such a culture, it is always deferred; it con-tinually cuts back to the start, in the musical meaning of cut as an abrupt, seemingly un-motivated break (an accidental da capo) with a series already in progress and a willed return to a prior series. (...) Black music sets up expectations and disturbs them at irregular intervals; that it will do this, however, is itself an expectation. This peculiarity of black music – that it **draws attention to its own repetitions** – extends to the way it does not hide the fact that these repetitions take place on the level of sound only. (Snead, 67, 69, emphasis added)

Stein actively disavowed this subtext of her work with commentary about the cultural and philosophical "nothingness" that "Negroes" suffered from in her view. On the other hand, she quite frankly accessed ownership of black material that blacks had no original claim to, according to her:

After 1925, Robeson's magnificent voice had brought him acclaim as a singer of spirituals in American and Europe, but Stein did not like to hear him sing spirituals. "They do not belong to you any more than anything else, so why claim them," she said. (Stein 1986 (1933), 257)

Both, reading Stein as a 'figure' and her writing, reveal a stunning complicity with the very Western teleology that, in terms of gender and literary creativity, she so ardently attacked. Her comment on African-American "nothingness" and her text's refusal to own its "debt" to black culture (Allinson 439) echo Hegel's "Geschichtslosigkeit" in no uncertain terms: For Hegel, as Snead summarizes,

the African, radical in his effect upon the European, is a "strange form of self-consciousness" unfixed in orientation towards transcendent goals (...) [He] overturns any European categories of logic. Second he has no idea of history or progress, but instead allows "accidents and surprises" to take hold of his fate. He is also not aware of being at a lower stage of development and perhaps even has no idea what development is. Finally, he is "immediate" and intimately tied to nature with all its cyclical, non-progressive data. Having no self-consciousness, he is "immediate" – i.e. *always there* – in any given moment. (Snead 63)[82]

Stein's double-faced strategy introduced a particular American racialized tension of attraction/repulsion to (white) modernism, a dilemma to last into postmodernism as well.[83] What was attractive to an intellectual mind acutely sensitive to the pretenses of historism, and the vacuity of bourgeois ideology, namely the being always there resurfaces paraphrased and abstractly aestheticized in Stein's "pounding" continuous present (and its many aesthetic successors). A sense of ethical commitment, or even a social desire to place oneself into American history and to ac-

---

82 I imply, of course, that for American intellectuals in the 1910s their conception of American black culture was synonymous with their ideas of "Africa" and "Africans." I base this implication on observations by North, and DuPlessis 1995, who have drawn attention to the metaphorical equation so much en vogue between even the most urbane African-American cultural production and the "Congo."

83 See Ross 1989 about white cultural fantasies.

knowledge black culture in the living materiality of its community was passed by with great nonchalance.

As much as her intimation of blackness helped Stein to initiate modernist writing, predating James and Woolf, it in effect added to her opacity for and disrepute with white bourgeois audiences at her time, but of course also created scandalous attention. It seems to me that black style as an anti-bourgeois "totem of the avant-garde" (North 66) functioned as a willed "representation of radical difference" (North), as long as to "become Negroes" (Huggins 93) could be exercised as a voluntary act of privilege. It did neither require a becoming white in the sense of acknowledging the privilege precisely of that subject position, nor any actual political or cultural closeness to or cooperation with black artists or intellectuals – if one does not count later intellectual habits of slumming. In terms of cultural politics, this idea opens the interesting speculation of how American culture could have been altered still, had the 20th century's white modernists[84] been willing and able to connect to black cultural producers in a purposefully creolized common and non-hierarchical agency.

While *MA* does not, for its inscription of a "queer" voice and its sheer artistic, if enigmatic brilliance partake in what Stallybrass and White call "the very blandness and transparency of bourgeois reason," in its whiteness (in the sense of a refusal of black agency) the text shares that bourgeois claim to superior "universality." The subject, in this view – and I want to analogize to the 'subjectivity' of Stein's text – is

> constituted through and through by the clamour of particular voices to which it tried to be universally superior. It is on this account that the very blandness and transparency of bourgeois reason is in fact nothing other than the critical negation of a social colourfulness, of a heterogeneous diversity of specific contents, upon which it is, nonetheless, completely dependent. (Stallybrass and White 199)

Dependency on "colourfulness" has a very particular resonance with the history of American (white) subjectivity, of course, and should thus, in the case of American writers, be taken with literalness. Any claim to universality within the American context has to be measured against its conscious racial 'inclusiveness' or lack/denial of it. Stein's appropriation of the figure of "Caliban" which I take to metaphorize both her self-conceived "illegitimacy" and its redemptive turn to black style should indeed be considered a transgression of sorts. In that it empowered her

---

84 DuPlessis' article on modernism's whiteness uses almost identical phrasing to make her point, writing of an "anxious desire for and resistance to black materials and sites" (DuPlessis 1995, 682); it speaks as much to a widely felt urgency for an investigation of whiteness as to the emergence of certain 'camps' within that debate. I see a willingness for a white acknowledgement of **debt** in DuPlessis work that very much echoes my own.

modernist authorship, it also reaches across the boundaries of an otherwise disrespected culture's creative repertoire. I read this ambivalence as a problematic momentum of Stein's work, as well as of American (white) modernism in general.[85] It raises aesthetic and ethical questions that should not be laid to rest by foreclosing the argument on simplifying grounds of either options for canonical (black) purity, or for a liberally, pluralistically owned American culture / history. Both ends of that specter eschew intricacies of aesthetic authorization, of ethical acknowledgement, and of the power relations at work within cultural mixing.

2.2. Josephine Herbst's Rope of Gold – *Trilogy: Radical Whiteness*

> It was during the 1930s that for the first time in American history the forms, roles, and functions of 'literature,' of 'American Culture,' of 'documentary expression,' of 'modernism,' of the institutions of 'Art' were fundamentally questioned, contested and redefined in the public culture at large as well as in critical thought. (Lenz)
> I have followed first the kind of haunting history of my family to its natural decay and end, that history only meaningful because of its wider implications (...) and those in turn carried me along to a point where an automobile worker in Flint, a peasant in Cuba, a soldier in Spain had become more real and moving than any memory of my buried family, but not obliterating that family or its meaning either. (Herbst)
> This weblike structure serves a number of rhetorical functions. First, it implies that one cannot build a monofocal narrative about history (...) Second, one cannot assume the individuality of a family, which is constantly being shaped by economics, history and politics. Third, although individuals feel atomized within American capitalism, appearing to drift along disconnectedly, they are interconnected by class. (Rabinowitz)

Critics have somewhat differed as to how to classify Josephine Herbst's *Rope of Gold*[86] trilogy: the terminology ranges from American realism, proletarian realism, radical writing, proletarian novel, a depression novel, to a materialist-feminist rewriting of typical Thirties' themes (Mayr, Bevilacqua, Rabinowitz, Foley, Newton and Rosenfelt); there is no controversy, however, about the re-canonization of this rather prolific writer/journalist's main fictional oeuvre within feminist, women's studies syllabi and within anthologies of radical writing in the USA.

---

85 Of course, the Harlem Renaissance brought forth exceptional moments of contact; the complicated and ambiguous issue of patronage is not covered by my argument.

86 The three novels are: *Pity Is Not Enough, The Executioner Waits,* and *Rope of Gold.* In the following as *Pity, Exe* and *RoG*.

Written under the influence of the greatest economic crisis this country has yet known, the 'Trexler trilogy' is not only an exploration of aspects of American experience that are often neglected in fiction, it is a protest against them as well. (Langer, *Pity* XII)

For the last ten years, ever since the re-issued paperback edition introduced by Elinor Langer and accompanied by her Herbst biography, the novels are being read again and have acquired some representative status as literary documents of the intricacies and contradictions of female authorship in the American left of the 1930s. As Paul Lauter remarks,

a novel cannot leap out of history, especially if it is committed to historical representation, like Herbst's. And none of the novel's concerns – the rise of fascism, duplicity and male chauvinism on the Left, the distant promise of a classless society – are resolvable within it. The recent revival of interest in Herbst (...) may suggest that the very ambivalence that kept her slightly apart from total commitments in the period's politics is appealing, in a way that forced conclusions are not, to a postmodern generation of readers. (Lauter 355)

The novels are being circulated, along with Tillie Olsen's work, with Meridel LeSeur's and Agnes Smedley's texts as icons of a female productivity that was struggling to find a fictional voice for feminist concerns 'before its time,' in a historical period unconducive to a prioritization of women's questions, specific demands and ideological challenges (Rabinowitz, Foley, Lauret).

The trilogy is an almost epical attempt to fictionalize American history from the end of the Civil War to the beginning of the Second World War, culminating in the Depression era;[87] although one finds a succession of male protagonists in the three novels, the trilogy's particular focus and vision is provided by the personal, sometimes rather intimate (historical) recollections of generations of white women. All the necessary observations about the formal properties of Herbst's writing have already been made, stressing its closeness to other experimental collage fiction of the 1930s such as Dos Passos, applauding her achievement at incorporating historical sources from the Herbst family archive like diaries, letters, newspaper scraps, and old bills into her narrative, as well as lamenting her strange insistence on her style, its obsession with the banal, gratuitous detail and its flirt with the melodramatic. For my argument, I will first comment on Herbst's use of multiple and sometimes conflicting points of view to puncture, and thus construct the narrative, since that formal feature is directly related to the novels' ideologically ambiguous perspective.

---

87 See Bevilacqua for a full length study of Herbst's oeuvre.

Herbst's express purpose is to use alternating narrative voices and perspectives throughout her novels as a means to fictionalize various, sometimes conflicting personal interests as well as antagonistic historical forces, to go beyond the 'local' biographical family intimacy, and to create a narrative holding up a mirror to American history as such.

If the text places such strategic value on multiplicity of perspectives, why did she restrict its range to those within reach of her white middle class and white working class protagonists? American history, in effect, is played out in only two adjacent fields: gender and class. One of Herbst's achievements, actually, was to probe into the overlapping and interactive oppressive mechanics of those two social contradictions. She constructs a gendered alternation of her individualist male protagonists' perspectives as 'makers' or direct participants of American history interlocking with female perspectives provided by closely generationally connected protagonists as chroniclers and observers of that same history. The conflicting choices these same already clearly gendered protagonists make about their personal, professional and social lives are overlaid and dominated by class interests. The work of 'race' or racialization in American history gets to be neutralized by Herbst's strategy of multiple perspectives despite the democratic claims of her technique.

History, in Herbst's novels, is double. All three texts struggle with a competitive juxtaposition of two historiographies. The quotidian, the small routines and events that, in sum, constitute social life which is remembered in private, personal, haphazard, associative and thus 'female' ways, is one. Diaries, letters, passed on conversations among family members are flattened out into a highly subjective narrative, an aggressively gendered version of historical memory. On the other hand, there is History as we know it from college history books: the Civil War's aftermath, the Frontier drive, the Gilded Age, World War I, sharpening class struggles and the Depression: protagonized by (white) men, on either side of the class divide. The middle class young man (Joseph Trexler) who goes west figures just as prominently as the capitalist villain (David Trexler) and the proletarian radical hero (Steve Carson); bourgeois historical illusionism, decadence and cynicism appear in the form of male characters Jonathan Chance and Lester Tolman. Generations of women chronicle that history via keeping records of men's lives. That dualism works **within** the novel but is effective also in the female author/narrator's admiring gaze on her favorite male character Steve Carson, or in the empathy for young Joe Trexler, both resulting sometimes in a complete symbiosis of point of view between the author's and the character's. **Female observation**, which is actually part of **small life**, is pitted against **male action**, which constitutes **big history**.

The novels' ambivalent, sometimes openly self-contradictory class politics displace this antagonism. The text seems carried by a tension between illusionary, sentimental longing for a good and peaceful middle class life of a supposedly socially healthier American past and revolutionary impulses to change the classist structure of American society. Again, these poles are gendered on a historizing plane: nostalgia figures in women; capitalist aggression (failed or successful), or its opposite revolution (in all cases: a desire for forward action) figures in the heroically symbolizing male characters Joe Trexler/ David Trexler and Steve Carson. Herbst's representation of the white lower middle class engulfs the reader in claustrophobia; it is dominated by antagonisms pitted against each other in ever repetitious moves without any hope of respite, redemption or flight, except in acts always already set up for failure, as is most clearly demonstrated in the case of the perennial adventurous loser, Joseph Trexler.

Male pioneer and frontier solidity gets to be aborted in sickness and is damned to the unfertility of mortgaged property on the first book's first page. The Trexler ancestor, in 1859,

had to lie on his sick bed (...) and know he'd not get up again and that his children and his wife were as stripped of all they needed as if he'd been improvident and drunk. (...) He died during the hard times of fifty-nine, along with John Brown's body (...)[88], but he was not really dead for a long time. (*Pity* 13)

From that point on, a struggle is set up between white men figuring easy, dirty, greedy and egoistic money versus white women's thrift, hard work, and family altruism – a textual economy of spending versus keeping, of waste versus lack. Seen in that light, Joe Trexler and David Trexler, for all their differences and conflicts in character, are just two sides of the same coin: they aim to make and spend. The real opposition is between them and their male entrepreneurial ambition and the female static schemes of keeping things for/in the family, perennially working hard, staying clean (innocent), economizing, making do, saving up. Racist allusions to the pressure on lower-middle class life in the North to stay on the "white" side of American history: white thrift against black lack of self-discipline are contained within but hidden under the conflict's engendering.

Both sides of this divide share an obsession of accumulation, an almost visceral desire for money which at times acquires a protagonistic prominence on its own and threatens to run the narrative into the ground. Joseph Trexler typically receives the narrative sympathy as the charming loser, whose material possessions grace the

---

88 This is a very early reference to blackness, and I will come back to it later: Why does John Brown appear here, and what is the function of the implied analogy between the two men being alive after death, supposedly in people's memory?

family forever, even though his greed kills his sister Catherine (*Pity* 165). Capitalist David Trexler becomes the focus of narrative scorn because he makes money but it does not materialize in visible cash for the family: he makes it to reinvest it, the ultimate reward to the family forever deferred. History becomes exclusively submitted to this perspective of craving tangible gains. The Civil War, for example, effects the narrative only as a founding moment in American society to have made the wrong (big) people richer and the right (small) people more vulnerable: "Big Business crowd out little men" (*Pity*,116) or "The war had changed everything" (*Pity* 67) are the refrains.

Women in their housekeeping mentality[89] are the true defenders of a healthy American middle class set against corporate capitalism's fraud, corruption, and greed. If "money was power, and power was freedom" (*Pity* 165), as Joseph Trexler claims, neither that kind of power nor that (male) kind of freedom interested those women. The double subject Joe/David is grounded in and tied to an omnipotent **desire** for money and things, fending off that other earlier American legend of decent self-sufficiency through hard work which becomes feminized in Herbst's texts. Middle-class (white) women are the always failing, but true keepers of the white American pioneer dream: work is the only reliable thing (*Pity* 138), and "steady ways were best." (*Pity* 119) Ultimately, the text's posture vis-à-vis American history is one of (white) female longing, obsessions and despair, with just very scarce interstices of other voices immediately drowned out.[90] The third novel (*RoG*) claims to introduce a transgressive perspective in the revolutionary forces of the late 1920s; however, it replays a variation on the former theme in Victoria's ambivalence between her attraction to radical change on the one hand, and her family attachment on the other. The individual want of money is at long last somewhat displaced, but the family keeping impulse is still operational. The trilogy's ambivalences about white middle class ideals reverberate in the text variously as nostalgia, obsession, disintegration, erosion and a romantic vision of transcendence. Herbst's antipode: the attraction of revolution in the (male heroic) flesh of Steve Carson – who, not accidentally, never worries about money – ultimately re-

---

89 See Gillian Brown on the impact of domesticity on various 19th century American discourses.

90 The most striking example is the "Oxtail" insert (Pity 80), that encloses Anne's memory of Miss Ferrol, who functions as the polar opposite to her own family's regime of "early worries and sewing and responsibility"; the most crucial attraction being her "laugh coming suddenly from her in the midst of gardening as she squatted on her haunches, throwing her head back and laughing and then laughing again as if the world were the best thing that had ever happened or thought of happening"and the "expansive way Miss Ferrol had for wasting time". Earthy laughter and wasting time were of course among the (black connoted) human qualities that a struggling white middle class could not afford to give way to.

mains projected into a vague future. This vision does not have a generation: Carson distances himself from his family life, Victoria loses her own. The question, if radicalized communitarian life among the working class masses (so strongly idealized in Victoria's impressions of the Cuban revolution) can possibly offer a social and individual transgressive alternative to the sentimentally enshrined white middle class (female) safety, is left unanswered by the final novel. In the end, Herbst simply overrules Victoria's disillusioned retreat into an emotional safety of family memoir, her self-acceptance as her female ancestors' daughter with Steve Carson's heroic social posturing.

Civil War

The trilogy constructs itself as white by using black people, matters of racialized/racist history and white perceptions of black culture as richly signifying, figurative **textual relief**. This structure is as much an integral driving mechanism within the text as it works as a shared impulse between text/author and readership.

Allusions that no American historizing text will fail to make to moments of American history intricately based on and connected to the oppression of black people may, however, not acquire a connotative potential of their own but have to remain safely bound into white perceptory agreements as to their 'meaning.' Paula Rabinowitz applauds Herbst's textual organization of her historical material in a "weblike structure" of great "complexity" and goes on to say:

This intergenerational obsession mirrors the mad frenzy of capital accumulation that followed the Civil War and continued until the threads unraveled after the 1929 stock market crash. (Rabinowitz 159,160)

To evoke the Civil War here serves the same function as it does within Herbst's text: it constructs a binary between a historical time before the Civil War and after it: the "before" evokes a somehow rational, even reasonable American history, whereas the "after" connotes wild, out of control, irrational. The observation mirrors the novel: its structure appears allegorically figured in the novels's episodes of Joe's adventures in a decadent, chaotic, money making post Civil War South which follows directly on the heels of a pre-Civil War pastoral of his childhood. The American economy indeed underwent a transformation from self-reliant, rather rural, not yet fully capitalized modes of production and social organization to rapidly industrializing, urbanized forms pushed by capital accumulation on a large scale, producing a massive change in the distribution of home and land ownership in the last decades of the 20th century, a process amplified and speeded up by the results of the Civil War. It is, however, crucial to distinguish critically between a historiographic account of these factual changes, even including a representation of the cultural, emotional consequences American society experienced through that kind of progress, and a nostalgic reverence for supposedly 'untainted,' uncorrupted and politically/socially **innocent** middle class life as in Herbst's text. Her condensation of pastoral versus madness split by the war's axis reveals a lot more about American mythological sentiment than it informs us about historical developments.[91]

The Southern episodes effectively based on this binary suggestively imply a narrative of American history somewhat contaminated by the freedom of black people. Those episodes insinuate that a lot of 'bad' capital could be made after the Civil War, as opposed to supposedly good, clean frontier money in an immigrant working people's America somehow void of blackness; as if that capital accumulation did have something to do with black people, was somehow infected by way of having been made in a new historical context based on their legal freedom: If it hadn't been for the Old South being 'freed,' being there for the Northern carpetbaggers for the taking, American ideals would not have been corrupted that quickly, or even that radically at all. One of the Yankee power brokers Trexler overhears in a conversation embodies the drive to profitable enterprise based on a contempt for the cause of abolition and for free black people; only the latter imprints itself on Trexler's consciousness **and** on the narrative.

[W]hy you'd think the fellow never get a wink of sleep for worrying about the poor black devils and their sorrows and how bad they'll feel if they ain't made free and equal with the vote. Now you and I know that Bullock don't give a little finger for the black man, but he wants his vote and he's cute enough to see if he can get business going with Yankee money, he'll keep his power. And Yankee money won't invest unless it sees the South humbled, humbled low, with nigger votes choked down its throat. There's not a handful of men in this country that care what happens to the Negro, if he starves or votes or what he does and the funny thing is that some of this handful is made up of the old masters. Yes sir, it ain't only the abolitionist but the same old masters right here in Geawgie that cares what becomes of ole Sambo. (*Pity* 26)

This cynicism implies a moral decay that equalizes perpetrator and victim, by staging this historical moment as a game being played between "ole Sambo" and the profiteers.[92] It leads us via readerly tolerance for Joe's admiration of the old Southern ways – since we know he is so naive – into subtle complicity with his point of view:

---

91 Michelle Cliff's *Free Enterprise*, for one, responds to that nostalgia by laying bare a narrative of ethical corruption settled into United States' foundational conceptions. For historical verification, see also Morgan 1972 and 1975.

92 Wynter's analysis becomes pertinent here (1979).

Fawcett was elected to the Senate. A bunch of Negroes came down from Chattanooga in the state elections and Joe went around to the polls with them to show them where to put their marks for Boss Fawcett's men. Afterwards he herded them on the train to Tunnel Hill and they made their marks there again. There must have been seven carloads made the trip down that day. (*Pity 47*)

The text itself as much as Rabinowitz' remark make use of arguably the most radically racialized momentum of American history; both are pulling a plug in their respective audiences' emotional repertoire to call up identification with an America that wanted to be good and pure; readers are positioned in a textual identification that sees American history as going downhill **after** and **by force** of post Civil War effects. Indeed, not for the first time, Northern capital in the United States was amassed by making use of racialization, or more specifically, by making racist use of black people[93] – a fact that Herbst's texts quite vividly, if unwittingly gives away.

This historical moment, however, becomes effectively obscured by Herbst's narrative strategy of focussing readerly empathy, if not sympathy, on "poor Joe." Herbst even blurs Joe's and the narrator's perspectives at the cost of any readerly distance with regard to Joe Trexler's racism against "niggers," to make her point. A real historical and aesthetic challenge for a novel that presumably takes on American history, namely the post-war South's free African-Americans, figure as stage props for the deluded white petty bourgeois hero and his post-pubescent ambitions. The narrative judges Trexler completely within his own parameters of success and failure: the innocent young man does not know how to play the big guys, how to win, the text says, but sees no other problem, historically. If one was not reading a supposedly progressive radical historical novel, she would not need to feel too surprised, but Herbst has raised the stakes of historical truth and moral righteousness too high for her narrative.

None of these textual maneuvers even comes close to basing the narrativization of Reconstruction on an **inclusion** of black people as legally free subjects and citizens to let them figure as subjects of American history, or to deal with any of the rather fatal political and social contradictions of the period. Moreover, this erasure from sight is actually doubled: once it works **within** the trilogy, and on a second level, **within** the negligence of critical commentary. A context of slavery, abolition and racial conflict is aggressively evoked and at the same time nonchalantly denied, by way of displacing the South, and the authority to speak about it, onto a tragicomical protagonist like Joe and his deluded anecdotes. Herbst does not compensate the vexing absence of the Klu Klux Klan, lynchmobs, voting manipulation and other Southern atrocities to her socially blind hero's eyes by any intervention of

---

93 See Goldfield 109-114.

author/narrator either but instead drowns readers in details given from the least pertinent perspective. Herbst's strategy of passing point-of-view around to the point of dizziness, to convey a democratic and as spread out panorama of the everyday as possible fails her with regard to black Americans. She does not employ her own strategy consequently enough to inscribe either black historical participation, or at least points-of-view directly confronting the racialization of United States history.

Nigger Heaven versus White Elefant

Very characteristically, in Herbst's writing, moments eminently pertinent to the narration are buried under gossipy detail, or appear as completely insignificant or inconsequential pieces of text. Insofar as that mirrors a non-linear, non teleological concept of narration in which 'meaning' is not authoritatively assigned, her 'female' voicing of a quotidian randomness that makes sense only in hindsight – a process she sought to reconstruct in her writing – seems a valid strategy.[94]

By this strategy, the text's whiteness appears almost completely neutralized, but is not rendered ineffective. The narrative signifies only in passive signs, as it were, an acknowledgement of American history as racialized but does not afford to foreground and engage that fact. The most crucial of those passive signs, is the juxtaposition of two 'locations' in the narrative (in the first and the second volume of the trilogy) as a complex racialized, blackened metaphor of the erosion of American white middle class life – one of these stunning textual instances that makes one wonder how something so crucial may on the textual surface appear so peripheral as to be merely atmospheric.

At its very beginning, *Pity* provides us with a miniature anecdote about Aaron, the third of the Trexler brothers, and the least spectacular one by the novel's own terms. Upon Joe's leavetaking for the South,

[T]hey stood waving handkerchiefs and Joe leaned far out waving. (...) They all turned homeward, Catherine to school to be a teacher, Aaron to the store to sell thread, a bar of soap and Dr. Ruff's Vegetable Compound and perhaps toward night to negotiate a quarter from the till and make an excuse to "walk out" after supper to Concross Dixie's Minstrel Show. Because of their mother's crying the children stayed clear of her that day. Her slow even determined tears had stopped but she sat there, a wooden figure with a wooden face. Aaron ate with a good appetite and read his paper, then cleared his throat and said he'd walk out, was gone, the quarter from the till heavy as a lead dollar in his jacket until it was safely slid under the window and he was stowed away in nigger heaven. There he let out a long sigh and hunched to the stage below (...) Mary Trexler sat

94   See particularly Rabinowitz for a detailed reading of Herbst's narrative strategy.

for hours ripping bastings and felling seams, found stockings to darn and darned them and after that, just sat, trying to read her Bible. (*Pity* 9)

From my vantage point of 1990s discourse on racialization, this passage almost works like a caricature of late 19th century middle class whiteness and it may thus look like a gratuitous exercise to read it again. Supposing that discourse did not exist for Herbst's contemporaries (and some later generations) however, I want to point out its significant potential to call up racist, or at least subconsciously racialized interpellations among white readers.

The effect is created by a series of binary oppositions. Staying: leaving; sitting: walking out; work (teaching, darning socks): having fun; stillness (for hours): activity (ate with appetite, read, went out); aggression turned inward (ripping, felling seams): release of emotion (letting out); uprightness (determination, figure): moral decay (Aaron hunched); thrift (darning old socks): expense (a nickel spent uselessly); motherly tears: male indifference; family safety: individual male safety (the money and Aaron stowed away); transparency (teacher): secrecy/lies (to negotiate a nickel); repression (wooden): sexual satisfaction (a long sigh); mother/daughter: son. At first sight, this is an almost overwrought condensation of innocent 19th century late Victorian gender conflict, sharpened still by oedipal overtones. Only the opposition between "Bible" and "Minstrel Show" reveals a distinctly American problematic displacement of that innocence.

The bad son's badness is not simply caught in the image of "walking out" on his good mother, but in a rather more threatening metonymic connection to blackness: he is walking out and down, actually descending into a "stage below," the hell of a minstrel show. Whereas a simple oedipal 'betrayal' would stay within the law of the (white) same, Aaron's hunching down to blackness displaces his actions' threat to his mother onto that very blackness. What the 'good mother' has to fear, then, is not so much the other gender's infidelity to family values, but the subversion, the erosion of a value system commonly held between her and the next male generation by an opposition related to, and in touch with, the other **race**[95]. That paranoid scenario does not materialize; however, as if to compound its anticipation, readers learn at a later point that is has been ineffective Aaron, of all the Trexler children, who led a fulfilled happy sexual life with actress Miss Ferrol, even if he – wisely – shrouded its illegitimacy in secrets.[96]

---

95 See Lott 1993 on blackface minstrelsy and male bonding.

96 Aaron's ultimate betrayal of Miss Ferrol in the transactions to force her to sell her house and lot to his mother and move out of his family's way to Philadelphia results in her death in childbirth, which reads like biblical punishment for his, **and her** bad ways.

I now suggest reading this passage in conjunction with its echoing coda, a passage in *Exe*. Up to this point, the novel has faithfully chronicled the erosion of the Trexler family's white middle class life standard and the disappointment of their assumptions, desires and confidence. Historical time is 1934: Anne Wendel, Mary Trexler's daughter, sits in desperation, trying to comprehend her daughter Rosamond's suicide in a willed car accident. She does not find consolation in the bible anymore, a secularized, disappointed version of Mem Trexler. She tries hard by keeping herself busy, but cannot avoid facing her loss of Rosamond to the dire times of the Depression years: "The White Elefant was really not a shelter for anyone anymore." (*Exe* 213) White Elefant, the name the Trexlers gave their house in Oxtail, has functioned throughout the narrative as a perfect metaphor for white middle class homeliness and comfort: big, strong, solid, perennial, stoic, undisturbed it was the guarantee of their existence. The white middle class family, the image now implies, will not save its Depression generation from economic and social onslaught.[97]

The two chronotopic metaphors frame a cultural social space of disintegration of white middle class existence wherein the **touch of blackness** in "nigger heaven" subtextually prompts the onset of disorientation that becomes fulfilled in the threat to or loss of white privilege (to feel homed in society) as social shelter. Moreover, the Herbstian metaphoric frame suggests in the evident binary complementarity of nigger = heaven and white = unhomed that white men went looking for physical and spiritual home in places that were officially despised and subjugated to moral and ideological taboo zones in white middle class ideology. The attraction of Minstrel Shows for white men contained moments of facing and re-joining suppressed desires in a projected "h(e)aven" of an undisturbed, uncontrolled environment loaded with connotations of sensuality, emotionality and highly contested non-productivity, that is, laziness.[98] Herbst capitalizes on the vernacular knowledge of this seductive force[99] even if she hides its potential in an episode ostensibly dedicated to Joe Trexler's departure.

Seen from this angle, there is again the shadow of Temperance[100] on Herbst's narrative: on a metonymic axis, white middle class women projected the **unhoming** of families onto a plane of social and moral decay that not incidentally conno-

---

97 I thank Jane Marcus for bringing the contemporary vernacular use of 'white elefant' as useless, unwanted, to my attention.

98 Roediger 1994, 63-66.

99 Morrison brilliantly inverts white enjoyment of black showtime in the country fair episode at the beginning of *Beloved* when the new family Sethe, Paul, Denver and Beloved join the rest of the Cincinnati Negroes watching white people making a spectacle of themselves.

100 See Evans 1989 for a brief history of the Temperance Movement.

tated blackness (or blackening) in a racialized cultural register: alcohol, waste of money, unreproductive sexuality, laziness, poverty, violence, powerlessness. This shadow keeps hovering over and against the quasi-Marxist narrative of big money as enemy, its hold on the picture re-enforced by an unresolved tangle of white pathology. It insinuated to American middle classes that contact with blackness might **cause** social degradation, a very effective ideological displacement of a factual experience of being accumulatively 'blackened' by proletarization and its hostile, violent, disempowering capitalist regimentation.

In Herbst's orbit, white female industriousness of guarding and saving pushes constantly, if unsuccessfully against temptation, distraction, and senseless curiosity and adventurousness: if desire ("nigger heaven") would not lure around every corner, if Joe had not fallen prey to the South's chaos, which seems in this novel intricately connected to intrigues made possible by "free nigger votes" – might the white elefant still be home, might the white middle class still be safe? This question runs through the novels like a strongly suggestive, if not explicit subtext, again furthered by Herbst's technique of dispensing with a distanced narrative voice, and her oftentimes blurred terms of address soliciting readerly identification. Her narrative as such comes all too close to the middle class paralyzing fear of dispossession that she allegedly sought to expose and transcend with a revolutionary script of "The Earth Does Move," the title of the trilogy's very last chapter. As a **protest novel** the trilogy of course exploits the tropes of (self-)possession and dispossession to the fullest. It employs a critique of class domination as well as it interrogates that leftist critique from a feminist point of view, especially in *RoG*, asking why and how women have been doubly dispossessed, within gender and class hierarchies. However, Herbst's empathy with her narrative's protagonists (based on autobiographical memories of her own family, after all) obscures the missing third term in American history, race. She does not examine how the ideological trope of possession / dispossession becomes altered within a racialized historical field to re-channel white middle class conceptions of social fear/social benefit, ideological em- or dispowerment into an arena of white versus black competition. What she chooses not to confront, however, will not be therefore evacuated from her text, as Morrison has pointed out in *playing in the dark*.

Charmed Lives and Wild Creatures

In fact, needless to say, African-American citizens had nothing to do with capitalism's structural changes, other than indeed being severely and adversely affected by them to the point of re-dispossession under Jim Crow rule. That development, however, goes unnoticed by Herbst, except for being mentioned in a passage that focuses, again, on Trexler's state-of-mind and is written from his perspective. In a chapter called "Charmed Lives," we read the following sentences:

Joe began to feel that nothing harmful could ever happen to him. Papers were full of terrifying news about other people and of poor creatures being hauled from their beds. Negroes were wandering around like wild creatures or else pushing themselves forward with their uppity way and getting lynched for daring to take their emancipation seriously and poor whites were sore and brooding for fear they would loose their jobs to Negroes now they were to be hired for next to nothing or just impressed in gangs for vagrancy. It looked bad all around and all the time the employees of the State Road were in a kind of magic kingdom were they weren't touched. (*Pity* 73)

Given Trexler's naiveté, his narcissism and completely self-delusional Weltanschauung, one is only mildly surprised to see lynched, chain-ganged or homeless black people lined up in one and the same series of "bad news" with white Southerners **afraid** to be robbed, or to lose jobs. Moreover, as the passage vaguely implies, these 'calamities' seem somehow connected: "poor (white) creatures" being "hauled from their beds" at the end of one sentence; and "wild (black) creatures" run loose in the next; the insinuation clearly being that the black creatures are getting the whites, if only because of their alleged "wild"ness: set the Negroes free, and the Congo will overrun the South[101]. This reading is enforced by the use of one of the most stereotypical white slurs against African-Americans: to be "uppity" certainly does not have any connotation of self-confidently enjoying citizenship status. The combination of that revoicing of a slur with the observation that Negroes "are getting lynched **for** taking their emancipation seriously" (emphasis added) serves to have a sentiment of scarcely veiled scornful envy at black people "pushing themselves forward," cancel out a somewhat resistant and not exactly emphatic acknowledgement of racist killing. Also, to say that African-Americans "got killed" (in a neutral form, disavowing white agency) **for** wanting to be free human beings, as a form of irony borders itself on racist glee.

The real problem with that passage, however, is not even young Trexler's racist misconceptions but the fact that we as readers do not hear any other voice in that chapter. We are brought to a point of seeing through Trexler as somebody who will be setting himself up for dramatic failure; we sympathize with a young innocent victim of mafiose power schemes he is not intelligent enough, and too self-aggrandizing, to detect. There is no vantage point however, outside Trexler's perception of his surrounding world that would enable white readers to distance themselves from it; the narrative does not revoke his sentiment at any point. Given an average historical ignorance, callousness or downright racism of the American

---

101 See DuPlessis 1995, for reverberations of this theme even among Northern intellectuals; also Harris, Davis, Fout and Tantillo.

reading public (not only in the 1930s) the text does indeed take reckless risks of relying on readerly identification.[102]

Trexler's story in the South contains a series of repetitions on that theme. The narrative point of this series relegates blacks to the necessary yet dispensable background of a white people's play, within the plot as also on the level of interaction between protagonist and readers. The "Yankee"-schemes of railway fraud and voting manipulation (that Trexler finds himself ultimately caught up in as victimized rather than being the major player he fantasized himself) depend on the new historical fact of a free black vote and a purely functional employment of that relation is the only narrative interest (*Pity* 26,47). Trexler, and readers, do not have to invest any direct confrontational interest in African-Americans as potential agents within that historical situation; on the contrary, we are allowed to share Trexler's contempt for the "handful of Negroes (...) that made the difference between Southerners and Northerners" (*Pity* 98).

The Social Topography of Blackness

In a certain uncanny way, the trilogy benefits from the ability of blackness to creep up on American texts. Black people, and associations of/with blackness function in the trilogy as a social topography to make and ground whiteness, white suffering and white humane qualities. Different narrative scenarios and scenes connected to black history are assembled into a scenic repertoire for the staging of historical, social and cultural conflicts that appear neutrally white: pertaining to a clash of interest between and among white people, acted out between white people, suffered by some and benefited from by other white people. The national drama of American history in Herbst's book – the ultimate rise of corporate capitalism, the repression of the American working class, the Stock Market Crash, and the Depression of the 20s and 30s – is **white** whereas the moment of American history that was already traumatic "before the fall" of/into corporate capitalism, namely the Middle Passage and slavery, is **black**, but not **American** History. It does not become even remotely interesting in her context, except to serve as a metaphorical repertoire from which to draw white working class stylization.

The narrative is propelled in a textual economy that has so-called black history figure as social relief, as a kind of milieu that makes, that is, describes and inscribes

---

102 That becomes shockingly obvious if we contrast the passage just quoted, in which black people figure as background to Joe Trexler with those passages in *Beloved* which do engage that specific American historical phenomenon: black people wandering the country bereft, homeless and mad have appropriately become the focus of empathy.

its white characters. Certain states of stress, emotional burdens and physical hardships linguistically connected to black history are so ingrained in white American thought and speech as to be virtually naturalized. That enables the text to have white subjectivity mirrored in black suffering without having to pay any interest in black subjectivity and historical agency at all. Moments of black history embody white distress, alienation, psychic and social displacement or desire and bliss.

Blackness is metaphorically incorporated into the text as one of its main, if unacknowledged, referential frames: the novelistic attack on the ruthless exploitation and oppression of the working class operates within texual metaphors surrounding slavery. That seems to me to be a very specific American cultural phenomenon in which vernacular language has been saturated with metaphors like "being sold down the river" that incorporate a very specific historical memory, but Americans not even a full century later do not feel compelled to engage the grounds of that figuration. All white characters at one point or another are marked in the text by a rather economical connection to black history, strangely taken away from its original bodies, without ever being made to confront their habitual parasitism – on the contrary, the narrative voice actively participates in and makes effective use of it. This maneuver works by equation, analogy, opposition and negativity. For example, impolite white behavior is encapsulated in the phrase "as if they went slumming", moments of happiness for Victoria and Jonathan are highlighted by black bodies in the background, either in pain, or in dull desperation.

In the first novel, the text tries to fend off the challenge of dealing with black history by erasure and a coquetterie with racism, except for occasional qualifications of hard work, for example about railroad workers "who work like niggers." (*Pity*, 58) The parallelizing hints keep coming faster in *Exe* and *RoG*, as if to mirror the 'blackening up' of the lower white middle and working classes during the Depression era, as if the narrative were underwritten by another register: a 'positive' blackness being more useful to white protest writing than to the white middle class fears of the first novel. The trope of being worked like slaves as applied to white male farmers and workers figures prominently in this linguistic scenario, supplied with its complementary opposite image of a white fight against slavery which allegorically ennoble white workers' plight. The desperation of "They had worked and slaved, where had the substance sunk to?" (*RoG* 207) his answered by "John Brown, I'm marching on" (*RoG* 270), uttered in fictionalized defiance by a militant participant of the Harlan County fight of 1935. One of Herbst's non-narrative inserts in *RoG* (81) is addressed as a rally speech in Washington to Abraham Lincoln, heavily capitalizing on abolition:

You're going to let us down, Father Abe. We're still here, another batch of men, wearing different skins, different clothes. We never forget what you said. We're making the same old fight, property versus human rights. (*RoG* 81)

The oscillation of the term property here deserves notice: of course, the point of this rhetorical piece is to equate the slave owners with the capitalist bosses, both only interested in their property (which here stands in, without ado, for financial profit), pitted against freedom. The crucial historical difference, however, between the slave's actual **being** the property and the proletarian's double freedom within a capitalist economy (according to Marx) is erased, just as much as in Steve Carson's statement "He thought he saw who was being sold down the river" (RoG 140) which serves to metaphorize his political awakening. The political point to be had from that equation was obviously not lost on the capitalists and their apparatus, either; the novel refers to various instances of IWW working class leaders or farm organizers being tarred and feathered. (*Exe* 121, 181). The metaphoric repertoire of 20th century class struggle, from both sides, is slavery; the props are complete, as Herbst puts it into the mouth of one "government expert" sent out to quench rebellion among the farmers:

My god, if they ever realized they were in the same boat, if they ever quit tearing at each other's throats, if the little storekeeper ever got it into his head that his friend, his only friend was the poor farmer, not the rich banker, where in the hell would the system be then? (....) So let the feuds brew and the **nightriders ride**, let them go to it. (*Exe* 198, emphasis added)

Black history is invisible – there is no way to know, how many of the small farmers, if any, might have been black sharecroppers or even landowners – and highly suggestive in the Ku Klux Klan threat in one and the same gesture. The effect is plain: the most massive threat hanging over the dispossessed, is to become 'Niggers'; the logical answer to that, a common confrontation of that threat which would have, of course, to be based on an acknowledgement of black agency, is an option Herbst does not even engage by way of narrative doubt vis-a-vis her text's reliance on social realism.[103]

The author's explicit claim – to establish a monument to the revolutionary potential of the American working class and to the need for radical change – culminates in the figure of working class Steve Carson, a hero undaunted, and in his fe-

---

103 As Langer writes in her Herbst biography, the journalist Herbst refused to go down South upon being commissioned an article on the Scottsboro case, and decided instead to do the assignment with other press material. The 'race' politics of American communism in the 1930s were ambivalent, if not in many cases merely rhetorical, an earlier variation of 'politically correct.' See also Goldfield, Foley, and Rabinowitz.

male opposite, journalist Victoria, an 'aborted' female white political activist. Both are revealed in a respectively gendered relation to blackness. Carson ultimately does not care for matters of personal, family life; he is operational, forward bound, not compassionate, strategic, not romantic, a fighter, a man in his bonding with white men in a war, the repertoire of slavery replaced by industrial imagery in the novel's epiphanic closure:

> Men shot men in a war. Make no mistake, we are now at war (...) we're only fighting for our human rights, better to die like men than live like dogs on the speedup. (*RoG* 429)

Victoria, the novel's youngest heir in a line of very white middle class women, who embodies feminist care written across masculine domination of the revolutionary movement, is at last 'blackened' in her contact with the Cuban peasant rebels: no matter how sensually, passionately involved she becomes in her political endeavors, however, the narrative resigns her to ridiculous and self-serving romanticism. Her intensive yet altogether wistful contact with (mostly black) Cuban militants, the text implies, only reinforces her gender, and maybe her class – she does not qualify as proletarian heroine – and as such, her ineffectuality:

> Then she scolded herself and said, only think if you were a silly timid woman who never had stirred from home, made crocheted doilies and believed in the Holy Trinity, Holy Matrimony and the Holy Mother of God. But at that she suddenly envied those who could pray. (...) From that distance her mother's love only reminded her that she was alone. (...) Her hands still felt like stumps that were bound behind her back and she was to wander in a grove with the pears always too high for her mouth. (*RoG* 406)

White Middle Class Romance Aborted

Economical and historical developments have undermined the perfect solidity of the "Snow Scene" of Steve Carson's youth; society does not "look like that **anymore** with a peaceful house resting on a hill and smoke like warm fur pouring from the chimney." (emphasis added) What scars this city-on-the-hill (snow) white replay is "big" and "black" (*RoG*, 429) but it does not seem that Herbst herself was able to read that signification on whiteness: by the time of the 1930s it had been rapidly losing a lot of its (material) privileges for many white people, and thus its presumed innocence was severely threatened.[104] The novel's white romance signifies a textual longing for a (white) togetherness that defined itself by its incorruptible predisposition for idealized emotional discipline:

---

104 See Goldfield 129-133.

And the thought of the string reminded her of her own mother who had never thrown string away. She had died with an attic full of things too good to throw away, with bags of old letters hanging from the rafter like beheaded corpses as if the written words of the dead somehow pledged the family to immortality. (...) [She felt] as if her mother had been looking at her again across the table. It was winter and her mother's hands (...) looked chapped and bruised (...) the book her mother had just looked up from was one Victoria had brought from the library. "How true." her mother had said. "How true that is. The **exquisite burden of life.**"(...) Something in the face and voice dissolved the contemptuous youthful "sentimental" that she was about to brandish at her mother. (*RoG* 170, emphasis added)

The text inscribes a desire for an unsoiled America that will somehow be re-incorporated into a postcapitalist society by way of doubled embodiment, as it were, in proletarian male heroism redeemed by female (middle-class) sentiment; this desire, however, tries to circumvent the questions of racial oppression at the very core of the 'pre-lapsarian' America. One of the textual maneuvers to achieve this evasion is the trilogy's narrative frame. Its constitution as personal, individual narration of family lore (reaching, however, nationally representative status) se-cures a controlling vision that keeps the occasional forays into 'social material,' like transcripts of newspaper clips, strike speeches or even the peasant rebellion in Cuba on a short leash, as it were.

In Cuba, not only is Victoria taken out into the larger world, readers are also at this point beyond an 'American family focus' for the first time. However, the guid-ing and binding moral intelligence of this foray is Victoria's. At the moment when she has stepped the farthest outside the confines of her class, gender and race, namely deep into the black Cuban rebellion[105], the text speaks its ultimate truth in framing her in a sentimental memory of her white childhood family life and its un-shaken faith. Rosamond's suicide, the loss of Victoria's own still-born child, and the death of the Cuban children of hunger are textually pulled together in a quasi-solidarity of suffering: "Life is hard with us. The children die" (*RoG* 405). Only thus may Victoria become the true heir to her female ancestry of perseverance, en-durance and love – a heritage of prayers, Sunday school, and motherly regimes evoked at the precise moment of her encounter with black people's oppression and resistance. Black suffering makes Victoria feel giddy, fearless, able to push her own sorrows way back in her head:[106]

---

105 Not surprisingly, at this point, the 'blackness' of the Realengo 18 Soviet is never ac-knowledged as in any way crucial; it seems not to have played a significant role to 'color-blind' American leftists that the Soviet leader, Alvarez, was a black Cuban; the fact only appears by way of en passant information in his description.

106 Elinor Langer's biographical text supports that idealization of suffering, as well as the erasure of blackness within the Realengo 18 Soviet. Langer 181.

> [Her trouble] had not vanished but it was remote as the **view of the sugarmill**... A light giddy happiness without rhyme or reason seemed pouring into her from no other source than the sun. She rode behind him, laughing to herself, everything saturated with delight. Perhaps I'm going clean daffy, she thought, **happily**, not at all deceived that this would last forever. Tomorrow or next day the other world down would have to be faced again. (*RoG*, 369, 370 emphasis added)

Ultimately, blackness brings her to herself, roots her (and us) in nostalgia, enables her to continue a self styled female tradition of "decent life" against overwhelming odds of loneliness and disrespect of her journalistic activity as a woman, but at the same time, it escorts her, as it were, out of the narrative. Rabinowitz' criticism mirrors the narrative again:

> Cuban women whose maternal suffering impels them to fight prompt Victoria's vision of her family, (as a) mythic vision of the collective. (164)

By contrast, I read Victoria's pledge not to forget the black Cubans, her determination in the line "She need not cry anymore because there were those who shed blood" (RoG 404), as a rather inconsequential textual instance of character embellishment, a romantic self-blackening, as it were. "She would not desert them, and they would not desert her", then, is as hypocritical as it is arrogantly deluded.[107]

Narrative Whiteness

> Yesterday's road... led through the crossroads where my own history intersected the history of our time. (..) a writer's way of learning through his(sic) own skin. (...) To insist on this point of the actual is, practically speaking, avantgarde. (Herbst)

Josephine Herbst's statements about her own writing offer an ironic frame to read her trilogy. The novel reveals its limitations in that very double claim, the presumption of white people to assume their **story** would provide them with full and actual access to **their time**, would make them avantgarde based on the perceptory reach of their own **white** skin. Black participation in the project of America, black people's victimization as well as their historical agency does not figure; but a 'his-

---

107 Compared to the biographical facts, Herbst's dismissal of Victoria is one of the stunning incidents of female protagonists deserted, or killed off in disaster by their female authors, who themselves negotiated ways and means to live quite socially and personally active, fulfilled lives. For example, Herbst actually wrote a series of radical journalistic pieces about her Cuban sojourn and the Realengo, and upon her return, continued to be a successful journalist, a career that we have a hard time imagining for Victoria at the point of her disappearance from the text.

torical memoir' based on this very effacement is passed off pointedly as a recuperative representation. Herbst's trilogy had a wide horizon, indeed:

> Her major literary undertaking was to be nothing less than a reinterpretation of America's social and economic institutions from the time of the Civil War through the Depression.

as Bevilacqua (13) has it. To revise American history in terms of a just portrait of the harsh realities of rural poverty, eroded middle class life, working class hardship, and to root this narrative in United States capitalism's turn to corporate power, without a single glance at how black people figured in that history, seems a contradiction in terms. To mourn and protest the betrayal of the American middle class idyll and its erosion in the decades after the Civil War without even raising questions about the meaning of both slavery and its abolition for the development of United States monopoly capitalism reveals foundational misconceptions of a (white) American leftist reading of history. All critics of the trilogy supportively reinscribe this crucial suppression, by investing a false universality in the novel's factual erasure of racialization of American history. The readerly space created for the trilogy upon its initial reception and upon its later recanonization contains an affirmation of white audiences' ethical empathy with the impulse to right/write the wrong of American history, quite unaware of its own as well as the novel's presumptuousness.

How the novel's deferment, its stillborn pull of melodramatic desire choking on impertinent detail, and its anti-narrative compulsion could be articulated with its evasion of racialization and racism, is a question not to have worried criticism.[108] The dilemma Herbst – who did not want to write proletarian kitsch, and thus refused revolutionary closure – was not able to solve was a contradiction between the

---

108 Bevilacqua focuses on leftist politics, Rabinowitz on incipient feminist narrative; both follow the approach that one reads writers only within their own parameters. That is, of course, valid and necessary, given the suppression of 'red' writing, and the marginalization of women's voices within it that Rabinowitz so clearly delineates; it is bewildering, on the other hand, measured by the dire necessity in American culture, even progressive culture, to face racism and the work of racialisation. The axis that Foley uses explicitly: feminist women are not to be criticized for race matters; if at all, race is for black women, is the controlling topos in all criticism. Rabinowitz anticipates criticism in her afterword but her defense is still deeply problematic: "I am afraid my study has reproduced (...) silences and omissions, and so I will leave aside what would amount to superficial discussions of the way race reshapes these two matrices of subjectivity in this brief outline for a literary history of white women's political fiction (or a political history of white women's literature)." She refuses "superficial discussions" but she does employ Sojourner Truth to trope the "working woman's body." (Rabinowitz 174)

genre exigencies of documentary realism and the white middle class myopic vision of Americans like her family that she so faithfully records. To engender her text as female – against a doctrine of class concerns as masculine – inscribes it within the realm of feminism. The text's attractiveness to white feminist critics thus resides in its insistence on the temporally and spatially disconnected narrative detail as a crucial signifier for everyday family life, written large against sacrificial male revolutionary fantasies; however, the whiteness of its femininity, one that particularly in the first two novels strongly reverberates a Temperance provenance, cancels out a narrative dynamic reaching beyond (family) nostalgia; as much as it whites out a social dynamic beyond its own limitations. John Brown's death, unwittingly maybe, but prophetically placed at the very beginning of Herbst's narrative, leaves but a sentimental narcissistic citation of another white America.

2.3. In Search of John Wayne: Joan Didion's Myth of American Innocence

> When John Wayne spoke, there was no mistaking his intentions; he had a sexual authority so strong that even a child could perceive it. And in a world we understood early to be characterized by venality and doubt and paralyzing ambiguities, he suggested another world, one which may or may not have existed but in any case existed no more: a place where a man could move free, could make his own code, and live by it. (Joan Didion)

Didion's moralistic rigor has been positively noted by most of her literary critics, as by Katherine Usher Henderson in her commentary on *The White Album*:

> Didion tells the story of the Sixties from the perspective of a woman who has banished the demons of the nightmare through the written record of their devastation. (K. Henderson 120)

With her entire oeuvre she indicts American postwar moral decay – from the loss of positive social cohesion and shared meaning to corruption at the core of civil institutions and corporations but also to spiritual deprivation and a decline of sincerity on the individual level. The Yeatsian allusions to apocalyptic disaster of *Slouching Towards Bethlehem* (1968)[109] are programmatic; they exhibit the typically Didionesque paradox of a seductive conservatism.[110] Her work taken as a

---

109 In the following as *Slouching*.
110 Recently, poststructuralist critics haven taken Didion on board, as it were, because of her style of fragmentation, her anti-narrative energy, and her distrust of easy realist teleology.

whole could be considered an extended jeremiad on postmodern terms,[111] which will not assume civic agency to be readily imaginable upon exhortation. As she herself said it:

You are getting a woman who somewhere along the line misplaced whatever slight faith she ever had in the social contract, in the meliorative principle, in the whole grand pattern of human endeavor.[112]

Didion does, however, assume the right to and obligation of superior witnessing. Her voice comes from the lone vantage point of priding itself on its incorruptibility by ideologies, or by materialistic interests. This voice's righteousness, her aesthetic precision, the sharpness of her register remain strikingly wedged to the American Dream of 'once-to-be-had innocence' and to the myth of an untainted American Eden.

Insistently, her texts raise the question of guilt: post-World War II conspicuous consumptions, political incapability, corruption of Christian values, liberal presumptuousness, United States' involvement in Third World Countries like El Salvador[113], its politics in Cuba and towards the Cuban exiles in Miami, and the disaster of Vietnam[114] figure in her catalogue of evils in telling conjunction with an alleged

---

111 See Hollowell.

112 Didion, quoted in E. Friedman 90.

113 See Kiley in Friedman; he seems d'accord with Didion's reading of the situation as absurd to the point of unintelligibility; whereas I would agree with his appreciation of Didion's observations of a terror beyond words, I disagree with a reading that ultimately obscures historical explanations of United States' economic and political interests in Central America and American responsibility for the situation Didion found upon her visit to El Salvador. That ambiguity is located within Didion's text which opens itself up to different 'interpretations' in its very insistence on the graphic particular, as can be seen in Kiley's commentary. (Kiley 182, 184) That Didion epigraphs her reportage with a passage of Conrad's Heart of Darkness, and calls "race [of the Nahuizalco Indians] the ineffable element at the heart of this particular darkness" is emblematic for the way problems connected to race, (of other, 'non-white' people) figure in almost metaphorical equation for darkness, confusion, angst and terror in her white American imagination.

114 See the most recent, post-Baudrillard reading of Democracy in Nadel: "[T]he novel, like foreign policy, has gotten out of hand. the policy that offers democracy has become a narrative that does not contain it (...) The basic narrative assumption creates a sense of inevitability and this allows a novel to manifest destiny. In rejecting that assumption, Didion makes clear, she is denying the manifest destiny of Democracy and of a foreign policy that resembles it. In so doing, she reveals the facts of American history to be the function of a dubious narrative convention. (...) As Didion presents it, democracy becomes one more signifier divorced completely from its signified, existing, as Jean Baudrillard has pointed out, simply to the extent that it participates in codes of consumption" (117, 118).

promiscuity of the 1960s, as well as with feminism's elitism and what she sees as reverse chauvinism. As her antidote, Didion clings to a mythical John Waynian American past and extols a *nostalgic* longing for frontier values and pioneer social reliability. I am making this point in contradiction of critics like Jennifer Brady, who asserts Didion's attitude is one of "love" for and "memory of its mythic past":

> H)er novels and essays return ineluctably to that promise of starting afresh that the American frontier once seemed to offer: the 'cutting clear, which was to have redeemed them' and us "all"(...) The perception of the relationship between the closing of the frontier and the dilemma of America's national destiny originated with the Turner thesis, and the assumption of their profound connectedness, both then and throughout our century, is key to Didion's work. (...) Didion has established a place for herself as the West's contemporary mythographer through her stubborn love for and memory of its mythic past. (Brady 43, 54, 58)

The most forceful positive image in *Slouching* that deserves a sad "Love Song" is John Wayne's maleness and westernness. Despite a tone of self-deprecative irony at the fabricatedness of John Wayne's iconicity and despite her very aloof adult acknowledgement of her own teenage dreams' futility, the longing for the better American past embodied in the Hollywood icon shimmers through and undermines Didion's detachment.

> [W]hen John Wayne rode through my childhood, and perhaps through yours, he determined forever the shape of certain of our dreams. (...) [I]nto this perfect mold might be poured the inarticulate longings of a nation wondering at just what pass the trail had been lost. (...) Since that summer of 1943 I had thought of John Wayne in a number of ways (...) of him telling the girl at the Alamo that "Republic is a beautiful word." [E]ven now I can hear [him], in another country and a long time later, **even as I tell you this** (*Slouching* 44, 45, emphasis added).

"Notes from a Native Daughter" establishes her leitmotif: the pioneer West metonymically comes to bear the weight of Edenic promise that the nation as a whole has accumulatively forsaken:

> (...) California is a place in which a boom mentality and a sense of Chekhovial loss meet in uneasy suspension; in which the mind is troubled by some buried but ineradicable suspicion that things had better work here, because here, underneath that immense bleached sky, is where we run out of continent. (*Slouching* 172)

The gesture to call her authorial I a "native daughter" refers to Didion's Californian upbringing as a pioneer family descendant[115], of course. It also implies, however, a

---

115 Her family had arrived West with the Donner-Reed party, but split from them before their disaster.

102

process of aggressively racialized connotation: her use of **native** for the white Californian woman alludes both to Native Americans and to Richard Wright's *Native Son,* as well as to James Baldwin's *Notes of a Native Son*, all of which Didion's acquisition of the name repudiates, claiming back the attribute of nativity and literary authority for the white girl. This very claim establishes Didion's self-assumed legitimacy as a witness to what she perceives of as America's "obsolescence"[116], its failure and loss. Didion's writing is driven by what she herself called "wagon-train morality," a bonding of (white) "primal loyalties" to "blood kin" (Brady 45) that grounds her nostalgia. By insisting on a difference between *nostalgia* and *memory* I am of course implying a serious objection: A mythography of the American (Western) past is always already based, even if not acknowledged, on a racialized displacement, since the frontier promise's reach did extend neither to the enslaved African-American part of the American population, nor to the victims of pre-frontier genocide of Native Americans. **Nostalgia** in this context works as a mental desire that screens over a kind of historical **memory** able to re-perspectivize the mythography. To locate the original sin, the "primal transgression" (Wilcox 77) of American history, in the Donner-Reed party's cannibalism committed to reach Sacramento limits Didion's writing to a myopic vision. Her America is self-contained as a white society; her texts do not acknowledge American history as thoroughly compromised and corrupted in its very inception. However faithfully she reports late 20th century white middle class "angst," her writerly intelligence stops short of naming one of its crucial conditions: the white denial and/or ignorance of oppression and exclusion structurally built into the social American fabric. Whiteness and its losses are brilliantly, if inadvertently highlighted in Didion's fiction and numerous essays, but she – until most recently – never squarely confronted the issues of race and white positionality.

However radically she might condemn (white) American political and social machinations, most expressly in *Salvador* and *Miami*, she refuses to acknowledge their rootedness in the very conceptualization of the American past's idealist project. Contrary to the desublimation of Didion's scathing, brilliant observational particulars, her moral commitment is to the "American Sublime" (Wilson 205-229), a national narrative that has, as Donald Pease phrases it, "always already evacuated its content" (Pease 12) but whose fragmentation and deterioration she eloquently mourns.

Her American fall is located in various nodes of American history[117] – a series of metaphors of disgrace strings her writing: be it the patriarchal entrepreneurial obsessions of the Gilded Age, America's greedy expansionism in Hawaii, the Aero-

---

116 A critical term recurring in all the essays in the E. Friedman collection.
117 See Wilcox for analysis.

space takeover in Sacramento in the 1950s, the "crisis" of Vietnam. But Didion does not engage a foundational "sin" – to stay within her vocabulary: the aggressively racialized access to democracy within US-America's historical self-constitution and its oppressive and destructive effects. To frame American history in terms of post-industrialization, post-frontier decay and failure – the two controlling topoi of Didion's oeuvre – amounts to the rather privileged self-delusion that it is Didion's ostensive purpose to defeat. For all her proclaimed indifference, and depressing dissection of the American Dream's wreckage, her writing partakes in it in the most crucial way. She indeed remakes mythology, limiting her historical loyalty to white kinship, and to white experiences borne by a belief in the redemptive qualities of the American wilderness.

Before her article "Sentimental Journeys," allusions to racial collision in American history appear more than scarcely[118]; they do have strategical allegorical value, however. "White" in *The White Album* for me not only alludes, via the Beatles' record title, to Sixties' helter-skelter, it also quite literally signifies a particular white catalogue of paranoia in a social "landscape of bleached lostness baked by the dead white blankness of a vacant sunlight, scorched by hot Santa Ana winds" (Wilcox 68). Indeed, the stress the particular combination of "white" and "blank" has to bear in Didion's prose, suggests a subterranean fear of an emptying out, a voiding of American society peculiar to its whiteness.[119] At this point, then, a fear of "blackening," of "dark chaos" becomes active, which most poignantly materializes in Didion's register of 1960s alleged social and individual degeneration. One part of Didion's take on the 1960s in *The White Album* and *Slouching Towards Bethlehem* is a glimpse of the Black Panthers by way of portraying Huey Newton's political posturing and generalizing rhetorics, and Eldridge Cleaver's eagerness in talking about (his) book sales figures. (*White Album*, 26-33, 34) These vignettes appear in line with Didion's record of public hysteria, neurotic obsessions, promiscuity, sexual diseases and inexorably spreading illnesses, abandoned and severely abused children, pointless and drugged hippies, immature student rebels and the ritual Manson murder; in line with her Yeatsian commentary on the "mere anarchy loosed upon the world":

> The center was not holding. It was a country of bankruptcy notices and public-auction announcements and commonplace reports of casual killings and misplaced children and abandoned homes and vandals who misspelled even the four-letter words they scrawled. It was a country in which families routinely disappeared, trailing bad checks and repos-

---

118 In *Miami*, it does become one, but she is mostly concerned with the situation of Florida's exile-Cuban population and the racial conflicts ensuing from there. In the novels, blackness, and for that matter whiteness, is not an open issue at all.

119 See in particular Wilcox, where white and blank keeps being repeated.

session papers. Adolescents drifted from city to torn city, sloughing off both the past and the future as snakes shed their skins, children who were never taught and would never learn the games that held the society together. (...)It was not a country in open revolution. It was not a country under enemy siege. It was the United States of America in the cold late spring of 1967, and the market was steady and the G.N.P. high (...) and it might have been a spring of brave hopes and national promise, but it was not (...)San Francisco was where the social hemorrhaging was showing up. (...) At some point between 1945 and 1967 we had somehow neglected to tell these children the rules of the game we happened to be playing. (...)These were children who grew up cut loose from the web of cousins and great-aunts and family doctors and lifelong neighbors who had traditionally suggested and enforced the society's values. (...)They are less in rebellion against the society than ignorant of it, able only to feed back certain of its most publicized self-doubts, Vietnam, Saran-Wrap, diet pills, the Bomb. (*Slouching* 84, 85,123)

The essays were written to mark a generation of young (predominantly white) adults[120] who refused to integrate properly into society. Some of them indeed did not stop short of violent abuse of their own children (*Slouching* 127), even if those cases should only be taken as a measure of the extreme – which remains obscured by the purposeful randomness of Didion's assembly. The essays discredit a morally legitimate cause and its proponents – however necessarily one might have to criticize Black Panthers' politics – by aligning it with a merciless depiction of white society's own young generation's most threatening misbehavior. Against that background her spotlights ridicule black resistance against white racism. By virtue of its metaphorical value for Didion's voluntary narrative, the peculiar positioning of blackness comes to figure as a meta-signifier for irredeemable social sickness.

Race in Excess

Only in her late essay "Sentimental Journey"[121] does Didion finally take on the issue of race and what it has to do with American self-definition. The occasion for her essay is the rape and attempted murder of a young white female executive in New York in 1989 – an instant of obvious and dramatically staged 'blackening' of New York contemporaneity. Race, for Didion, becomes of chronotopic interest at the moment when the 'other' race goes into excess, as it were, when it becomes visible beyond a frame of American mythography's 'normalcy.' A group of young black teenagers eventually were indicted in a trial which kept New York's media on the run for months and which was used, in Didion's view, to create a racialized melodrama complete with all the quintessential props of sentimentalism:

---

120 The continuous use of "children" in the essays is already a pathetic ploy.
121 In the following as "Sentimental"; in the latest published collection of essays under the same title. (1994)

The convention assumes, finally, that the victim would be (...) the natural object of prurient interest; that the act of male penetration involves such potent mysteries that the woman so penetrated (as opposed, say, to having her face crushed with a brick or her brain penetrated with a length of pipe) is permanently marked, 'different' even – especially if there is a perceived racial or social 'difference' between victim and assailant, as in nineteenth-century stories featuring white women taken by Indians – 'ruined'. ("Sentimental" 261)

It is the purpose of Didion's essay to uncover publicly veiled agendas of the conflicting parties and to reject the hysteria of most of the press coverage.[122] (She makes no distinction in her indictment between black and white media.) Underneath its surface of being a – however self-disruptive and meta-critical – New York elegy, the essay may be read as an extended white meditation on the metropolitan "race question" and how its configurations can be traced back to historical constellations. The essay does refuse plotted media sentimentality:

It was precisely in this conflation of victim and city, this confusion of personal woe with public distress, that the crime's 'story' would be found, its lesson, its encouraging promise of narrative resolution (*Sentimental* 260).

Narrative resolution being something that American society, for Didion, precisely does not offer unless borne by insincere narrative constructions:

[T]he imposition of a sentimental, or false, narrative on the disparate and often random experience that constitutes the life of a city or a country, means that much of what happens (...) will be rendered merely illustrative, a series of set pieces, or performance opportunities. ("Sentimental" 296)

Pitted against this sentimentalism, the essay records New York's urban fragmentation and the civic default of rational dénouements. With her very own journalistic acuity, Didion unerringly spots the lacunae, irresponsibilities and blatant lies of the media's scandalizing campaign and New York political players' complicities in those schemes. Quoting a news commentary on the prosecutor as the "jogger's avenger," Didion writes:

Do this in rememberance of me: the solution, then, or so such pervasive fantasies suggested, was to partake of the symbolic body and blood of The Jogger, whose idealization was by this point complete, and was rendered, significantly, in details stressing her 'difference,' or superior class. ("Sentimental" 276)

---

122 For a reading of the complex relations between the city and its gendering at work in the media, see Bronfen 413-421.

To support her point, she turns to describe a white on white abuse case that went basically unnoticed in the media: "no one, it was said, wanted to crucify the guy," and turned out to be "[n]ot a shriek the city wanted to recognize," (as opposed to Cuomo's "shriek of alarm" after the jogger's case).

Didion explicitly displays an awareness of the historical precedents of black-white conflicts like the "jogger's case"; her language at some points implies empathy with the black New York community's anger. She criticizes the media's "unflagging resistance, even hostility, to exploring the point of view of the defendants' families and supporters"(308), and, by contrast, investigates the "historical freight" of alleged rape of white women by black men. This passage is one of the very few moments in Didion's American mythography to acknowledge "American black history" – even though she has to qualify it clearly as the distinct property of African-Americans:

Rape remained, in the collective memory of blacks, the very core of their victimization. Black men were accused of raping white women, even as Black women were, Malcolm X wrote in *The Autobiography of Malcolm X*, 'raped by the slavemaster white man until there had begun to emerge a homemade, handmade, brainwashed race that was no longer even of its true color, that no longer even knew its true family names.' (...) There has historically been, for American blacks, an entire complex of loaded references around the question of 'naming': slave names, masters' names, African names, call me by my rightful name, nobody knows my name; stories in which the specific gravity of naming locked directly into that of rape, of black men whipped for addressing white women by their given names. That, in this case, just such an interlocking of references could work to fuel resentments and inchoate hatreds seemed clear, and it seemed equally clear that some of what ultimately occurred – the repeated references to lynchings, the identification of the defendants with the Scottsboro boys, the insistently provocative repetition of the victim's name, the weird and self-defeating insistence that no rape had taken place and little harm been done the victim – derived momentum from this historical freight. ("Sentimental" 263, 264).

Didion's language, at its most understated, manages to inscribe a trenchant reading of racism, almost by way of a throw-away insight. Referring to the white ridicule of Reverend Al Sharpton, to the rumor that he paid demonstrators to show up at his rallies, and the various white sources' bids on how much, she writes:

This seemed on many levels a misunderstanding, or an estrangement, or as blacks would say a disrespect, too deep to address, but on its simplest level it served to suggest what value was placed by whites on what they thought of as black time. ("Sentimental" 316)

The textual intelligence at work here is indeed aware of the specific American legacy of historically entrenched racism; to me, "Sentimental Journeys" marks a point for Didion's writing where her former myopic confines have been transgressed.

The focus of my critique, then, is a sound of white ambivalence that refuses to be contained by her strategy of dialogic orchestration of "two narratives, mutually exclusive" for the "city's distress":

> One vision, shared by those who had seized upon the attack of the jogger as an exact representation of what was wrong with the city, was of a city systematically ruined, violated, raped by its underclass. The opposing vision, shared by those who had seized upon the arrest of the defendants as an exact representation of their own victimization, was of a city in which the powerless had been systematically ruined, violated, raped by the powerful. ("Sentimental" 300)

The essay's point seems to be to make space for an intellectual position that distances itself as much from ignorant, aggressive white racism as from Afrocentric orthodoxy and black sensationalism in the media. The success of this move is contingent, however, on a subtle blurring of distinctions between black intellectual positions (she quotes Malcolm X on African cultures as 'great, fine, sensitive civilizations') and a rather propagandistic, self-discrediting idealization of one of the indicted youngsters as "African king" by the audience in the courthouse. **Both** signify to her the

> fragile but functional mythology of a heroic black past, the narrative in which European domination could be explained as a direct and vengeful response to African superiority. ("Sentimental" 301)

This yoking together of two very different moments of blackness belies Didion's white and indeed disrespectful reservation vis-à-vis a black history of the United States that has brought forth its own intellectual traditions (of which Malcolm X's thinking is but one part). The essay screens black social and political voices 'de raison' by surrounding them with obvious irrationality, and by a subtle quasi neutral reportorial distancing that reserves detached insight for the white commentator:

> Among a number of blacks, particularly those with experience with or distrust of the criminal justice system was such that they tended to discount the fact that five of the six defendants had to varying degrees admitted taking part in the attack, and to focus instead on the absence of any supporting forensic evidence incontrovertibly linking this victim to these defendants, the case could be read as a confirmation not only of their victimization but of the white conspiracy they saw at the heart of that victimization. ("Sentimental" 300)

In low key typical of Didion, she implicitly assumes a critical position, attacking the role of media stories (279) devised to obscure not only the city's actual tensions of race and class but also, more significantly, the civic and commercial arrangements that rendered those tensions irreconcilable. ("Sentimental" 280)

Her position appears attractive in that it integrates the class question, being aware of growing class contradiction within the black community:

Unlike Bensonhurst here was a case in which the issue not exactly of race but of an increasingly visible underclass could be confronted by the middle class, both white and black, without guilt. Here was a case that gave this middle class a way to transfer and express what had clearly become a growing and previously inadmissable rage with the city's disorder, with the entire range of ills and uneasy guilts that came to mind in a city where entire families slept in the discarded boxes of refrigerators. ("Sentimental" 310)

She does not examine the question, though, why there seems to be a shared a priori public consent to appropriate a moment of racialized confrontation to vent (after all, mostly white) middle-class anger. Toni Morrison's observation in *playing in the dark* applies poignantly; speaking of a "denotative and connotative blackness" as a quintessentially American trope, she notes that it allows a

way of talking about and a way of policing matters of class, sexual license, and repression, formations and exercises of power, and meditations on ethics and accountability. (...) It provides a way of contemplating chaos and civilization, desire and fear, and a mechanism for testing the problems and blessings of freedom. (Morrison 1992, 7)

Alleged black violence provides the occasion for white moral catharsis, signifying a moment of excess at which properties connected to blackness – poverty, illiteracy, violence, homelessness, drug abuse – spill over, as it were, into whiteness. Middle class anger at New York City's poverty, mismanagement and corrupted administration erupts precisely at the point where a growing number of white families sleep in discarded refrigerator boxes, too. Behind the fear of black gang violence – real or imagined – lies the more complicated historical white fear of a dissolution of racialized borders policing social, material and political privilege. The fact that parts of the growing black middle class share those fears does not mean, as Didion implies, that race is no longer the real issue (as opposed to class). Quite the contrary: the class distance within the black community only enforces (by way of a supposed justification of white interests) middle class' anxieties of keeping privileges conditioned on whiteness, like, for example, a civically satisfying city government, a functioning regular garbage collection, or the reliability of pap smear tests. Staying clear of impoverishment and down-slide into a social situation historically conditioned on blackness is clearly a late 20th century white middle-class conservative imperative, however futile the attempts might prove to be. A *Wall Street Journal* op-ed, reprinted by the *Philadelphia Inquirer* under the title

"The Emerging White Underclass and How To Save It" vividly illustrates this anxiety on more outspoken terms than Didion's sophistication:

> The brutal truth is that American society as a whole could survive when illegitimacy became epidemic within a comparatively small ethnic minority. It cannot survive the same epidemic among whites.[123]

Voodoo in New York City

> [T]his illustrates how a familiar urban principle, that of patronage (the more garbage there is to be collected, the more garbage collectors can be employed), can be reduced, in the bureaucratic wilderness that is any third-world city, to voodoo ("Sentimental" 288).

If cities like New York become gradually undistinguishable from Jakarta or Mexico City, as Didion's scenario implies,[124] the "essential criminality of the city and its related absence of civility" (289) have become its distinguishing features. What characterizes this analogy as a white subject position is the historiographical ease with which correct observations about a metropolitan Western center's decay and corruption are carelessly named by way of 'blackening' them: using the (black) Third World metropolis as a meta-signifier for chaos and urban disaster. It obscures the white Western political and social responsibility for much of the urban hardship in the Third World as much as it ignores the fact that bourgeois white "civility" has at no historical moment prevented a capitalist economy from following rampant laws of accumulation, no matter at what social or ethical costs. Only by way of this evasion may a city policy governed essentially by white capital interests – which appears threateningly unable to provide for the needs of its (mostly white) middle class citizens – be "reduced" to the point of black magic.

This is the moment at which New York in Didion's essay achieves strongly allegorical value for the rest of the country, in the same move that the essay wants to keep the allegory's implications at bay; her sarcasm in her last words about the "inevitability" of New York makes the city appear indeed as much unwanted but indestructible as Third World cities (by implication black), seen from a Western white point of view:

---

123 This quote by Charles Murray, op-ed page November 15 1993, A 15 is taken from Judith Stacey's article on rightwing family politics concerned with what the 'moral majority' considers a growing erosion of family values caused by the proliferation of single parent households and extra-marital sexuality and pregnancies (Stacey, 51-71).

124 A liberal cliche that to my experience does not withstand the test of reality.

[A]mong the citizens of a New York come to grief on the sentimental stories told in defense of its own lazy criminality, the city's inevitability remained the given, the heart, the first and last word on which all the stories rested. ("Sentimental" 319)

Thus, when I spoke of American self-definition, it should be put in quotation marks: one of the crucial points Didion's argument pursues, is the non-representativeness of New York for the United States that is itself connected to the way racial conflicts are played out in New York City. In that sense, her eventual 'owning' of the issue of racialization is at once also a disowning since how the New York public and the city government deal with their city's problems is so distinctly New Yorkish as to be un"normal," foreign, in fact "Third Worldish" to the rest of the United States:

What is singular about New York, and remains virtually incomprehensible to people who live in less rigidly organized parts of the country, is the minimal level of comfort and opportunity its citizens have come to accept. The romantic capitalist pursuit of privacy and security and individual freedom, so taken for granted nationally, plays, locally, not much role. A city where virtually every impulse has been to stifle rather than to encourage normal competition, New York works, when it does work, not on a market economy but on little deals, payoffs, accommodations, **baksheesh**, arrangements that circumvent the direct exchange of goods and services and prevent what would be, in a competitive economy, the normal ascendance of the superior product. ("Sentimental" 284, 5, emphasis added)

The way she employs the concept of "normal" here bespeaks Didion's own liberal sentimentalism. Inasmuch as capitalism at any historical stage ever offered "normal" competition, and the "normal ascendancy of the superior product" – which seems a particularly 19th century American myth in itself – the economic processes of monopolization and globalization certainly destroyed those presumed mechanisms, not only in New York. Whereas Didion distances herself from the "romanticism" of crucial American topois like "individual freedom," she lacks that distance vis-à-vis the economic structure of American society, and thus alludes, again, to the notion of an untainted America. The destructive influence on cities like New York, according to Didion, has not sprung from a globalized market economy that has its crucial base, after all, in US-American capital, so that it would thus have to be regarded as 'homemade.' Instead, the use of the word "baksheesh" instead of using the English word corruption, relies on an undercurrent of racist assumptions easily shared by Didion and prospective readers: the practice of buying services and of rendering competition obsolete by a "proliferation of payoffs" (285), in this view, does not belong to a civilized (white) history, and functions as alien influence on New York as part of the Western world:

Groceries, costing more than they should because of this absence of competition and also because of the proliferation of payoffs required to ensure this absence of competition (...) are carried home or delivered, as if in Jakarta, by pushcart. ("Sentimental" 285)

Black Poetry?

This white civilian anxiety becomes audible in Didion's resentment against black agency within a New York, or any other urban metropolitan social environment. To equate a historically sound consciousness of racism, a particularly urban justified black fear of race prejudice, police violence and state discrimination, with a pamphlet *Countering the Conspiracy to Destroy Black Boys* under the heading of "suspicions of conspiracy increasingly entrenched among those who **believe** themselves powerless" (303, emphasis added) indeed transgresses from journalistic irony into white contempt. Didion evokes a black "emotional deep core where whites are seen as conspiring in secret to sink blacks in misery" (305) in intimate textual connection to a long passage that ridicules the notion of "conspiracy" via instances of obviously unsound propaganda. The possibility that the black anxiety of white racism borne by the ghetto experience in metropolitan cities, including lethal drug wars, might have any other grounds than paranoia, is not entertained. The textual slippage in Didion's passages moves readers directly from a *New York Times* poll revealing a deep-seated black anticipation of racist government to sensational rumors around the Jogger's case, to black militancy against an assumed white drug conspiracy to destroy black inner city communities[125]. The passages are framed by her phrase of "conspiracy" on one side and by the sarcastic commentary "more secrets, more **poetry**" (emphasis added) on the other. The essay repeats the very phrase "conspiracy" ten times within a passage of six pages. The effect of this might well have escaped Didion's textual control. For example, the poll result

that 77 % of blacks polled believed either that it was 'true' or 'might possibly be true' (as opposed to 'almost certainly not true') that the government of the United States 'singles out and investigates black elected officials in order to discredit them in a way it doesn't do with white officials,' ("Sentimental 303)

---

125 I think she lets herself off the hook too easily here, also. Drug traffic may not be run by conspiracy in the classical sense but that does not mean, it is not a lethal problem for black communities, nor will suspicion of political involvement on the highest level be rendered mute by this kind of sarcastic ridicule. See the most recent news about a election campaign dinner thrown by candidate for vice-presidency Al Gore in Washington that raised media objections because a known drug mafia leader was one of the sponsoring guests, in *Die Tageszeitung*, 5.11.1996. I see a justified historical ground for black communities' anxieties which Didion's passages do not engage, or directly deny.

which reflects a quite understandable anti-government resentment backed by a history of racist betrayal and discrimination, qualifies as "suspicion of conspiracy" in Didion's register. This kind of disproportionate language deployment unsettles the essay's sovereignty of judgement on conspiracies and poetry: that which has to be rejected most forcefully, as psychoanalysis has taught us irrevocably, might well have the strongest claim on reality and will not be laid to rest by being discredited as poetry, as invention.

In the same vein, Didion uses the example of the militant Reverend Sharpton and his "demonization" (310) in the media. Her rational rejection of the scandalizing media campaign against Sharpton allows her to figure her own racial position as a white person wishing for racial reconciliation. As opposed to other white journalists, who did not escape his trickster strategies, she considers herself able to see through his political schemes of his (self)-staging as the ultimate "Outrageous Nigger" (313).

> What seemed not at all understood was that for Sharpton, who had no interest in making the problem more tractable [the Bensonhurst case], the fact that blacks and whites could sometimes be shown to have divergent interests by no means suggested the need for an ameliorative solution. ("Sentimental" 314)

According to her, Sharpton wants to keep the conflict smoldering in the interest of more "poetry":

> Such divergent interests were instead a lucky break, a ready-made organizing tool, a dramatic illustration of who had the power and who did not, who was making it and who was falling below the line; a **metaphor** for the sense of victimization felt not only by blacks but by all those Sharpton called the 'left-out opposition.'("Sentimental" 315, emphasis added)

The strategy here might best be characterized as beating the messenger in order to hit the message, which seems a logical consequence of Didion's approach. If a centuries-old history of racism and white/black conflict shall be kept reduced to the "sometimes" of "divergent interests," any instance of black militant agency which might be "articulating a great deal more of what typical attitudes are than some of us thought" (315) has to be contained in the disrepute of its supposed poetical nature[126].

---

126 This rhetoric has tradition in American history, scenarios of the black boogeyman come to mind. And tradition in Didion: from Huey Newton's limitedness to a rhetorics of the "autodidacts for whom (...) safety lies in generalization" (*The White Album* 30) it is a short step to black poetry of paranoia. This does not imply a judgement on Sharpton on my part.

Ultimately, the whiteness of her contempt against black radicalism subverts Didion's informative inscription of American history's racial oppression. The text is carried by a momentum that conjures up but has to evacuate the unresolved urgency of past and present racism, to be swallowed in Didion's wishful, prototypically American narrative of "ameliorative solutions" between parties that "can be said to have divergent interests," all arrangeable within "normal" capitalism.

3. Terms of Engagement

3.1. Flannery O'Connor's Mysteries

> I am always having it pointed out to me that life in Georgia is not at all
> the way I picture it, that escaped criminals do not roam the roads extermi-
> nating families, nor Bible salesmen prowl about looking for girls with
> wooden legs. (...) We find (...) that there are strange skips and gaps which
> anyone trying to describe manners and customs would certainly not have
> left. [The characters'] fictional qualities lean away from typical social
> patterns, towards mystery and the unexpected. It is this kind of realism
> that I want to consider. (...) In any case, it is when the freak can be sensed
> as a figure for our essential displacement that he attains some depth in lit-
> erature. (Flannery O'Connor)
>
> [W]hen she sat her pen to [characters] not a whiff of magnolia hovered in
> the air (and the tree itself might never have been planted), and yes, I could
> say, yes, these white folks without the magnolia (who are indifferent to
> the tree's existence), and these black folks without melons and superior
> racial patience, these are like Southerners I know. (Alice Walker)

Critical interest in Flannery O'Connor's work has not abated since she became a young author elect by the New Critics in the Iowa's Writers Workshop in the early 1950s. For the most recent anthology on O'Connor, Sura P. Rath and Sarah J. Fodor have compiled and discuss four decades of critical evaluation of and institutional marketing strategies for this highly controversial, yet securely canonized writer's oeuvre. (Rath and Neff Shaw)

As the essays in this anthology demonstrate, O'Connor's subject matter, her style, her Catholic "outsider" vision and engagement still provide ample 'writerly text' in Barthes' sense, to engage re-imagination along more recent critical lines of gender criticism, of Bakhtinian readings, of new insights into the relations between O'Connor's immediate social, historical context and her literary representations. My reading here is supposed to help fill a gap in criticism that Sura Rath herself acknowledges at the end of her introduction; in her words, "the question of race (...) needs to be followed" (Rath 11). In an essay already written in 1975, Alice Walker had put this question on the agenda with a kind of enraged homage to O'Connor, which, while it unabashedly registered Walker's black anger at O'Connor's white privilege, claimed O'Connor's literary qualities and insights for a heritage of de-segregated literature:

Standing there knocking on Flannery O'Connor's door, I do not think of her illness, her magnificent work in spite of it; I think: it all comes back to houses. To how people live. There are rich people who own houses to live in and poor people who do not. And this is wrong. Literary separatism, fashionable now among blacks as it has always been among whites, is easier to practice than to change a fact like this. (...) She destroyed the last vestiges of sentimentality in white Southern writing; she caused white women to look ridiculous on pedestals, and she approached her black characters – as a mature artist – with unusual humility and restraint. (Walker 1983, 59)

While I agree with Alice Walker's "shock and delight" (52) mostly at O'Connor's mercilessness with her white Southern characters, "whose humanity if not their sanity is taken for granted, and who are miserable, ugly, narrow-minded, atheistic and of intense racial smugness and arrogance"(Walker 1983, 52), I want to suggest an evaluation that goes beyond O'Connor's successful seduction of me as a reader.[127]

My focus will be on O'Connor's reading of Southern history, guided by the question to what extent her texts – however conflictedly – share in white memory's mystification of the South, and to what extent they self-deconstruct and create a readerly urge and space for demystification at the same time. Peculiar for its extreme ambiguity, her writing has offered to generations of critics a repertoire of discussing human alienation and social decay, in which the factual history of the region, grotesque to the extreme, figures but as an occasion for universalizing moral speculation. Critical vocabulary is loaded with references to "tragic isolation," "disruptions of modern life which alienate man from his world and from grace," "visions of a dark and incongruous world" and "harsh discontinuities of history";[128] O'Connor's South, to those critics, is a violent landscape that lends itself to "premonitions of disaster" (Muller 7).

My argument, then, hinges on the word "premonition," which purposefully reads past O'Connor's inscriptions of past, not pending disaster. Those inscriptions are, however, only readable against the grain. What seems to me the most challenging quality of O'Connor's stories, is precisely their capacity to **contain** Southern violence in the grotesque, which, on one hand, shreds white illusions of rationality, superiority and innocence but on the other hand does not acknowledge the particular white agency of/in a history reaching from the Middle Passage to slave breeding to lynching. What critics have termed the grotesque's "play with the absurd," the "attempt to invoke and subdue the demonic aspects of the world," achieves its own

---

127 Yeager addresses the same difficulty to read O'Connor against the coercive force of her viciousness, which she calls writerly "torture." However, I disagree with her profoundly about her use of this term, as will become obvious in this chapter, see Yeager 183-206.

128 See, for example, the discussions in Muller, Feeley, or Coles.

particular effects under conditions of the quite secular "dissolutions," and "distortions" of Southern post slavery society:

> Suddenness and surprise are essential elements. (...) The grotesque instills the fear of life rather than the fear of death (...) [I]t presupposes that the categories which apply to our world become inapplicable. We have observed the progressive dissolution (...) the fusion of realms which we know to be separated, the abolition of the law of statics, the loss if identity, the distortion of 'natural' size and shape, the suspension of the category of objects, the destruction of the personality, and the fragmentation of the historical order. (Kayser 184-188)

Human (white) evil is pervasively debilitating in the most literal sense for O'Connor; she refuses to engage its particular Southern historical genealogy, however. The most stunning absence in her stories – given their extraordinary moments of aggressive defiguration and dismemberment – is the fact of lynching. If one follows Stallybrass' and White's discussion of the grotesque body as a body turned inside out,[129] the most horrifying imaginable grotesque – a living body killed over a fire or swinging from a beautiful tree, his "insides" bulging or being separated from him in the most literal sense – was, in Southern history, not a gift of poetic, carnivalistic imagination but a real scare.

The grotesque violence (and the violent grotesque) in O'Connor's writing bids the question if it might not function as a fantastic, sometimes an absurdly comical bogey that by calling attention to its very excessive presence gestures as much towards its own allure as to the absence it is meant to overpower. In O'Connor's own critical vocabulary this absence re-surfaces as a prototypical Southern trope: the burdening ghosts of the past:

> [Our present grotesque] heroes seem to carry an invisible burden and to fix us with eyes that remind us we all bear some heavy responsibility whose nature we have forgotten. (...) The South is (...) certainly christ-haunted. (...) What is pushed to the back of the mind makes its way forward somehow. Ghosts can be fierce and instructive. They cast strange shadows, particularly in our literature, for it is the business of the artist to reveal what haunts us. (O'Connor 1988, 860, 861)

"To reveal what haunts us" is precisely what her writing refuses; it haunts with a strange terror, but it does not reveal the actual terror within Southern history. O'Connor was too much a white Southern woman[130] herself to translate the

---

129 Stallybrass and White 9.
130 On O'Connor's own existence as a somewhat estranged white woman too inappropriate and too odd, and too seriously Catholic to aspire to Southern Belle status, as well as on her literary handling of gender, see Walker 1983, Reesman, Gentry, and Giannone in Rath and Shaw.

"mysteries" of Southern identity into unmannered facts. Even though she would not ignore white social and individual deformations she stopped short of exploring their possible historical connection to her contemporary South's legacy of the (im)moral absurdity of plantation slavery. History, to O'Connor, is what passes; what remains, is incontingent "evil":

> The South is struggling mightily to retain her identity against great odds and without knowing always, I believe, quite in what her identity lies. An identity is not made from **what passes, from slavery** or from **segregation**, but from those qualities that endure because they are related to truth. It is not made from the mean average or the typical but often from the hidden and the most extreme. (...) What has given the South her identity are those beliefs and qualities which she has absorbed from the scriptures and from her history of defeat and violation: a distrust of the abstract, a sense of human dependence on the grace of God and a knowledge that evil is not simply a problem to be solved but a mystery to be endured. (...) [W]e have had our Fall. We have gone into the modern world with an inburnt knowledge of human limitations and with a sense of mystery which could not have developed in our first state of innocence – as it has not sufficiently developed in the rest of our country. Not every lost war would have this effect on every society but we were doubly blessed, not only in our Fall but in having a means to interpret it. (...) In the South we have, in however attenuated form, a vision of Moses' face as he pulverized our idols. (O'Connor 1988, 861, 847, emphasis added)

O'Connor shares in a white nostalgia of a feminized South and its victimization. Her "Fall" is not caused by slavery, but by the Civil War defeat. Behind the "mystery," though, in the stern image of mosaic punishment, might lie an acknowledgement of guilt, however veiled by her Catholic rhetoric of a society blessed by suffering. O'Connor's ambivalence, again, is striking: to allude to a white Southern historical responsibility for oppression moved her out of reach of those "traditional manners" which to her, were better than "no manners at all" (O'Connor 1983, 200). But to use the collective "we" bases her moral perspective within a community that – at O'Connor's lifetime – still evaded or negated the "blessings" of the old South's defeat.

The Black Body as Historical Excess

The grotesque in O'Connor is located anywhere and everywhere imaginable except where one would logically expect it: the grotesque white violence executed on black humanity and black people's very bodies. Drawing on an immense white Southern historical and contemporary potential for violence, embodied socially and individually, O'Connor exerts a vitriolic aggression on – and through – her characters. The **dismemberment,** in the most literal and in a socially metaphorical sense, that white supremacy rule brought onto the South's black population is hitting home, as it were, taking apart white individuals,

118

families and communities, with a vengeance. I read O'Connor's glee in sentences like: "She would of been a good woman, if it had been somebody there to shoot her every minute of her life" in "The Misfit" as a seismographic signification of a latent dangerous aggression that becomes readable through and against O'Connor's Catholic efforts to narratively swallow it in "mysteries" of the human soul. However inadvertently, sentences like this attest to a white mentality that was grotesque enough to support or tolerate the Ku Klux Klan. O'Connor's unsympathetic narrators act as literary perpetrators of intra-white violence directed indiscriminately against innocent white children, well-kept white ladies, proper farm owners or 'poor white trash' – a violence which was in real life fact, by general social agreement, addressed to and enacted upon black people.[131]

However, this strategy of displacement also serves to remove the entire history of the violated black body from readerly sight. What we as readers **are** able to see, though, are insistently visceral remainders of this eclipsed history: "Niggers" populate the landscape of O'Connor's stories to the point of exasperation. O'Connor's use of the word itself is irritatingly inconsistent: at some points she obviously assigns the racist pejorative to her characters' voices, at other times it comes directly from the narrative voice – a fact that again bespeaks O'Connor's ambiguous position vis-a-vis her subject matter. I disagree with Shaw's opinion that the "heteroglossia" at work in O'Connor's fiction is only an aesthetic question (Shaw 142). For me, O'Connor's oscillations reflect not only a narratological decision to "suspend her narrator's authority and deny her narrator's omniscience" (Shaw 150), but in the tension between letting her characters see the South – and themselves in it – as they want to, and her authorial, sarcastic intrusions on that perspective, I see her own white undecidedness.

Stories begin and end with "niggers," they perform services necessary to the development of character, or to the plot's machinations; they are occasions for arguments, insights, initiations and revelations on the part of white protagonists (and readers). Toni Morrison's observations apply once more:

Such analyses will reveal how the representation and appropriation of that [Africanist] narrative provides opportunities to contemplate limitation, suffering, rebellion and to speculate on fate and destiny. They will analyze how that narrative is used for discourse on ethics, social and universal codes of behavior, and assertions about and definitions of civilization and reason. Criticism of this type will show how that narrative is used in the construction of a history and a context for whites by positing historyless-ness and contextless-ness for blacks. (Morrison 1992, 53)

---

131 As well as against some of the few white people who refused to exhibit unquestioning loyalty; see Hodes for a discussion of the political and ideological post Civil War campaigns against white women living with black men.

The narrative status of "niggers" is intriguing: they do not function as integral part of the setting, they do not fade into the landscape; they, or white commentary about them, engage readerly attention constantly, insistently, but they never accede to protagonism, either. They move through the geography of O'Connor's fiction like embodiments of a Southern peculiarity which can neither be named nor be repressed, which, on the contrary, O'Connor wants to activate for her own narrative of rewriting Southern history as grotesque, connoting a particular genre as well as a particular historical sensibility. "Niggers" signify by way of their numerous and rather opaque presence the "mystery" of Southern history. As such, they must be present literally because they have not and will not disappear. However, "niggers," and what they **embody**, in the truest sense, cannot be represented; this 'darkness' becomes something like an excess meaning lurking as a subtext behind O'Connor's deconstruction of Southern society.

In "The Artificial Nigger"[132] – with even its title being a blatant provocation – the word "nigger" appears 23 times; "Negroes," "dark women," "colored people" or "blacks" an added 35 times over the space of 21 pages of its entire length. Looking at this proliferation in psychoanalytical terms would provide an exemplary case study for the return of the repressed; what is rejected most will resurface with the strongest force. Not only is the story overwhelmed by the sheer grotesque number of rather unwarranted references to real "niggers," its ultimate collapse is achieved by one plaster "nigger." Does this mean that **even** as fakes, as mere representations of historical guilt, "niggers" hold the power to redeem whiteness, or does it, quite contrarily, imply that **only** as hollow caricature of subjectivity will "nigger" be allowed to have a human effect?

Criticism has looked past the white characters' nausea of "niggers" as if the story's black bodies do not matter, which might be seen as a proper response to the plot's implicit invitation to regard only a plaster statue as matter 'mysterious' enough to bring about Mr. Head's and his grandson Nelson's reconciliation, based in their finally shared recognition of blackness. **What** the conceited old man and the cocky child have been arguing about has gone generally unrecognized; the story's problematic of their intergenerational male competition about ignorance and the possession of knowledge is generated by and **based** on the question whether or not and how one is able to see "niggers" – which, in the characters' ideological register, is directly equated with seeing reality.

The reality, of course, that neither Mr. Head nor the boy will be able to see is Atlanta's reality of a huge black population and how they themselves historically and presently relate to it – even though they fight verbal battles over almost every black person they encounter. What they ultimately see in the artificiality of the

---

132 In the following as "Art."

plaster figure (complete with watermelon and grinning mouth) is not the "wild look of misery" of a black life but their own humbled but still narcissistic reflection.

For O'Connor herself, this scene functioned in a register of revelation. She intended the "humble" plaster "nigger," one of her "terrible symbols of what the South has done to itself," to suggest "the redemptive quality of the Negro's suffering for us all" (*O'Connor* 1979, 35, 140). That is to say, the author at this point partakes in her characters' narcissism: to see black suffering as a symbol of a (presumably white) self-destruction, to claim the victim's suffering for the oppressive agent's redemption has indeed been a marshalling white and quite parasitical trope of historical denial. In contrast to most of her critics, then, who have been concerned with the universal meaning of grace and redemption, I want to deal with the "niggers'" significance. I would like to open up a site that makes it possible to see the text's self-deconstruction at work, to account for my own appreciation[133] which runs counter to the story's racist appropriations of history.

If one reads against the criticism and against O'Connor, what does the text do? Self-righteous, arrogant old racist Mr. Head, living with his grandson in some backwoods little town in Georgia, takes naive presumptuous Nelson on a trip to the big city, to Atlanta. He aims at teaching the boy a lesson, to force him to acknowledge his own superior social wisdom and authority. They both get lost in the city streets and end up in the ghetto; when the boy contemptuously attacks Mr. Head for losing direction, the old man sets him up for public disgrace and betrays him by not acknowledging him as his own. Both are about to stay fixed in their mutual hatred and despair when they hit upon a plaster statue of a black man. Only in and by this moment are they able to recognize each other as kin, as connected in their shame and fears, under the penetrating, if humble gaze of the black figure.

Nelson has accepted his position; his rebellious dreams of the city violently destroyed, he will settle himself securely under Mr. Head's authority who has been himself brought to a humbler acceptance of his own limitations. Finally, the (white) male intergenerational order, threatened by the city's seductions, is safely restored by force of a black deus ex machina.[134] The lacunae here – between the story's rendering the two protagonists completely alienated from their world and from each other, and its confident denouement of mutual and self-acceptance at the end – have been remarked by critics (Shaw); however, how the relation between the plaster figure's blackness and the narrative's real life "niggers" could be pertinent to this jarring significant gap within the text has not been commented upon.

---

133 As well as, for example, Alice Walker's delight.

134 It is an interesting aside to read that O'Connor claims the plaster statue was the first thing she had, by way of having heard an anecdote about it, and she made a story to go with it; thus unwittingly furnishing proof for Morrison's theses that Africanism has literally, in this case, occasioned much of American literature. See Feeley 124.

Before their eventual redemption, the boy is seen as being torn between ac-knowledging his grandfather's power as a white adult – Nelson feels pride in him upon his perversely inhumane joke against blacks a cockroaches ("Art" 218) – and his anger at this very power to treat him in his alleged childish stupidity like a "nigger": "'Yes,' Mr. Head said, 'this is where you were born – right here with all these niggers'" ("Art" 221). To finally be able to confirm each others' white 'reality' in opposition to the "nigger's" artificiality, assures the foreshadowed acquiescence on the boy's part. He is eventually tamed by his grandfather's superior whiteness that was dramatically thrown in doubt and could not be assured in their encounters with real black people:

"An artificial nigger!" Nelson repeated in Mr. Head's exact tone. (...) They stood gazing at the artificial Negro as if they were faced with some great mystery. Some monument to another's victory that brought them together in their common defeat. They could both feel it dissolving their differences like an action of mercy. "They ain't got enough real niggers here. They got to have an artificial one." ("Art" 230)

The story successfully frames a white initiation rite. The self-possession Mr. Head wants to teach the boy[135] depends on **seeing** the (black) other as a means of self-empowerment; the seeing being a specular practice to fix the other in his/her place[136]:

"You may not like it a bit," Mr. Head continued. "It'll be full of niggers." The boy made a face as if he could handle a nigger. "All right," Mr. Head said, "You ain't even seen a nigger. (...) There hasn't been a nigger in this county since we ran that one out 12 years ago and that was before you were born." He looked at the boy as if he were daring him to say he had ever seen a Negro. "How you know I never saw a nigger when I lived there before?" Nelson asked. "I probably saw a lot of niggers." "If you seen one you didn't know what he was," Mr. Head said, completely exasperated. "A six-month-old child don't know a nigger from anybody else." "I reckon I'll know a nigger if I see one," the boy said. ("Art" 213).

They continue their quarrel as to whether or not the boy would recognize a black person, and of course, the boy "loses" the game, not being able to describe a black person on the train to Atlanta as black:

---

135 Critics have argued about the problem as to whether or not Mr. Head does in fact possess any wisdom of his own, that is, how to read the heteroglossia in the story between his own assumptions of himself, and the narrative voice's interventions. See Shaw 139-151.

136 See feminism's explorations of patriarchy's cultural insistence on its ability to 'see woman.'

"That was a nigger," Mr. Head said and sat back. Nelson jumped on the seat and stood locking backward to the end of the car but the Negro had gone. "I'd of thought you know a nigger since you seen so many when you was in the city on your first visit," Mr. Head continued. "That's his first nigger," he said to the man across the aisle. (...) "You said they were black," he said in an angry voice, "you never said they were tan. How do you expect me to know anything when you don't tell me right." "You're just ignorant is all," Mr. Head said. ("Art" 216)

For Nelson, it will be essential to know his place as racialized and gendered in intricate connection: Nelson's dead mother therefore does not play any role in this story, but a huge black bosom does. It affords him with a first glimpse of an initiation waiting for him as white male, for whom the "pitchblack tunnel" he is afraid of and anxious for at the same time, has not only sexual, but also racial connotations. After a faulty public scale has given Nelson his wrong weight on a paper slip with the ominous advice to "beware of dark women" ("Art" 220) he recklessly asks a black woman in the street for the way back to the station. She tells him to catch a car, and Nelson

understood she was making fun of him but he was too paralyzed even to scowl. (...) His eyes traveled up from her great knees to her forehead and then made a triangular path from the glistening sweat on her neck down and across her tremendous bosom and over her bare arm back to where her fingers lay hidden in her hair. He suddenly wanted her to reach down and pick him up and draw him against her and then he wanted to feel her breath on his face. He wanted to look down and down into her eyes while she held him tighter and tighter. He had never had such a feeling before. He felt as if he were reeling down through a pitchblack tunnel. ("Art" 223)

Angrily, Mr. Head accuses him of having no sense and pulls him away; Nelson burns with shame.

The sneering ghost he had seen in the train window and all the foreboding feelings he had on the way returned to him and he remembered that his ticket from the scale had said to beware of black women and that his grandfather's had said he was upright and brave. He took hold of the old man's hand, a sign of dependency that he seldom showed. ("Art" 223)

Thus, the narrative negotiates the terms of entry into male (white) bonding against black mothering, symbolically and literally, as a prerequisite for successful historical (re)generation. For Nelson and his grandfather, the black female body, consequently, is not allowed to figure but as grotesque excess.

Read against its universalizing grain, then, "The Artificial Nigger" becomes an allegory for the social contract of segregation, for the white Southern necessity to acknowledge identity over and against "niggers." The real black people in the story, however, seem pretty resistant to these white necessities – O'Connor allows them to just **be** there, rather undisturbed, doing their thing. Apart from the plaster figure, who is attributed with sadness and misery (logically, because he has to bear the incredible burden of white redemption), none of the black people in the story seem the least concerned with the two white people, except for exhibiting a meandering urban curiosity. Moreover, readers get to see the city, standing for reality here, as blackened in a manner rather unconcerned with whiteness, in an undramatic, anti-sublime register. The "niggers" do not appear as victimized but as concretely hip: they, metaphorically speaking, possess a map of urban reality, which the two white people do not. They are not miserably abject but occupied with their own daily, banal activities: working, playing, riding trains, eating.

In their self-concerned blackness they are left to be the others; as such, by way of a – for the white characters impenetrable – presence, the overwhelming repetition of "nigger" in the story 'niggers' it in turn, blackens it in probably unintentional ways. The fact that Mr. Head and Nelson can hardly talk to each other without communicating "nigger" bespeaks an intense presence of alive blackness that its relegation to plaster cannot efface. Ultimately, the two white people's obsession with "niggers," their unfounded fear and revulsion are given away as completely myopic; no black person in the text does anything in the least to warrant even a subjective white feeling of being disrespected or rejected. The "niggers'" indifference exhibited towards the white people's existential angst of identity, as in the black woman's lazy "sugarpie"-ing (Art" 223) of Nelson, undermines the pompous – indeed artificial – message the statue is made to bear. A potential objection would be to see the story's "niggers" as perfect instances of Morrison's "contextless-ness" for blacks, which is certainly the case. For my case here, however, it is more important to see how that very disinvestment on O'Connor's part defies her closure's "proper" purpose of meta-investment, as it were, in blacks' redemptive potential. Black bodies' quotidian materiality stands in aggressive opposition to the title's claim of fictionality for blackness; thus subverting the plot's claim that blacks in the South still only function as useful symbols. History is not the "mystery of existence" that Mr. Head feels implored by Nelson's "hungry need" to "explain once and for all" ("Art" 230). Its mundane consequences are hurtful for black people, who have to suffer grotesque white initiation rites – as the humiliating scene in the train goes to show ("Art" 217) – but it is no higher force of grace, as the story's closure tries to suggest.

"A Late Encounter With the Enemy"[137] introduces O'Connor's readership to one
of her most hilarious white figurations: "General Sash was a hundred and four
years old" ("Late" 252) His granddaughter Sally, 62 years old, is expecting him
to grace her evening classes' graduation ceremony, which will turn out to be the
focus of the story. As a fictional character, the general becomes an embodied allegory for Southern white readings of history and Flannery O'Connor's ambivalence with respect to it. His monologic recollections to himself reveal as much of
his individual confusion as of a particular Southern corruption of the terms history,
memory, nostalgia, and fantasy:

> This was not the same uniform he had worn in the War between the States. He had
> not actually been a general in that war. He had probably been a foot soldier; he didn't re-
> member what he had been; in fact, he didn't remember that war at all. (...) He didn't have
> any use for history because he never expected to meet it again. To his mind, history was
> connected with processions and life with parades and he liked parades. People were al-
> ways asking him if he remembered this or that – a dreary black procession of questions
> about the past. ("Late" 253)[138]

Almost sadistically, the general himself, then, gets to be paraded through the story
by a narrative voice that can hide neither its fascination with a persistence that "had
no more notion of dying than a cat" ("Late" 257) nor its disgust at the necrophilism
supporting its endurance:

> Every year on Confederate Memorial day, he was bundled up and lent to the Capitol
> City Museum where he was displayed from one to four in a musty room full of old pho-
> tographs, old uniforms, old artillery, and historic documents. (...) In the spring when the
> old homes were opened for pilgrimages, he was invited to wear his uniform and sit in
> some conspicuous spot and lend atmosphere to the scene. ("Late" 257)

At the graduation, eventually, the speaker serves the audience the quintessential
Southern mythology of its intimate connectedness to history which, supposedly,

---

137 In the following as "Late".
138 The repetition of the term "procession" for the graduation's keynote speakers (all
 addressing Southern history) echoes Virginia Woolf's "procession of the sons of
 educated men" as much as it calls to mind Walter Benjamins victorious processions:
 "Whoever has emerged victorious participates to this day in the triumphal procession in which the present rulers step over those who are lying prostrate. According
 to traditional practice, the spoils are carried along in the procession" (Benjamin
 256). To let a white old man, fake general, die of the effects of such a procession, is
 a supreme irony in O'Connor's story that lets a victorious procession kill one of their
 own.

will assure a commonly shared future way of existence: "If we forget our past we won't remember our future and it will be as well for we won't have one" ("Late" 260). The general's death, however, symbolizing the lack of future for a Southern history as fake as its incarnation "general," reveals the corny falsity of that claim. The general indeed will not have a future anymore, but not because of forgetting – it makes him actually happy not to think of history and have wet dreams of "Miss Queen Cotton" parade girls ("Late" 252) instead – but because of the past swallowing him up as (and in its) mythology:

> He couldn't protect himself from the words and the words were coming at him fast. (...) As the music swelled toward him, the entire past opened up on him out of nowhere, and he felt his body riddled in a hundred places with sharp stabs of pain and he fell down, returning a curse for every hit. (...) Then a succession of places, Chickamauga, Shiloh, Marthasville rushed at him as if the past was the only future now and he had to endure it. Then he saw that the black procession [the general's phrase for the college honorables preaching Southern history] was almost on him. He recognized it, for it had been dogging all his days. He made such a desperate effort to see over it and find out what comes after the past that his hand clenched the sword until the blade touched bone. ("Late" 261)

So far, one could settle in with his death, smugly contemptuous of the South's self-righteous legend (in the double sense) and perfectly delighted at its vitriolic demolition, but O'Connor's narrative voice has waited to complicate her textual scenario until the very last paragraph. After the general's death at the height of the ceremony, his nephew, a child in khaki clean Boy Scout uniform

> bumped him out the back way and rolled him at high speed down a flagstone path and was waiting now, with the corpse, in the line at the Coca-Cola machine. ("Late" 262)

This last sentence unravels the entire story. With uncanny slyness, O'Connor takes apart and reassembles a vision of Southern history that again inscribes her (white) doubleness.

Significantly, the only thing really relevant for the general's memory is the one time that he "had received the general's uniform and had been in the premiere." He gets to be paraded himself at a movie opening patterned upon the Atlanta premiere screening of *Gone with the Wind* ("Late" 256). For the conceited old man, white Southern history provides but an opportunity for himself to bask in the borrowed glory of the "Confederate Battle Hymn" ("Late" 255) he is supposed to illustrate. After having him deliver a totteringly silly contribution – he keeps yelling at the audience about kissing "pretty guls" ("Late" 256) that kept him young – O'Connor lets him sleep through the movie's presentation, though.

His granddaughter Sally has her own designs on him: she wants the "general" at her ceremony

for 'what all was behind her' and was not behind them. This them was not anybody in particular. It was just all the upstarts who had turned the world on its head and unsettled the ways of decent living. ("Late" 252)

Sally, too, in her pathetic, inappropriate desire for the "[o]ld traditions! Dignity! Honor! Courage!" ("Late" 253) elicits but a contemptuous ridicule by author (and presumably readers). At the movie premiere's climax she discovers that her "two brown Girl Scout oxfords protruded from the bottom of her dress" ("Late" 256). The same contempt is heaped on the academic graduation ceremony where the "graduates in their heavy robes looked as if the last beads of ignorance were being sweated out of them" ("Late" 259); a narrative voice oscillating between authorial perspective and the "general's" annoyance tells us that "[t]he speaker was through with that war and had gone on to the next and now he was approaching another and all his words (...) were vaguely familiar and irritating. ("Late" 261) The last in line, the nephew, selected by Sally to magnify the "general's" allure, gets to be called a "fat brat" ("Late" 260) by the old man – no objections by the narrative voice – and eventually figures as the executioner of his demise.

O'Connor seems to satirize everybody: the story deflates Sally's nostalgia for better times, the guardians of Southern culture who are faking the general like they fake history, the "general's" willful forgetfulness (he does not even remember his own family) as well as the boy's complete lack of historical consciousness and humane piety symbolized in his greedy affinity to the coke machine[139]. The last sentence invites one potential reading as a pleading of a respect for the dead Southern past's "corpse" that nobody else seems to be willing to deliver. The last paragraph's unnerving coupling of corpse and coke could imply O'Connor's indictment of a body-stripping of Southern history, her grotesque intervention to stop the "regular volley" of emptied out "words" on the Southern past ("Late" 261).

"The past and the future were the same thing to him, one forgotten, the other not remembered". This phrase appears twice, first in the above sentence that interrupts the "general's" interior monologues with a shift into the narrator's perspective. The second time, displaced and hollowed, in the context of the graduation ceremony, its words have become ritual exercised by the people in the "black robes (...) telling something about history" ("Late" 260). This ambiguous rephrasing seems to me to offer a key to O'Connor's own take on history. Being aware of her dedication to the South as **violated**, I read the doubled phrase as her insistence that however falsely appropriated the topos of Southern history has become, Southerners still should retain heartfelt remembrance of their legacy. This version of remembrance,

---

139 On the most obvious level, of course, coca cola – and the company's influence on the city – figures as a potent metaphor for the 'new' Atlanta, part of a commercialized, industrializing, consumptive South.

then, remains a completely ingrown white-on-white affair: O'Connor's critique of false historical representations occasions a moral admonition to remember a white Southern indestructible dignity of blessed suffering and failure.

This sentiment, as always in her writing, is undercut by what one could call her sarcasm of whiteness. O'Connor critiques low culture's mass marketing of past, present and future, its movies and its coke; the story satirizes a mythologizing sell-out of the past, as well as the youthful, unhistorical, disrespectful bumping of the corpse. The surprising sound of her last image, its serves-them-right-all-of-them-fakes leaves the reader with a profound disinvestment of white historicization of any kind. In her cynical lining up of movies, processions, corpse and coke, the parody of Southern whiteness is unbeatable.

What seems missing, however, is something to interrupt that strange liaison, a third term outside a quite chivalrous competition between *Gone with the Wind* (the college speeches, as the immediate doubling in the story suggests, are only a similar spectacle minus girlie glamour, but indebted to the same ideology) and Coke. Nostalgia and the reckless forgetfulness symbolized by the Coke machine's attraction are actually on O'Connor's display as two sides of the same coin of white idealization. In "Late", the Coca Cola-upstarts are feeding on its corrupting sweetness and on Southern narcissism in a consumptive alliance of oral, sensual and visual immediate satisfaction, which Hollywood may serve up as a national white spectacle. With her unfailing, chilling sense for imagistic precision, O'Connor cuts to the white bone, as it were; beyond that textual operation, she refuses assistance and leaves the reader in the suspension of shredded whiteness without relief.

Only later in her career, as Alice Walker has also suggested, she cautiously references blackness as an agency potentially able to disrupt this complacency: "The added quality is rage, and (...) O'Connor waited until she saw it **exhibited** by black people before she recorded it." (Walker 55, emphasis added). It is true that finally, in "Everything That Rises Must Converge," for example, the absent term of the black Civil Rights Movement which backs up the impertinence of the big black woman refusing to be humiliated, hovers like a shadow commanding definitely more readerly respect than the young white Southerner's solipsistic fantasies. Certainly not by happenstance the incident takes place on a bus – O'Connor's sly double edged homage to the Montgomery Bus Boycott. I am stunned, though, by Walker's implicit assumption that black people did not exhibit any contentious agency worth recuperating or referencing before the Civil Rights Movement. I would maintain that texts like O'Connor's[140], in over and again re-inscribing the myth of black "historyless-ness," in overwriting a history of black rage against

---

140 She refused to connect with Baldwin, for example, maintaining her status as white belle dame des lettres sans merci.

white supremacy with a white claim to Southern history precisely by way of an appropriation of metaphors of violation, partake in a white racism that reaches far beyond O'Connor's gorgeous white Georgia house.

3.2 Lillian Smith's Strange Fruit and Killers of the Dream: History, A Shadow Three Centuries Old

> We sound like missionaries with a powerful solemn purpose but we do own up to a love for the South that makes us want to do a little to help pull it up by its own bootstraps. (Smith 1939)
> If the liberals in the South do not turn to the constructive act, if they continue to "solve" deep fundamental conflicts by silence and evasion, pep talks, quiet pressures, or by criticism of Negroes who are attempting to pull their race toward freedom, much of the responsibility for the violence which may result may be theirs – as it has been theirs in the past. (...) If we profoundly believe that the Negro is as important as the white man, that his happiness and security are as essential as ours, we shall not be so quickly alarmed about "race trouble" by which is meant trouble for the white man. The Negro is always in trouble, a trouble which does not seem to concern many white people until the contagion spreads from the Quarters to White Town. (Smith 1942)
> That is what most of us mean when we talk of race relations: a more harmonious adjustment by the Negro to the white man's pattern. (Smith 1944)

There is a Lillian Smith icon, recently.[141] Adrienne Rich addressed her essay "Disloyal to Civilization: Feminism, Racism and Gynophobia" (1979) to her legacy, quoting Smith from a 1962 article:

Freud said once that woman is not well acculturated; she is, he stressed, retarded as a civilized person. I think what he mistook for her lack of civilization is woman's lack of loyalty to civilization. Southern woman have never been as loyal to the ideology of race and segregation as have southern men. (...) Many of them have been betraying White Supremacy for two hundred years but most who have done so could not reason with you as to why. (Smith 1962, 191)

Smith has since then become an "ancestor" for a number of white lesbian writers and activists who have, spurned by their own alienation, renounced adherence to (Southern) regimes of whiteness and racism (Segrest 1985, 1994; Frye, Bulkin et

---

141 A scholarly conference was devoted to her work in 1994, the proceedings of which I haven't been able to discover; the *Village Voice* featured her admiringly in 1994, a sure indicator for cultural hipness; she gets as of late quoted in prestigious cultural studies anthologies like Stam and Shohat.

al.). Her life and work seem to be very much to the contemporary point, even though it took her texts roughly 30 years to be re-discovered by white (feminist) scholars. In the middle of *Gone With the Wind*-hysteria[142], Smith confronted the legacy of slavery squarely. Battling the "creeping paralysis of anxiety" (Smith 1944, 42), she unflinchingly criticized segregation and racism in/of her beloved South:

> Most of us still want the privileges which we have under the White Supremacy system and we know that when segregation goes, White Supremacy will go with it. Most of us are incapable – having calloused our imaginations with the daily rubbing of one stereotype against another – of realizing what we are saying when we say calmly that 'these things must be changed very slowly,' (...) that 'the Negro must prove himself and then he will be accepted by the white man.' (...) We are willing for black children to be humiliated, bruised, hurt daily, subjected to a psychic brutality that would arouse us to fury if our white children were subjected to it – that *has* aroused our fury when it has happened to Jewish children in Germany. We are willing for these things to go on and on, because we cannot bear to change our own feelings, because we cannot endure the thought of tackling the most immediate task before us: the white man and his love for himself and his skin color. (Smith 1944, 34)

What characterized her work and her political engagement most of all was great moral integrity and courage, to the point of having her house burnt down repeatedly by militant young segregationists.[143] Among African-American civil rights activists of her time (and later) she earned herself a reputation of sincerity and unfailing supportiveness mainly by her social activism that included public addresses at rallies, the editing of *South Today*, the first white Southern journal to publish the work of black scholars and artists, and by her work for interracial civil rights groups like the "Committee of 100," and later CORE, as well as the early SNCC until its change to black militancy in 1964. Morton Sosna explains her unwavering commitment with her strong religious engagement:

> Stressing 'regeneration' of the South, these people [activist Southern liberals] found in evangelical Christianity not only an answer to the region's long dilemma over race but a possible bridge between racial liberalism and the concerns of the typical white Southerner. They would end up supporting the civil rights movement in the 1950s and 1960s. (Sosna 173)

To deal with limitations of whiteness in her writing, then, might almost be considered an act of bad faith. I am not at all interested, however, in dishonoring

---

142 She was acutely aware of the mass media's power, in "Humans in Bondage" she writes about pressuring Hollywood to stop making racist movies (Smith 1944).

143 The fire destroyed, among others things, 13.000 letters; for biographical information, see Sosna, 172-197.

Smith's work or disrespecting her personal integrity. On the contrary, I do want to reread her earlier texts because nothing reveals the **difficulty** to unthink white supremacy more tellingly than a rereading of an anti-segregationist mind at work. That, in turn, provides not only invaluable assistance for a contemporary project of denaturalizing whiteness, it also raises the ante of the debate particularly within feminism. I will read *Strange Fruit* "through" Smith's theoretical/ autobiographical essay *Killers of the Dream*; genre does not separate these two texts as much as they are united by a common cause, the novel prefiguring the essay, as it were.

In *Killers of the Dream* (1949)[144], her "troubled" South's Jim Crow regime becomes submitted to a thorough indictment bolstered by Freudian influences, traces of Ghandian teaching[145] and Southern bourgeois 'well-bred' Methodist upbringing. The text is driven by a series of metaphorizations of the social reality of her time. "Haunted childhood," "darkness and distance," "shadows of the past" are fully established as leading signifiers in the first few pages of *Killers*, as if racism were a problem of modernization not promptly and fully realized, a belatedness to the "moving times," a change withheld for the sake of ghosts: "The South walked backward into its future," (*Killers* 68) and "the old signs are still over the minds of men" (*Killers* 43):

These ghost relationships still haunt the southern mind to such an extent that many of today's most urgent problems cannot be dealt with rationally, even though the outcome of the world's crisis [of white supremacy] may depend largely upon how they are solved. They are ghosts that must be laid. (*Killers* 116)

Killers' significations of "waste" and "loss" of its human potential effect a profound, Faulknerian sense of gloom and frenzy, a disturbing picture of mental sickness, irrationality and destructiveness that, however, gets to be countered by a strident pragmatism, a call on elites, and a religious optimism combined with relentless trust in modernization so that the tragic element is countered by an uplift tale. As much as it was groundbreaking – and a self-endangering provocation for Ku Klux Klan minds – to call white southern racism mentally and psychically debilitating in its effects on white people and madly murderous for blacks, it is also a limited and in a sense misleading metaphor. Historically speaking, the Middle Passage, slavery and post Civil War American history were not elements of a ghost story, neither did these "events" follow the irrational scripts of madmen. Her narrative

---

144 In the following as *Killers*.
145 She read Ghandi during a stay in China as a missionary music teacher. Her life in China, and her observance of the way white ex-colonists behaved, also schooled her in cosmopolitism and in a keen perception of segregationism and hermetic caste systems; see Sosna.

thus moves in the shadow of an American gothic that Fiedler and Morrison, among others, have later come to characterize poignantly.

The intertextual connection to *Beloved* appears striking; in both, Morrison's and Smith's writing of the South, the territory seems stricken with haunting presences. Morrison has taken up the Southern gothic topos[146] of the region's ghastly benightedness to give it a distinctly different twist. Smith's texts are as much nostalgically drawn to Southern "darkness and distance" and its ghostly remembrances because they represent a childhood her writing personas do not want to separate from, as they argue for an overcoming of the ghosts by scientific knowledge and a truer Christian sense of agape than a Southern bigotry of preaching love and racism under one breath. The ghosts in *Killers* and *Strange Fruit* not only represent a dispensable past, they also function as Smith's metaphors for a kind of evil caused by a lack of rationality in Southern society's self-conception and may thus be banned in the interest of a common humane future for white and black people. In this combination of historical naiveté, pragmatic optimism and political will, the Southern ghosts can indeed only be mere shadows serving as metaphorical drive of a narrative that is constructed itself as a paradigmatic act of ghost-banning. The impulse here is on turning towards a better future, on getting out of the past, going beyond immature evil.

Morrison, on the contrary, writes of ghosts of dispossession, torture and visceral and spiritual dismemberment with an interest of **putting the past in memory**, of making it come alive against forgetfulness. Her ghosts are painfully vivid presences, not of a past characterized by irrational evil but by calculation, interest and rational motif: Sethe's confrontation with Schoolteacher's power of, literally, writing on her back a project of categorization, measurement and judgement functions as a severe indictment of the underside of the "rationality" that Smith finds the South so much wanting. There seems to be not only four decades of historical difference between these two positions, but also, notwithstanding Smith's decidedly anti-segregationist and anti-racist political activities, a difference of black and white subject positions. Morrison may not allow for the ghosts to be banned before they have been **met**, as much by her protagonists as by her 1980s readership. Looking back on Smith's writing from the 1990s vantage point, it seems to be an inscription of whiteness to be able to take the past for granted enough to dismiss it, as much as the impulse to do just that can be considered ethically sincere.

---

146 For a particularly contemporary and apt re-reading of Southern Gothic, see Joan Dayan 109-143.

Smith's conception of American history includes the Civil War, the old South, the 'new South,' and Jim Crow segregation[147]. However, the Middle Passage – as the quite purposefully enacted condition for a slave system in the Americas – becomes eclipsed in the parentheses of a passage which unabashedly shares in a voyeuristic sentimentalizing gaze on African people's entry into Anglo-America, and which is overwritten with an eroticization of their adaptive survival as southern "back-yard temptation":

By the historical 'accident' of slavery, our slaveholding puritan ancestors were juxtaposed to a dark people, natural, vigorous, unashamed, full of laughter and song and dance, who, without awareness that sex is 'sin' had reached genital maturity. (...) Laughter, song, rhythm, spontaneity were like a campfire in a dark tangled forest full of sins and boredom and fears. So bright, so near... (*Killers* 116,117).

Even in Smith's essay – definitely one of the most radical Southern texts of her time – the particular narrative of black people's arrival to the New World gets glossed over in two sentences, to reappear incorporated as a rhetoric of "our" black people. *Killers'* plot of historical developments contains but two actors: Northern and Southern white people in a "family feud" over possession, control, profits and political power. The essay's quite selective approach to history hinges on one rather inconspicuous metaphorical condensation: "[T]hen the black man fell into their design" (*Killers* 168). Gallantly, Smith here sidesteps an American heritage of building 'freedom' on human cargo. Slavery is taken as a given that needs no further scrutiny; neither *Killers* nor *Strange Fruit* deal in any way with historical reasons for black captivity and constitutionally forced servitude, they rather evasively accept that location.

Black agency is a historical factor Smith only waveringly appreciates. She does acknowledge that "Negroes had organized in protest" (*Killers* 195) in her narrative of the history from the 1915 Supreme Court's decision against the unconstitutional voting requirements for Negroes (the "grandfather clauses") to the New Deal, but on the other hand, the text displays a concern framed by black suffering and endurance:

[F]or the Negro never knew he had a bargain. All he did was keep going... (sic) singing, dancing, working, lying and stealing, fighting himself... and thinking... studying about things till he knew them, studying about ways till he found them, making things with his mind and his hand and his heart that the world knew were important... and, yes,

---

147 Müller Hartmann, Sosna et.al. all comment on the particularly aggravated situation for Southern Blacks in the 1930s and 1940s. One factor Smith credits with raising her own awareness was the dichotomy between a US moral and military victory over fascism, and its segregationist politics at home; there are repeated references to the Holocaust in *Killers* and her other work.

sometimes bowing, bowing and scraping and laughing, laughing easy at the white man, laughing easy at Mr. Poor White and Mr. Rich White, laughing loud at Mr. Negro, laughing belly laughs at Mr. Negro to hide his sorrow and his fear and his anger and his shame that nothing was due him. (*Killers* 187)

The NAACP, or other antiracist organizations, even though Smith was an active supporter herself, never exceed textual attention as a mention in a white polemics against the Northern Yankees. (*Killers* 185)

One of the scariest ghosts Smith is trying to exorcise is the terror of lynching: her metaphorization of it, however, effects obscurity and a very ambivalent positioning of the reader with respect to it. Smith judges the number of lynchings as "infrequent" (*Killers* 163), even though she volunteers numbers like 5,000 lynchings over the eighty-year period after the Civil War (*Killers* 68); the pertinent passage gives the following information:

From 1890 on, white-colored, white-colored grew into a regional chant that swells when tensions come, diminishes when tensions go, but there is always chanting... (sic) Minds and hearts were aroused by political greed, and sadistic fantasies spiraled higher and higher. Almost anything could happen and much did. The Atlanta riot in 1906... more and more lynchings of more and more sadistic nature, more white women succumbing to fantasies that they had been raped and sometimes there were actual rapings... more rumors and gruesome tales of brutality. Although 3,148 lynchings took place in the South from 1882 to 1946, no member of a lynch mob was given a death sentence or life imprisonment. Only 135 persons in the entire United States (according to records of years 1900 – 1946, during which time almost 3.000 lynchings took place) have been convicted of being members of lynch mobs. (*Killers* 201)

One of Smith's irritating strategies in *Killers* is not to quote any sources of her documentary evidence, so that there is no way of checking her personal authority. Black activists against lynching, and the black press circulated vastly different numbers. Ida B. Wells-Barnett's pamphlet "A Red Record" (1895) spoke of "over ten thousand lynchings" for the years 1865 – 1895 alone (Davis 184,185). Wells-Barnett and other scholars/activists, over decades, have consistently pointed to the voluntarily constructed relation between supposed rape and lynching, in which the specter of rape was propagandistically employed to justify the post-Civil War terror of lynching[148] – a relation that Smith's text equivocates about. Robyn Wiegman focuses on the relations between the political and psychosexual functions of lynching:

With the advent of Emancipation and its attendant loss of the slave system's marking of the African American body as property, lynching emerges to reclaim and reassert the centrality of black corporeality, deterring the now theoretically possible move toward

---

148   See also Giddings, and Harris on the politics of lynching.

citizenry and disembodied abstraction. Through the lynching scenario, 'blackness' is cast as a subversive (and most often sexual) threat, an incontrovertible chaos whose challenge to the economic and social coherency of the nation can be psychologically, if not wholly politically, averted by corporeal abjection and death. That lynching becomes during Reconstruction and its aftermath an increasingly routine response to black attempts at education, personal and communal government, suffrage and other indicators of cultural inclusion and equality attests to its powerful disciplinary function. As the most extreme deterritorialization of the body and its subjective boundaries, lynching guarantees the white mob's privilege of physical and psychic penetration, grants it a definitional authority over social space, and embodies the vigilant and violent system of surveillance that underwrites late nineteenth- and early twentieth- century negotiations over race and cultural power. (Wiegman 1993, 233)[149]

Smith even comes close to allowing a reading that would sanctify the argument of actual rape (as black retribution) being the justification for lynching. Without any historiographical substantiation she claims:

But a few angry bitter ignorant Negroes did fight back and in the only way they knew how: by assaulting white women. It did not happen often but it happened and it was a powerful and suicidal revenge. White men had ruthlessly used Negro women for a hundred and fifty years and carelessly abandoned their children. It was natural that a few Negro men should try to hurt the white race in the same way they had been hurt. But it was like pouring gasoline on a fire. And every mind in the South was scorched by the heat. (*Killers* 69)

Her discussion of lynching appears clearly to be one of the areas where she must have ignored available black contributions to the problem; it seems implausible that she had not known any NAACP material and thus reduced herself to downplaying lynching by way of numbers[150] and incorporating the centrality of the 'institution' of

---

149 I mostly agree with Wiegman 1993, except that her privileging of "the white mob" somewhat obscures the fact that lynchings might have been enacted by the white mob, but strongly benefited the massive political, social interests of the white dominant class of ex-aristocrats and newly bourgeois Southern white male gentry.

150 The second and only other time in the text she claims documentary status with numbers is a piece of strange figuring with respect to the slave population – it is not evident to me why Smith's authorial position in the 1940s should have excused such insincere moves. On page 168 in the chapter "Distance and Darkness" we find the following passage, as an extension of the narrative of Southern history begun in her dialogue with the child: "By the time of the Civil War in 1861, only one-tenth of one per cent of these old refugee [that is what she calls the European settlers, the "rejected of Europe", 166] owned as many slaves as did Scarlett O'Hara's family; only two and one-half per cent owned four or more slaves. But 200,000 families out of 5,600,000 whites did own at least one slave and the ownership of one human being as slave is enough to put a Christian's conscience and mind in bondage for a lifetime." The numbers the text offers at this point do not add up to her own calcu-

lynching into an sarcastic analysis of the psychological deprivations of 'white trash' Southerners. Describing rural boredom and isolation with no small amount of empathy, Smith continues:

> Sometimes a man sat on the front steps, talking a little about the crop or the next day's farm work, whittling on a stick, maybe just thinking, now and then aiming his spittle to hit the bull's eye of a totally imaginary spot. Have you seen that? That is rural adventure, rural fun. **No wonder a man-hunt took on zest, with no more thought given the running, frightened human being than to a running, frightened animal.** (...) Such a man-hunt is a journey into all that has been forbidden by religion and by women, a group flight into a strange free land of fury which the rational mind finds hard to understand. (160,162, emphasis added)

However, if one turns to Smith's discussion of the white Southern ladies who dared organizing against Jim Crow's terrors, founding the "Association of Southern Women for the Prevention of Lynching" in 1930,[151] one hears quite a different voice: that of the involved activist, not that of her vulgarly psychoanalytical ruminations.

These ladies went forth to commit treason against a southern tradition set up by men who had betrayed their mothers, sometimes themselves, and many of the South's children white and mixed, for three long centuries. It was truly a subversive affair, but as decorously conducted as an afternoon walk taken by the students of a female institute. (...) They set secret time bombs and went back to their needlework, serenely awaiting the blast. (...) Insurrection was on. White men were unaware of it, but the old pedestal on which their women had been safely stowed away, was reeling and rocking. (...) [T]hese men went on with their race-economic exploitation, protecting themselves behind rusty shields of as phony a moral cause as the Anglo-American world has ever witnessed. In

---

lation; also, they differ from the number for the post Civil War black population of 4,000,000 that the Freedmen's Bureau counted. (A number Smith herself provides on page 61). To follow her calculation through leaves more questions than information: adding up her slave population data, one cannot arrive at a clear figure because she does not give the numbers of white families owning more than one slave, percentage is absolutely irrelevant here since we don't know of what. The information value of "as many as Scarlett O'Hara's family" is also irrelevant, – an evocation of a pictorial scenario of large numbers of field hands does not stand in for numerical clarity. On the other hand, she does give the number of 4,000,000 ex-slaves contacted by the Freedmen's bureau, a number about which there seems to be no scholarly disagreement because of the Bureau's records.(60) 4,000,000 Black people implies, though, that almost half of the South's entire population had been black through the Civil War, given her number of 5,6000,000 Whites, whereas in her employment of surprisingly low percentage rates there is at least the tinge of a hardly countable minority. This is not just a different numerical ratio but also a different social and historical scenario.

151 See J.D. Hall, and Müller Hartmann.

the name of sacred womanhood, of purity, of preserving the home, lecherous old men and young ones, reeking with impurities (...) whipped up lynchings, organized Klans, burned crosses, aroused the poor and ignorant to wild excitement by an obscene, perverse imagery describing the 'menace' of Negro men hiding behind every cypress waiting to rape 'our' women. (...) The lady insurrectionists gathered together in one of our southern cities. (...) They said calmly that they were not afraid of being raped; as for they sacredness, they would take care of it themselves. (...) [T]hey would personally do everything in their power to keep any Negro from being lynched. (*Killers* 144,145)

Here is the voice of scathing critique, the call for insurrection against violent racism and the misogynist myth of the Southern Belle – echoing finally the Grimké sisters' appealing advocacy and sounding a pronounced "lack of loyalty to civilization" as Smith herself phrased it (Smith 1962, 191). Given the strength of her moral infuriation and her unhesitating support for the ladies' politics, it is not easy to follow Smith's textual oscillations on the lynching question; does she adopt two different voices to appeal to different clienteles? Does she emplot lynching in two different narratives so as to serve different audiences?[152] The duplicity of the essay's narrative voice remains with the reader as a haunt, indeed; the ambiguity of a point of view that could either be tactically employed to cater to a white conservative audience's reservations or could bespeak Smith's own residue white projections will not be resolved.

"Our South" calls for a textual strategy trying desperately to contain alienation, to keep a home, to redeem personal recollections, to – in a certain way – integrate horror, so that a common heritage might be lived. The very notion that history could have an alienating effect strong enough to cause disruption, a break with home, a disinvestment, is not imagined by the text – it would have transcended even her race traitor's imagination. Smith's pathos at times borders on euphemism, inviting identification with a history that would need distance, instead of binding readers into a closeness to oppression as human evil, as explicable, if not condonable human erring. The bulk part of the text is written in the autobiographical voice of a teacher straining to reduce complex history to a basic narrative for the understanding of a white twelve-year old Southern girl, without offending her sensibilities and her sense of loyalty. For Smith, "[t]he South was in trouble." *Killers'* first sentence becomes her controlling topos that she uses almost as one would speak of

---

152 Biographers and critics have commented on her successful ability to camouflage, as Sosna calls it, her radical politics with 'Miss Lil' Southern genteel behaviour, resulting, e.g. in the relative success and the unrestrictedness of *Strange Fruit* sales in the South, her continuing neighborly embeddedness in her hometown Clayton, and in the unbroken history of the summer camp for elite white school girls she maintained until 1948. To offer to her wealthy camp patrons that their children ought not to read *Strange Fruit* might bespeak that kind of shrewd tactics.

a troubled, and troubling, child refusing to mature. Smith's narrative voice is voicing these troubles from within:

> We southerners had identified with the long sorrowful past on such deep levels of love and hate and guilt that we did not know how to break old bonds without pulling our lives down. Change was the evil word, a shrill clanking that made us know too well our servitude. Change meant leaving one's memory, one's sins, one's ambivalent pleasures, the room where one was born. (...) We who were born in the South called this mesh of feeling and memory 'loyalty.' (*Killers* 26)

The speaking I in *Killers* wants to remain unsplit from her childhood; the text thus constructs a parallel between her own (narrative, autobiographical) persona and a "dark," infant, irrational South that finally has to grow up and face its problems as adult, as a rational, enlightened human being. Accordingly, the implied reader in *Killers* is a result of pedagogically complex considerations, of an eventually matured intuition for a reluctant audience and how to satisfy it: positioning us variously as a white Southern child straining to understand, and as a liberal white (Northern) adult who needs his/her superior post-abolitionist suspicions answered.

The construction of "I"/"we" as Southern versus "they," "city people, townspeople" (*Killers* 159) – a priori Northern – mirrors a split in the national consciousness. Northern urban whites have felt doubly free (in the sense of lack and gain) of blackness – the North constructing itself as heir to the Abolitionist movement and Lincoln's proclamation, thus conveniently glossing over the racism and ghettoization of urban development after World War I, leaving Northern white middle class life largely untouched by intimacy with blackness. Smith lets her text be driven by an emotional forcefulness that not only attacks the South for segregation but also caters to particular Northern convictions of its own moral superiority. She discusses racism as a "dark doctrine," a system bespeaking a benighted consciousness – which ignores the fact that racism was written into the core of enlightenment ideology itself. (Nelson) With her embedded narrative about the two brothers' (North and South) rivalry and various hints at Northern political machinations to support re-segregation after the Civil War, she criticizes that particular Northern mythology. At the same time she curiously reaffirms it by pitting an enlightened Northern urban consciousness against the backwardness, mental "darkness" and isolation of the South. Even that opposition, though, is not clearly held because there is also the undertone of Southern defensiveness and anti-Northern sentiment. In her story to the young girl, the North appears as rather slick as opposed to an embarrassing idealization of the deep and "complex" inner life of Southern white people that appeases a most prototypical Southern white self-pity:

"[Black people] filled [their] small lives with work and raising their families and their hope for heaven and a struggle for education, and dancing and razor fights and dreams and laughter. And there was singing, the saddest singing in all the world, and the most beautiful. And sometimes we who caused the sadness would weep with them as they sang." "The North can't understand that," [the girl] interrupted softly, "but I do. And I think it makes us seem a little more decent." "Maybe it only makes us more complex." (*Killers* 69)

Smith's emplotment of Southern history in *Killers* stages a very calculated disruption of white Southern consciousness; one that may, and must, as Smith's narrative control forcefully enacts, be carefully contained. The textual signposts of this containment are a dream of human freedom, Christian faith, belief in love and nonviolence: a clear demarcation against black militancy, a refusal of communist 'temptation' and a positive understanding of the South's 'human dilemmas.' Smith's caring white motherly femininity – as opposed to the racist frivolous white Southern Belleism that was her anathema – reveals itself in sentences like:

Knowing that bitterness is a poor bent key to unlock the future, I wanted her to begin her search for answers with sympathy for those who had not found them. I knew it would be hard enough for her who so passionately loved her ideals and a family that did not share them. (*Killers* 74,75)

The maternal measure here seems to be how much radical critique can a white consciousness bear without paying the price of complete alienation from their white culture. The very text that voices Smith's indictment of her cultural and social legacy thus embeds a problematics of white narcissism – seeing Southerners as "tortured" – something that no discussion of whiteness by white people can escape, it seems.

"But is it never to end?" she said. "It's like a nightmare everybody is having together! (...) But how can a person like me do anything! No matter how wrong you think it is, laws are against you, custom is against you, your own family is against you. How did you begin? (...) If you hated your family, it would be easier to fight for what is right." (...) We had made the circle and were beginning that old treadmill route that the **tortured** southern liberal knows so well. (*Killers* 72, emphasis added)

To re-name the emotional challenge, the doubtlessly enormous difficulty to unthink and to resign supremacist privilege as **torture** bespeaks to me a prototypical white position: it is precisely those gestures of metaphorical self-victimization that have historically underwritten the power of white subjects to name, categorize, and criticize history.

Given this privilege though, Smith has made a quantum leap in writing and acting herself out of the cultural script Southern society had waiting for women like her. To her, white women should be the first to break the domination of irrationality, religious stupor, authoritarian, puritan family structures and white racist superiority in dealing with their families and the immature South. She assigns historical responsibility to women in two ways: not shying away from calling them to task for Southern segregation and discrimination, she urges them to invest their lives in radical change.

Strange Fruit

> Smith] stated that she was using college-educated blacks in the story inasmuch as she did not want to carry on the 'old tradition of quaint Negroes.' (...) [S]he was "intensely interested" in exploring the family relationships of Southern blacks. (...) Once on radio [Smith] insisted that the novel was not really about race prejudice and lynching but rather a fable of sons, mothers, brothers and sisters searching for love.[153] (Sosna)

Lillian Smith's novel of a tragically failed relationship between a white man and black woman in the Georgia of 1920, *Strange Fruit*,[154] became a bestseller[155] and a cause célèbre upon its publication in 1944. (After seven publishers had rejected it before.) It was banned in Massachusetts, allegedly for using the phrase "fuckin" twice, which led to a landmark free speech case. The United States postmaster refused to allow it through the mail because of its "obscenity" – a decision to be later revoked by the White House upon an intervention by Eleanor Roosevelt herself.[156] The topic of interracial romance, or miscegenation has of course occupied North and South obsessively, and the title's unwitting[157] allusion to Billie Holiday's

---

153 That might – given the recent critical acceptance of Lillian Smith's life as a lesbian with Snelling, be more correct than people could know: the race plot in a certain way hides the lesbian plot within the mother-daughter conflict; that plot being, for Smith's autobiographical reasons, the ultimate unsayable and therefore to be only subversively included. What does it mean for a culture that white Southern lesbians can rather 'come out' **for** the Negroes than for their right to their own sexuality? That would be a topic for another study, however, and one would have to trace the working through of Smith's legacy in Bulkin's, Pratt's, Segrest's and Frye's work to cover the question.

154 Hereafter as *Strange*.

155 It sold over 3 million copies and was translated into sixteen languages.

156 Reception was varied in the progressive camp also: Communists attacked the novel, because a black character is burned to death by a white mill worker's mob, as divisive to class solidarity; Walter White, among other black intellectuals, criticized the portrayal of the young black heroine, a Spelman graduate, because of its lack of realism – no black college woman would carry on with white men the way Smith has her do (Sosna 190).

157 See the introduction by Fred Hobson to *Strange Fruit* in the 1985 edition.

mourning of black bodies (lynched for alleged interracial sexual trespassing) certainly furthered its overwhelming popularity. Notions of the black male sexual "aggressor" must have been so entrenched even among the most progressive white people that Herbert Aptheker, in his edition of W.E.B. DuBois' correspondence, introduces Lillian Smith as the author of a novel whose "plot was the love of a Black man and a white woman in the South and the eventual lynching of the man" (Aptheker 1976) – a telling misreading of the actual text.

The novel is framed by a shadow, literally: on the first and last pages of the novel, respectively, history appears but eclipsed in metaphorical short hand. When black Ed Anderson on a visit to his home town meets white Tracy Deen, even a chatty conversation between them is impossible: " 'So,' [Ed] whispered. 'So,' his mind echoed. 'So,' three hundred years shouted back at him." (*Strange* 13) In a scene towards the novel's closure, white liberal Tom Harris and black doctor Sam Perry have an argument about how and how fast (or better, how not so fast) to overcome segregation that is interrupted by the news of the plot's lynching, and again: "White man, brown man, stared across the shadows of the room, across three centuries of the same old shadow" (*Strange* 343)

That construction – to evoke history but not to engage it directly – precisely enables Smith to unfold her psychodrama of black and white relations, as a kaleidoscope of parts that are exact fictional precursors of her autobiographical lay-out in *Killers of the Dream*. *Strange* assembles all the available Southern positions on segregation, ranging from a black woman's embittered rage to the Ku Klux Klan lynchers; all these points of view are allowed their own voices in the text. In widening circles that multiperspectival participation spirals out from the core conflict of interracial sexual relations. First the protagonists and their families alternate in their mutually reflective points of view, churning in their segregated ways; next we meet the characters that will gain narrative importance in the conflict's unfolding: Sam Perry, Henry, Dessie, Tom Harris, the KKK members; at last, the commentators Reverend Dunwoodie, Captain Rushton, Prentiss Reid, Charlie, Harriett, Miss Sadie, Miss Belle: stand-ins of Southern beliefs and politics. The plot is pushing forward to the lynching of innocent Henry with frightening implausibility. After Ed Anderson kills Tracy Deen in his hurt rage about Deen's sexual abuse of his sister he disappears to New York; the Anderson women remain untouched by white revenge – nobody even comes bothering them.

Smith drives her point home forcefully: the social act of burning a black man alive is not a retribution for actual guilt (horrible in itself as that would be) but a ritualistic human sacrifice to keep the white order in place. As she puts it in Sam Perry's words:

But he stands for something – his living stands for something. And they'll get him. Bound to! Got to hate something and kill it. Got to! Things couldn't keep on like they are down here if you didn't kill something. To keep from killing your own kind (...) (*Strange* 340).

Black Memory, White Writing

The novel raises the specter of Southern history by different means: one is of course the very event to set the plot in motion – the affair between almost white Non Anderson and Tracy Deen, son of one of the most respected white families in *Strange*'s prototypical Georgia town. That relationship echoes a history of white men raping black women, or using them sexually, and the compounded tragic end of a relationship so oppressively doomed, seems to be inevitable: Tracy's ultimate betrayal of Non in order to remain a good white son is as predictable as lonely Non's decision to keep his baby as somebody to love, even if that might ruin her own life.

Strange's two protagonists act as if living out a historical script that allows no other options, thus embodying the author's convictions of the South's deadly psychological sickness. Readers have to extrapolate, however, Non's and her mother Tillie's actual history at the hands of white men from textual hints, as in father Anderson's restless suspicion of his wife's possible "traffic" with white men (*Strange* 281). Rape of black women actually never becomes an issue, even though, again, we find a covert allusion to it in Tracy Deen's drunk and guilt-ridden assault on Non the last time they meet.

The other, more 'resistant' presence of history in the text is black memory possessed by Bess Anderson, who in turn seems to be consumed by it in Smith's allegorical claim on her. Bess's troubled spirit is the only signifying trace of a black family's history in the turn-of-the-century South. In *Strange*, hardly any mention of slavery is made by any black character in any direct way (which is all the more confounding since Tillie Anderson must have been a girl or young woman before the Civil War and thus lived in slavery). Bess's desolate outcry: "Maxwell holds no good memories for a Negro" does not lead into textual explorations of what that might actually have meant for the Anderson family. Nor does the text seem able to let her insistence that Maxwell is indeed home for her – based on her love for its beauty, serenity and natural bounty – appear as permissible feeling:

You don't know why you stay in a place where you were born! How can you be sure! There're a thousand reasons why it's easier to stay than to go. 'Maxwell holds no good memories for a Negro.' You lied. A thousand good memories, Name them, girl! All right. I'll name them. Moss... (sic) trailing in your face when you're little... you'd make great pillows of it (...) Oak trees you couldn't reach around. (...) Thickets of yellow jessamine...

and violets... everywhere sand. (...) It's more than sand then, it's you then... some of you you couldn't leave behind, forever. (*Strange* 36)

The text has Bess ridicule and denounce her own desire for memories that empower her to feel human in the face of oppression: "You stay for that? Cypress and branch water, sand and wild flowers?"[158] The real reason she wants to stay, we are told, is to be close to Sam Perry, the man in her life she loves but could not marry. For Smith, the sexual narrative – jealousy, desire, rejection – is always articulated with, and sometimes undermines her interest in, the racial narrative. *Strange* thus evades a narrative focus on history, even though the phrase "no good memories" evokes implications beyond individual hurt only to be translated into a "personal" realm of frustrated love. Bess's black memory, instead, is inscribed only as a subtext in a script of sexual sisterly envy, to indeed shame the character. Bess's pent-up uncorrupted radicality – the one mature black consciousness in the novel to oppose the more conciliatory black decency and cooperativeness embodied by Sam Perry – explodes as violent bitterness, propelling itself forward in a frenzy of self-hatred.

Sometimes I wonder if there is something in the Negro – Ed killing, Nonnie pregnant – what's the matter with us! Is it Negro? Is it Anderson? What's the matter with people like us? (...) And I don't see how any colored woman would want to bring another Negro into this world! (*Strange* 292)

Bess's voice, the one who insists on keeping track of violation and humiliation, will be effectively silenced for the rest of the novel by Sam Perry's verdict: "'Bess,' his voice was sharp and angry, 'there's something about you that makes a man sick!'"(*Strange* 294). The sexual narrative – Sam feeling attacked by Bess's jealousy of Non and not being able to hold out to her enraged articulateness as a woman, either – overrides the racial narrative again. Measured against Smith's idealization of black mothers in *Killers*, Bess's painful psychic contortions sound, in *Strange*'s inscription, the despicable "ambivalence" Smith wants to evacuate from her historical narrative of a people "restive under severe restraints and humiliations":

But throughout slavery [Negroes] possessed a psychological quality that could maturely withstand the temptation to take revenge. Their record during the Civil War and later during the chaos of Reconstruction is one of the most honorable in human annals. To call them cowards for not being vengeful, as some do today, is to ignore the dynamics of personality. Cowards would have been the first to let their hate feelings break through: it would not have required much bravery to kill and burn and rape helpless women and

---

158 *Beloved* again has an intertextual answer to that: it "shamed" Sethe to think of the beautiful sycamore trees on Sweet Home; she is, however, not lead to denounce her reminiscence as ridiculous.

children left isolated on the big plantations. I think the answer lies in the home, in what happened between mother and child in those tiny slave cabins. Those of us who in our childhood knew a few of these strong old women – the children of slaves – can never forget their wisdom, their capacity for accepting life and people, their deep laughter, their unashamedness. They had strong instinctual feelings, not all of them loving, but they rarely let hate or fear master them. And I cannot imagine one of them feeling guilt in the way in which their 'white folks' felt it, nor do I remember their suffering from that sickness of the soul we call ambivalence. (*Killers 119*)

That focus on self-identity and endurance precisely keeps black memory contained in white admiration, to be thus passed on – within the narrative, and to readers as well – as a normative legacy: in Mamie's motherly whippings of little Henry for dangerous foolishness around white girls, for example, or in a repeated narrative exposition of Tillie Anderson's larger-than-life strength. What Alice Walker would later call "contrary instincts" has no legitimate space in Smith's writing. *Strange* enacts this containment, even if it manages to let a reader feel some of Bess's maddening anger as excessive to it, but it cannot finally take Bess's position.

Likewise, even when Sam's cooperative poise breaks up upon realizing that he too (as well as the Anderson family) will be complicit in the lynching, and when he finally loses "control" (*Strange* 341) in an argument with his liberal white "friend" Tom Harris, black memory, the genealogy of his anger, is never confronted directly. It remains a threatening shadow (*Strange* 343). The unspeakable might not be uttered, at the cost of a terribly precarious balance; the threat of race riot is almost viscerally present in the narrative anticipation of unmanageable danger:

He'd have tried... (sic) shown he had a little manhood... You'll make it worse for the rest of us... That's what they always say... you'll turn it into a race riot... That's what everybody tells you ...Manhood's for powerful folks, you can't afford it, they mean. (*Strange* 343)

The Black Woman as White Prize

The one story that is actively **unwritten** in *Strange* is Non Anderson's. Her very existence as a black woman within a black family is in doubt, she is indeed a "non" Anderson: her white features, the mystery that surrounds her 'uppity' behavior and the striking apartness from her siblings function as coded signifiers for a (black woman's) history of miscegenation, in this case, the rape of her mother by her white master. On the very first pages of the novel, before Non has uttered a word, or has had a thought of her own, she is engulfed by veiled envy, hatred, sexual greed and the white male gaze of "old Cap'n Rushton":

And white boys whistled softly when she walked down the street and said low words and rubbed the back of their hands across their mouths, for Nonnie Anderson was something to look at twice, with her soft black hair blowing off her face and black eyes set in a face that God knows by right should have belonged to a white girl. And old Cap'n Rushton (...) would rub his thick red hand over his chin slowly as he watched her (...) sit there watching the girl, rubbing his hand over his chin, watching her (...). (*Strange* 2)

There is more than a hint of a paternal incestuous interest in Smith's representation of the old white man here,[159] but the narrative does not exhibit any interest in exploring the connection. Non is a static and somehow vacant embodiment of the tragic mulatta, who, as a "neither/nor" figure (Spillers 1989 "Notes") cannot have a position, a voice of her own. She is the white enough prize that everybody, white or black, covets, textually loaded with fantasies and interpretations. She, however, does not speak herself, and thus moves through the plot as rather stereotypical enigma of miscegenation. Her signifiers are "waiting, good, quiet and giving" (*Strange* 146), and she appears impenetrable, focussed on herself and narcissistically beyond the materiality of her blackness. Even when the plot conflates humiliation, hurt and loss for her in Tracy's death, Ed's disappearance and the inevitable outing of her pregnancy, we read her mind as crowded out by other people's utterances; she is only the zombied receptacle of the confused human feelings participating in the interracial dilemma, Bess's and Ed's voices warring in her frenzied, dreamlike associations with Tracy's phrases. In the most literal sense, she narratively embodies Smith's conception of Southern history's tragic sickness.

Smith's narrative, then, reaches its own limit in a black historical experience "too terrible to relate," as Morrison has put it. (Morrison 1987, 109) There is a specific white cultural pressure not to **say** history directly, but to metaphorize, allude to, or displace it. I see Smith's novel partaking in that pressure, in its overwriting of historical dynamics with vulgar psychology, its ambiguous conflation of sexual and racial oppression, and its emblematizing of black characters. Her emplotment of the "bad nigger" trope signifies to this white pressure's ideological hold most clearly.

The Bad Nigger

Strange capitalizes massively of the semantic potency of the "bad nigger"- trope. Why does the novel need the flesh of a stereotypically oversexed, loose, bad and stupid "nigger" to burn? I sense a jarring tension in the text: On the one hand, Smith carries on a moral debate through her characters' conflicts and the verbal commentary from all sides involved; the obvious structural principle being to have racist, segregationist, and humanly insincere behavior reveal itself in confrontation with a radical Christian humanity. On the other hand, the effects of the

---

159 And there is a later echo of it in the scene when Ed Anderson meets Rushton.

plot stripped of its narrative articulations share in the white supremacist paranoia Smith so ardently attacks.

If a black man has to be sacrificed, he may be innocent – which supports the liberal moral point of her narrative – but he, for the same reason, must certainly be a "bad nigger":

> Henry watched her. His big wet mouth hung open. His big black hands hung deject-edly between spraddled legs. His eyes moved over her face, to her little pointed breasts, down her body, lingered over the curve of her little belly. 'I'm hongry sho,' he said abruptly and heard his words with surprise. (...) He laughed, drank of it again, reached out a big lazy hand, pulled her to him. He drew her between his legs as he sprawled in the chair and locked her within them like a vise. (...) After he had had his satisfaction Henry stretched out on the warm sand, gave one deep body-resting sigh and was almost at once sound asleep. (*Strange* 238,9)

Henry thus appears to readers as a possible sexual threat (which might always already also be a lure) in a white feminized gaze which cannot hide its own pro-found disturbedness. The narrative construction and function of the trope invites a perverse complicity calling to mind Spiller's "pornotroping" of black bodies:

> [A]s a category of 'otherness' the captive body [which might legitimately be equated with the black body, in the context of the segregated South, S.B.] translates into a poten-tial for pornotroping and embodies sheer physical powerlessness that slides into a more general 'powerlessness' resonating through various centers of human and social meaning. (Spillers 1987, 67)

The "bad nigger" is held suspended, in this racist mythology, in the schism of a factual absence of power unto himself and the attribution of (sexual) omnipotence unto him in a white projection. These two pressures on his personality perversely feed and condition each other. In this scenario, Henry's "inevitable" aggression – which is narratively answered by his fatal powerlessness – is not directed against a real white woman (even though that possibility lingers in the text) but to young, in-nocent Non. His attack, not incidentally, serves to whiten up Non, in a supposed empathy of white readers, precisely because of a spiritual (if not sexual) purity re-served for the white man she loves as opposed to mere genital sexual attraction). Non is, in Southern fact, a black woman, which means the same codes of black permissiveness and "primitive" genitality would apply to her as to childish and sexually easy Dessie. The narrative allows her, however, to be split from the other black woman and feel dirtied and hurt by Henry. She may act, as it were, as a white woman; thus, her narrative effect is to shore up feminine white identification against Henry, whose black genital monstrosity is again furthered massively:

[Non] was seeing Big Henry, she was breathing his sweating stench, she was looking at his big open mouth with his upper gold teeth, feeling his hot breath on her lips, her ears rang with his deep-bellied laugh, her thigh felt his wide gripping fingers. She was remembering when she was eleven. (...) "Say," he said and grinned, "say, how about fuckin with me?" (...) "You knows," he grinned, "fuckin," and opened his pants. She had begun to run and he had run close behing her saying, "Say, what's the matter? Are you skeered?" Suddenly she had turned on him and whispered (...) "Don't you come near me, don't you come near me!" (...) "Shucks,' he called after her, "whassa matter wif you? Even white girls does dat." (*Strange* 225,226)

The figure, and most of all, the extremely sexualized **body** of Henry calls up a complex, and racially invested field of readerly response: A grinning "Negro" who so obviously cannot keep his always bursting sexuality in check is not only an embodiment of the "black boogeyman"- threat to morally upright white Christians, he also reigns supreme in the repertoire of their envious or desirous most secret fantasies. White Southern women whose upbringing severely restricts them in their sexual rights and their imagination are entitled to use the figure of the black potent, yet powerless body either as a symbol for their own abjection, or as "strange fruit," an incarnated object of threatening desire. However unwittingly, Smith herself gives away this unacknowledged sentiment in a corresponding passage in *Killers*:

These so-called primitives (whose culture had so many sophisticated elements in it) were not (...) brought into this country and hidden away in ghettos. They were brought into our back yards and left there for generations. They were everywhere and highly conspicuous not only because of their color but because of their liveliness which the chains of slavery never subdued. From all that we know of them they seem to have had, even as some have now, a marvelous love of life and play, a physical grace and rhythm and a **psychosexual vigor** that must have made the white race by contrast seem washed-out and drained of much that is good and life-giving. (*Killers* 117, emphasis added)

Smith, as a white woman, narratively constructs a black male body that – via her aggressively humiliating figuration of him – has to bear punishment for the white desire palpable in her rhapsodic lines to black people's playfulness, grace and vigor.[160] Correspondingly, for white men, lynching a black man becomes an act to keep control, as Paul Hoch observes, "over the bestial supermasculinity he has projected outward on to the black male (which) would threaten the racist's control over his own suppressed sexuality." (Hoch 54)

The black male body, in Smith's scenario, inadvertently becomes an incarnated historical reminder of a white racism legally and morally declaring African human beings as beasts. In offering up Henry to a cruelly voyeuristic narrative perspective

---

160 Smith's lesbianism does not negate this reading; an imaginary eroticism between the races is not necessarily tied to general sexual choice.

that actually dispenses with Henry's humanity before the actual lynching, Smith partakes in that legacy despite her best liberal intentions and effectively mutes a history of lynching.

The plot's foundational sacrifice of a "bad nigger" is doubled by lethal punishment for Tracy Deen for not having been able to cut his ties to blackness timely enough. Smith later analyzed the complex of desire/rejection that binds white Southern men to black women psychically, even if that remains a cultural taboo.

> Because white mother has always set up right and wrong, has with authority established the 'do' and the 'don't' of behavior, his conscience (...) ties its allegiance to her and to the white culture and authority which she and his father represent. But to colored mother, persuasive in her relaxed attitude toward 'sin,' easy and warm in her physical ministrations, generous with her petting, he ties his pleasure feelings. (*Killers* 132)

As a young boy, Deen himself had depended completely on Henry's mother for creature comforts, emotional acceptance and spiritual balance, a fact not only due to her nursing both boys as if her own sons, but also to his mother's extreme anti-sensuous rigidity and frightening parental distance. With Non, he finds a kind of happiness he has been lacking since Mamie left the house: the unconditional acceptance she seemed to have lavished over him.[161] To grow up white, however, means to cut these tender ties.

It is acceptable to fool around with black "girls" but a man has to know the limits of public decorum – Smith does reveal the ugly, abusive hypocrisy of this type of masculine white honor and how much Tracy Deen, in spite of some more sincere feelings for Non, shares in it. Ultimately, Tracy has to die because he cannot make sure the decorum be kept before Ed comes home. Tracy has refused to cut his oedipal ties to both his mothers – a social/individual predicament that a segregated society keeps nourishing on the one hand, and tabooing and punishing on the other. The only real man is a white man, and vice versa, only if one agrees to be white, may he be a man at all.

Black Ed Anderson, then, keeps the white community's time for masculinity which Tracy fails to meet; he re-establishes the ground rule of segregation: racial purity. Smith portrays his murder of the white offender with considerable empathy as morally wrong but humanly understandable act of black retribution.[162] In a stunning twist of an old script, Ed Anderson gets away with murder whereas both

---

161 Smith in both texts is not very eager to explore this tangle from a black woman's point of view; the possibility that for many black Mammies loving white children like their own did not play the role white people maybe wished for, is not really entertained.

162 See slave narratives' enraged laments about the impotence of black men to defend the women of their communities against sexual assault.

white Tracy, guilty of too much visceral and psychic closeness to two "niggers," **and** his alter-ego black Henry have to die. Mamie's two "sons" Tracy and Henry are killed in a kind of crossover execution: black man kills white man Tracy, white men kill Tracy's black "brother." Latent in that plot effect is a white revenge for remaining too much a black woman's son. Tracy refused to become properly white in time, so blackness kills him with a vengeance, but this killing paradoxically results in a twofold white victory of death.

In the narrative passage coming to meet the plot's climactic fulfillment of lynching, Sam Perry gets to voice the entire respectable (white **and** black) community's share in the ritualistic practice:

> You know who's lynching him? It's you and me! That's right. White man and brown. Respectable white folks don't like to get mixed up in things like this. No. And respectable colored folks don't either. So we shut our eyes, you shut your eyes, I shut my eyes and –
> (*Strange* 339)

But his confession is as belated and thus as ineffectual as Tom Harris' intervention to stop the burning; both of the men will – as the text implies without doubt – keep their mouths shut and not raise more trouble at cotton-picking time. Both Tracy's and Henry's "dirty" sexual lives are ultimately exorcised from the community, White Town and Quarters. I read this belatedness as an acknowledgement of white paranoia running its course; a readerly position thus being opened for a voyeuristic gaze on transgression and punishment, with all the fascination that implies. By basing the plot on the two men's sexual "badness" by the laws of a racially segregated community, a history of racist murder becomes tinged with an attractivity of scandalous trespassing and righteous catharsis. This plot result thus bespeaks once more Smith's preoccupation with Southern psychosexual compulsion; a (white) perspective which screens an investigation into a racist social structure perpetuated by material interests, political investments and historically empowered subject positions. (Hodes)

Laura's Love

Immediately after Tracy's body has been found by Henry, in a cutting transition, the novel moves to the conflict between Laura and her mother. Henry's fearful anticipation that the lynchmob will get him is mercilessly abandoned in favor of Laura's sexual narrative: her mother has stolen (and destroyed), first, a little sculpture of a naked woman Laura made after the model of her beloved friend Jane Hardy, and then a letter between them. Laura's insight: "She hates what I like! (...) It had seemed now that she had known this for a long time without telling it to herself" (*Strange* 241) becomes confirmed by her mother's homophobic and disrespectful intervention against her relationship with Jane:

> There're women, Laura, who aren't safe for young girls to be with. (...) There're women who are – unnatural. They're like vultures – women like that. (...) They do terrible things to young girls. (*Strange* 243)

Not only does that reveal a motherly possessiveness in the extreme – the mother is said at one other point to have given up her own life to live Laura's – it also barely hides an inscription of lesbianism.[163] Women as **vultures**: the language of devouring is richly explicit underneath Mother Deen's prudeness and it – unbeknownst to her – bespeaks her own fantasies. Sexuality (with her husband) is something dirty and dispensable in her register, but not only does she in fact devour her daughter's life, she creates a fantasy symbiosis that is loaded with unacknowledged eroticism:

> And occasionally, oh most rarely, she had slept in Laura's bed, escaping Tut's masculinity. Feeling at times a desperate need, she would slip into Laura's room. And on those nights her sleep would be dreamless and peaceful. (*Strange* 67)

Laura appears nearly suicidal after finding out about her mother's aggression and betrayal of her daughter's integrity and has only one idea left in her, to leave her mother. She feels close to her rejected brother for the first time: "Why had he always failed and you succeeded? It made you (...) feel that you had climbed to success by standing on his failures" (245).

Only getting away from Maxwell would enable Laura to build her own life. After Tracy's and Henry's death, however, she decides to stay home; the perverse catharsis of sacrifice and mourning binds her, instead of Tracy, into the community as a returned prodigal daughter. She will take on her responsibility as a good white woman, following her mother's model, banishing any possible social compassion with a housekeeping practicality, a Southern Belle reliability: "Someone must remember to shut the door [of Henry's cabin]. Someone must remember to write Mamie" (*Strange* 364). Shared white shock and grief restore the mother-daughter balance; Laura will not go "anywhere" – the sexual threat (of lesbianism) kept at bay on the back of the racial sacrifice.

---

163 The strange mis-relation between Smith's factual lesbian relationship with Paula Snelling, the inscription of lesbianism as ostracized by Southern culture in *Strange*, on the one hand, and her virulent anti-feminism in *Killers*, on the other, merits a discussion that also exceeds the space of this work.

Strange wants to represent a "realistic" portrait of Southern segregation played out in family conflict. It can be inferred from its amply provided moral commitment, as in Smith's strategic deployment of the revivalist "Wash me, I'll be whiter than snow" to characterize the Southern frenzy for racial purity, that its melodramatic construction was meant to **mourn** the inevitability of segregation's human losses. The novel's undercurrents though, acknowledge the white order which the ostensive empathy for the conflict's tragical result is supposed to attack. As the introduction to the 1985 edition has it:

> If *Strange Fruit* qualifies as tragedy, however, it is of the deterministic variety, for the characters seem trapped into society into which they are born. (...) Her characters are anything but free agents: they are trapped by social forces, by patterns of conditioning, and their actions are nearly predictable. (Hobson XIII)

I see not only a naturalistic limitation but also a reflection of Smith's own white subject position. In her literary imagination Smith refused to imagine black agency as a historical force capable of disrupting the schizophrenic Southern determinism. In her own life, she was connected to black intellectuals like DuBois[164] who – as she knew perfectly well – labored precisely against paternalistic white theories of black pathology and victimization, to constitute black historical, political and cultural subjectivity; this factual interracial engagement did not carry over into her novel, however.

The fact that all three Andersons went to college ends up as an occasion for self-derision, buried in Bess's cynical ravings against "niggers":

> "Yes, nigger," she whispered (...) "It's caught up with us. It was as if the Anderson's had been running away from it, getting a little whiter and whiter with each generation, running hard. But it's caught up. As it catches anybody, sooner or later. (...) Going to college won't help you run any faster – all that stuff they tell you there makes it worse. Be proud of your African heritage, they tell you! Yeah... (sic) music... rhythm... all that... Proud! When you're pushed around through back doors, starved for decent friendliness and respect, they tell you about Benin bronzes – things like that. (...) When all that matters to you or any other Negro is that your folks were slaves and you're still slaves. You can't run away from that shadow..." (*Strange* 279,80)

One of Bess' arguments with Non contains a reference to intellectual creativity. However, it immediately deconstructs itself in Bess's envious mockery and her offhand dismissal of black authorship as a white scheme:

---

164 He once wrote a letter of recommendation for one of her research projects, see Sosna.

Once [Non] tried to tell Bess what the night meant to her but Bess said, "Listen. If it's good, don't waste it on me. Put it down and sell it. They'll buy anything a Negro writes these days, so surprised we can spell." (*Strange* 121)

If Smith's personal reality was largely motivated by the desire for establishing interracial contacts – one of her most often repeated admonitions to white people was to get to **know** black people personally – her literary self-restriction to knowing them either as nobly inflicted by their blackness or as quintessentially sexualized bodies, that is as tragically good or tragically bad characters, begs the question of Smith's residual whiteness.

To make her psychologizing points, she seems to have found it necessary, given a Northern liberal readership mainly influenced by Myrdal's *American Dilemma* (1944) to portray black people in a historical void, bereft of any rational, successful social and political agency. As David Levering Lewis has suggested:

Predictably, there was now a steady supply of "exemplary" Afro-Americans (athlete Jackie Robinson joining the Dodgers in 1947, poet Gwendolyn Brooks winning a Pulitzer and jurist William Hastie appointed to a federal judgeship in 1949, diplomat Ralph Bunche receiving the Nobel Peace Prize in 1950) – racial paragons whose lives rebutted inferiority stereotypes, on the one hand, and, on the other, diverted attention from the distressing Marxism of W.E.B. DuBois, Paul Robeson, and Benjamin Davis, Jr. Thus, in the Myrdalian decade after 1944, that article of faith of such civil rights leaders as James Weldon Johnson, Charles S. Johnson, and Walker White that the race problem was essentially not so much institutional, or even economic but, rather, a phenomenon of collective psychology, now seemed verified. (...) The impact of *An American Dilemma* was so potent that it controlled racial thought and politics for at least a decade. For all its impressive sociological panoply and perdurable insights, the Myrdalian analysis was imbedded in Hegelian idealism. Right ideas would gradually transform wrong institutions; the American Creed would ultimately reify itself because the compounding tensions between high ideals and ignoble realities would compel white Americans to reexamine the status quo. (Lewis 8, 9)

It seems to me that Smith, in translating her childhood memories into a literary form, reached the intellectual boundaries of her own Southern (family) background. The focus of *Strange* remains a disturbance, an imbalance of the white historical order and its subsequent restoration. Even though Smith herself saw a "therapy" in writing *Strange* that "removed a long amnesia about (her) hometown," (Smith, quoted in Hobson XV) her particular emplotment of the story belies a white innocence of, and dis-interest in history which thus consequently may only haunt her text as a shadow.

3.3. Rosellen Brown's Civil Wars: Can Feminism Integrate Historical Memory?

> The energy of the seventies is very different from that of the previous
> decade. There's a different agenda and a different mode of struggle. The
> demystification of American-style "democracy," the bold analytical and
> passionate attention to our condition, status and process – the whole ex-
> perience of that era led us to a peculiar spot in time, the seventies. Some
> say it's been a period of retreat, of amnesia, of withdrawal into narcissism.
> I'm not so sure. I'd say the seventies is characterized by a refocusing on
> the self, which is, after all, the main instrument for self, group and social
> transformation. (...) We were trained by the sixties to perceive activity, to
> assess movement and progress, in particular modes – confrontation, un-
> compromising rhetoric, muscle flexing, press conferences, manifestoes,
> visible groups, quasi-underground groups, hitting the streets, marching,
> singing, marching etc. On the other hand, the workings of the seventies,
> while less visible and audible and less easy to perceive, to nail down and
> define, were no less passionate and no less significant. (Cade Bambara)

In the American novelistic imagination the Civil Rights Movement appears to
have been swallowed up almost entirely by oblivion. The only prominent excep-
tions to confront that particular phase of American history are Alice Walker's
Meridian, Ernest Gaines's *Autobiography of Mrs. Jane Pittman* and Rosellen
Brown's *Civil Wars*[165]. As the bibliographical appendix in a collection like Charles
W. Eagles' *The Civil Rights Movement in America* (1986) indicates, there has been
considerable historical and social scientist research of the movement despite the
relatively short time lapse, as well as autobiographical writing and biographical
studies, but few scholars have "analyzed the literature and music of the movement
itself or later fictional treatments of it" (Eagles 177). Indeed one could read
CW (1984) as an intimate companion piece to *Meridian* (1977); the concerns of
Walker's black protagonist being – with delicate and ambivalent honesty – echoed
and displaced by Brown's white movement memories.

Whereas Rosellen Brown's novels in general have been well received by a
feuilleton readership, *CW* has not received decisive attention in feminist literary
criticism and has certainly not entered a feminist canon of "must teach"- ables. One
can but speculate about the relatively low (critical) success of, or response to, the
novel: One problem seems to be related to the very distinct boundaries that English
departments – despite all the rather faddish flirts with Cultural Studies – have
erected against critical readings of contemporary novels that sell well. The seduction of trivia still seems to be everywhere and has to be warded off except for either
an avantgarde posturing vis-à-vis camp, or an occasional theoretical inquiry of
dime romances. This verdict seems to be rendered mute only if there are some very

---

165 Published 1984; hereafter as *CW*.

rewarding academic gains to be made, as in the case of the *Color Purple*-industry; shadows of 19th century suspicions of the Sentimental Novel still loom large. Another reason might be *CW*'s unusual combination of author and subject matter: a contemporary novel by a white (feminist) writer about a period in American history that only figures as a black topic obviously fell through the cracks of curricular interest.

A fate the novel clearly does not deserve: Taking up Beecher Stowe's and Smith's legacy, it is one of the rather few white texts reflecting on the convergence of racism and sexism in American society. It addresses a series of particular American problems in its overlapping of an exploration of the (white) Civil Rights Movement generation's social, ethical commitments in the late 1970s and early 1980s with an unflinching inquiry into the individual patterns of (white) male-female relationships. The failure of the protagonists' Jessie and Teddy Carll's relationship, in Brown's most intimate, almost visceral representation of it, is directly related to a conflict between the two characters as to how to relate to history, that is, the Civil Rights Movement; it is also enacted and read as a repetition of the unresolved conflict between Jessie's parents, Communist Party members Jack and Elisabeth Singer, in the 1950s.

The text's forays into everyday gender struggle are narratively punctuated by way of metaphoric mirror effects, as it were, by Brown's close-ups on American history's 'other' impasse: racial oppression and the tragic of black and white miscommunication. The way Brown writes these two characters' gradual falling apart is characterized by a rare precision in imagining their psychic life, a mimetic emotional exactness of register that does not elide the minutest detail. The text's strength is its properly understood textual integrity, an enactive language that seeks to come to terms with America's 'blackened' history reaching into white characters' lives. In speech painfully magnifying white investments, Brown's language makes things by and about white people sayable that American cultural memory prefers to keep as a suppressed subtext of whiteness. She manages to represent Jessie's and Teddy's personal struggles mostly without sliding into feminist kitsch or cliché, by counterweighing them throughout the text by the larger social-political dimensions and implications of their personal disagreement: their opposing views on their own immediate racialized history (their common involvement in the Civil Rights Movement) and what to do with it almost fifteen years later clash along the lines of gender.

The novel's plot turns on a family crisis: both, Northern Jewish Jessie and Southern born and bred Teddy Carll – a race traitor to boot – participated in the Civil Rights Movement. Over a decade later, Jessie teaching in an alternative school, Teddy working as a campus traveler for textbooks, their marriage suffers from a nagging unease whether or not to leave the black neighborhood they have been living and raising their two children Andy and Lydia in for years, by way of commitment to the cause of anti-segregation. Jessie wants to leave, Teddy refuses. At this point, they are given the sudden responsibility for the two children (Helen and O'Neill) of Teddy's sister and her husband, who both died in an accident. The children move in with the Carll family, and both sides have to adjust not only to a household suddenly doubled in size and changed by strangeness but also to their political/cultural differences – the new children having been raised on white supremacy and class privilege. With the inherited money, the Carlls buy a suburban house more appropriate to their spatial and emotional needs; when they are ready to move in, however, the marriage has fallen apart irreparably. Helen, after having been involved in a Ku Klux Klan bomb threat on her integrated school, tries to commit suicide because she cannot deal with her alienation in the new family. The novel culminates in Helen's rescue in the midst of a flood having hit Jackson, Mississippi, because of bad weather. Jessie and her four children are a tentatively redeemed family; Teddy Carll – it is implied – will not be part of their suburban white future. The narrative is told almost entirely from Jessie's point of view, even though it is delivered in large parts as a series of dialogic scenes. The text is interrupted in intervals by Helen's diary, which readers know large parts of before the other characters do; this mirrors the lack of communication between Helen's loyalty to her parents' values and the progressive family, between the "old" South and the "new."

Brown stages a confrontation between Teddy Carll's male idealistic sense of his own (white sacrificial) heroism and Jessie Carll's home centered loyalties. Teddy sees himself as a late movement martyr; he is the one literally resurrected from the dead, after a Ku Klux Klan attack had left him clinically dead for some time. Nostalgically and without success, he longs to carry over his engagement into a moment of slackening, or nonexistent, social activism, a narcissistic desire that takes him to a renunciation of his family's more immediate, rather apolitical needs. Jessie becomes characterized by her female resolve to accept the facts of historical change and a different Zeitgeist, tame her nostalgia, direct her cares and loyalties closer to home, as it were and invest her psychic and intellectual energies and wants in the ones closest to her: her husband and children.

Even though Jessie is not written as a corny feminist heroine who can do no wrong, and Brown goes to lengths to make her visible as a character with her own biographically and temperamentally conditioned limits and frailties, the textual sympathies, in terms of mostly plot (Teddy's desertion of the family at a high point of crisis) but also via dominant narrative perspective, tone and the strategic use Brown makes of the teenage girl Helen's diary, are clearly with Jessie. That perspectival control is loosened up to allow Teddy's voice to claim but little space; the narrative gist and dynamic are obviously with the female principle, as it were;

Brown has the male hero exit himself from the plot to be finally abandoned by a woman-centered household.

This, the text implies, is not a victoriously happy moment for feminism, much rather a result of irresolvable gender conflict as inevitable as historical change on another plane: Jessie's and Teddy's very lively, sensuous and intellectual mutual love and trust just as "dead" as the Civil Rights Movement (and, by implication, that historical moment's convergence of black and white interests). The novel constructs both of these relations' bygone good times and success not only as past experience but also entertains a risky, if melancholic flirt with relegating them to the realm of historical and personal naiveté, of youthful, transitory urgency.

Memory and American history

> If in fact the goal of the freedom movement was to achieve a situation in which each individual could stand alone to compete as best as he or she could, despite the residual and collective impact of gender, race and class, then it must be said that the freedom movement of the 1960s achieved, at least in law, the substance of its aims. But if the goal was rather to assure equality as a result, not just as an idea, then collective measures are essential – measures that specifically address the ways in which class, gender and race have functioned in the past, and function today, to deny freedom and opportunity. Both in the history of its own goals, and the history of its efforts to implement those goals, therefore, the civil rights movement provides a case study of both the limitations and possibilities of reform in our society. (Chafe)

I want to argue that *CW* is structured and driven by a tension between two different positions on the course of history, particularly the success, decline and eventual demise of the Civil Rights Movement and the decades following it. At a conference at the University of Mississippi in 1985, one year after the publication of Rosellen Brown's novel, a number of historians gathered to assess the movement and its impact on American society. Editor Charles W. Eagles introduces the collection of essays produced by the conference with a sentence that sheds ironic light on Rosellen Brown's title for her novel:

> Though the Civil Rights Movement did not solve what Gunnar Myrdal termed the "American dilemma," it did alter the status of blacks in southern society; it so changed relations between the races that C. Vann Woodward has called it "the second **reconstruction**." (Eagles IX, emphasis added)

If, for Brown, the gendered strife dominating her novel's white protagonists as a late consequence of their involvement in the movement may be encapsulated metaphorically as civil **war**, the post Civil Rights Movement 1970s are signified as erosive, destructive and characterized by loss, not by reconstruction. I read this opposition as produced by and characteristic for white and black American subject positions respectively, both of which *CW*'s narrative manages to inscribe even though its plot and its narrative control favor a white position.

Characteristic of the black position is an effort to establish a responsibility to/for history, a commitment to own up to the history of blackness in/of America. That commitment would entail a radical ideological scepticism as well as an individual location of respect for memory, a purposeful acceptance of a categorical imperative not to escape from the Middle Passage that regards forgetting as an unaffordable privilege.[166] Andrea's becoming a lawyer to further the interests of southern black communities and Varona's choice to remain the black mayor of her backwoods little town against all odds, narratively embody this particular agency, however marginalized by *CW*'s plot it appears. I will return to these two characters' function for the novel in a moment.

The position I will call white here is characterized by a different dynamic: for white people, like, for example, the white students who took part in the Mississippi Freedom Ride – the focus of the novel's memory – the same imperative does not exist. How to relate to American history's racialization and racial conflictedness is a question left to shifting individual and collective decision making. The white position affords an opportunity to get out of the ethical constraints of memory in a way that might not directly result in its erasure, but certainly in its relegation to a past safely sealed off from any given present tense's priorities. Memory, in that case, always already borders on nostalgia, which, as the novel demonstrates, however inadvertently, is the case for both its protagonists. Nostalgia's ground and address, as I have argued before, is a longing to own history narcissistically, as a mythological mirror to the self's desires without which disintegration threatens.

Jessie is nostalgic for the Civil Rights Movement because she misses its enabling connections to people, its spiritual exhilaration, the sense of purpose and belonging, the effectiveness in pushing for social change, the bridge it built across the racial divide at least while its momentum lasted. She is able, however, to put those times behind herself in favor of more urgently pressing concerns and is realistically minded enough to see and accept this phase she went through as valuable for her personally, but as clearly terminated. Her personal credo is delivered at the novel's very beginning:

All the free-floating sensuality of her first few years in Mississippi blended: approval, relief, concern, loneliness, terror, fury, and pleasure in hearty company. To have lost it

---

166 Of course, this is not to say that, in real life, forgetting would not be possible for individual African-Americans in the United States, which is not the point of this argument.

was like, at the other end of the scale, having lost the very particular touch of Lydia and Andy in their infancy, mouth on her breast, light fingers on her cheek. She could still miss it so sharply a weight inside her would shift, it was keen as a stitch of pain when she let herself. But she did not let herself. Not very often. Her children were half-grown and the days of Earnest White Girls for Integration were over. Even if it weren't that *Time* magazine and its accomplices tended to think in terms of The Year Of and The Decade Of, history, public and private, did move in its own natural waves, peristaltic, Jessie supposed, as real time digested them and reduced them to ash and offal. (*CW* 19)

Teddy 's position, if one looks at it from this angle, is not as diametrically opposed as it may seem: he wants to retain the Civil Rights Movement as a reservoir of personal enlargement, a permanent challenge to his always threatening white corruption, a continued call to social action and rootedness in alternative, non white, non quasi-aristocratic social location that can stay the tide of racism and Southern backwardness. Since his own investment in the struggle has been so much more complicated (being a deconstructed redneck) and involved (to the point of occupying leadership positions) and almost cost him his life, he logically does not find it as promising as Jessie (for whom the Civil Rights Movement's premises have become endangering obstacles) to draw a line between past and present, between memory and the quotidian life of white people in post Civil Rights Movement racialized Jackson.

The novel, via Jessie's staunch opposition to her husband, makes it quite clear that his affections for and interests in the Civil Rights Movement have more to do with his own ego reflection than with a realistically measured and exerted engagement in solidarity with black needs and interests. At the point, then, when the futility of re-staging the movement for his own sake hits him, he, too, is able to make it into a past that can be had, used, and even capitalized on (in the most direct sense of making money, privileges and a love affair). He writes a book about its failure, selling his own and the movement's iconicity to an American liberal public; his past does not threaten to deconstruct the present tense any more.

Significantly though, there is hardly a moment in the text where readers are allowed access to Teddy's mind directly; so tightly does Jessie's point of view control the image we are offered:

Well, and now here was Teddy, her hero with his one outdated song to sing. (...) It wasn't kindness that he lacked, or compassion or, God help him, earnestness, it was the capacity for honest reflection. (*CW* 372)

and also, on an even more destructively angry level:

I know that every time anyone tries a passion and exhausts it – I mean, the whole country even, fashion, politics, anything – that's a passion they can't experience for a long time. (...)But I just can't believe that looking back to the old victories is going to help you get on with your life. You're not a historian, I swear you're a goddamn necrophiliac. (*CW* 363)

No matter how much Jessie and Teddy seem to embody conflicting stances about the movement's meaning, its consequences and its possible legacy, what unites them is the respective whiteness of each position that allows both of them to feed on its gains and losses for their own present purposes. The novel allows these two white people to confront each other by way of using the (black) movement as territory of war. Whereas their real conflict is caused by a clearly individual and intimate challenge to their family life, the novel lets both their former participation in the movement and their competitive readings of this experience occupy center stage of their mutual accusations.

The white position both characters ultimately prefer to take is sustained by and manifested in a plot that draws all momentum, interest, and readerly investments onto a personal conflict within the white family, in which Jessie's and Teddy's temporary involvement in black history becomes first a pawn, and accumulatively but a part of the repertoire of their infighting. The black position is left, to no surprise, with the text's black minor voices, Andrea and Varona, both embodying in their lives the 'burden' of history. More importantly, though, blackness also hovers in a peculiarly insistent manner behind the plot's focus, around the plot's edges, by way of the novel's gripping textualization of the arguments, disagreements, invokings and celebrations of and speculations about the Civil Rights Movement – a textual field, as it were, that refuses to be absorbed by plot and the novel's denouement. This presence repeatedly succeeds in teasing the reader into her own memories of, and opinions about the Civil Rights Movement, thus calling up the blackness of American history against its being seductively drowned by[167] the plot's interest in the reorganization of white family life after personal trauma hit it.

This site of black memory in the text, however much compromised by Jessie's personal investments that we are invited to identify with, shores up a resistance against a political, social development that one could summarize in William Chafe's words as follows:

Ironically, the gains of desegregation have made even less likely the opportunity to forge a united campaign for improvement based upon racial identity alone. The well-educated, upwardly mobile beneficiaries of changes in the 1960s tend to move out of economically deprived neighborhoods. The home base of church, school and community organizations that had existed during the era of segregation is gone. And there is an increasing distance between those who are able to take advantage of the opportunities in the mainstream society, and those who are increasingly pressed to the margins of that society, living a life of misery, no longer linked to those better-off than themselves by neighbor-

---

167 It is no happenstance that the plot finally turns on a quasi biblical flood.

hood bonds, common institutions, and the shared commitment to racial advancement. (Chafe 145)

The Civil War in Civil Wars

By virtue of being about two white Americans whose narrative origins are as much in their very different family biographies as they are – for them as a couple – in the Civil Rights Movement, the text inscribes racialized US-American history in its very center. Inasmuch as a title is the first controlling lever for any reader, it is clear from even before the first page that Brown's conception of American history is not one of innocent origins but one of conflicting interests of what America should be, fought out over the very bodies of black people. Adding to this critical historical perspective is the fact that through novelistic flashbacks on the protagonists' respective childhood Brown juxtaposes Southern gentry – successors of a defeated planters' class – with Jessie's growing up as a Red Diaper baby in Jewish New York City in the late 1940s, early 1950s and with her memories of her father going underground for the CPUSA in 1954.

That juxtaposition, however, does not in the least serve or imply an idealization of 'good' (Northern/ leftist) versus 'bad' (Southern/reactionary) Americans. Jack Singer's characterization is constructed along the lines of Jessie's feminist and resolutely anti-heroic sensibilities, underwritten by her mother's and her own feelings of being lost, abandoned and betrayed. Her post black contact re-readings of her own impressions of Communist Party sessions when she, as a child, witnessed subtle discrimination against independent black opinion and a repeated failure to live up to Communist anti-racist standards undercuts any simplistic oppositional evaluation of the American past. What does emerge from these layers of slanted and mutually critical historical address is a picture of American history thoroughly compromised and complicated by the momentum of race, class and gender **conflict**. American history does not deliver one smooth narrative, nor does it offer – to *CW's* protagonists or us as readers – a vanishing point of desire for an identification with a 'usable past.' US-American past in *CW* does not appear as a generative source of national adhesion – however much embattled – but as series of interested, quite antagonistic fictions written upon and against each other that do not refer back to a unifying transparent telos of emphatic Americanness.

That kind of Un-American scepticism is as much due to feminist disillusionment with patriarchal self-righteousness, social and personal containment strategies and assumptions of contentment (Jack Singer and Teddy) as to an almost cynical, however desperate detachment vis-à-vis the masternarratives of race, class and, to some extent, gender, which have shaped America's cultural memory. To "sanction amnesia within the project of memory" (Castronovo 187) is what Brown's inquiries

160

into these masternarratives, always obsessing with the most mundane and irreverent human detail, try to avoid.

Within that comparatively radical scenario, however, a question remains nagging: given the implications of the title – the connotations include the Civil War, the class struggle in the fight between Jessie's parents, the Civil Rights Movement, **and** the marital war between Teddy and Jessie – what does it mean for the evaluation of each to put them, metaphorically, and by way of fictional plotting, on one level of pertinence? The civil war here but functions as key metaphor for American conflicts: does the novel thus disown a particular blackness of American history – of a war fought over the freedom of its black population – by way of its acquisition of this meta-signifier? If all possible conflicts in the American name, of gender, politics, history, private relations, between children and parents, between the generations, are being subsumed under that controlling image where does that leave this generative trauma of America's public and private "Gestalt"? This question becomes particularly pertinent because the text's avowed integrationism is so much on the edge (or over it) of surpassing social trauma by personal redemption – a redemption, in which blackness no longer figures but as historical shadow.

Civil Wars and Civil War Fiction

> The Civil War challenged this boundary [the distinction between battle-field and the homefront] constantly, fought as it was by definition on "home" territory – both within the domestic boundaries of the nation and, at times, literally inside domestic space. (E. Young 297)

As Elisabeth Young points out (293) scholars have counted about 2,000 novels directly addressing the Civil War and its aftermath, which – if read as a continuum – produce a veritable American subgenre with its own topoi and formal conventions. Even though the reference point of the actual Civil War – as opposed to all different sorts of "war" – has receded to a very far horizon in *Civil Wars*, the novel conjures up not only the war itself turned into an all-purpose metaphor, but also, perhaps more importantly, civil war fiction. If the conventions of those white-authored war novels are to "foreground heroism in combat" (Higonnet 80), *CW* functions as a rather satirical deflation. Brown appropriates, yet redirects the logic of civil war fiction's controlling metaphors.

Margaret Higonnet speaks of a "metaphoric transfer of civil war from an external, political realm to inner conflict over sexual choice and the proper gender roles," and maintains that in civil war fiction that transfer actually works both ways, in that "political relations acquire the color of gender" (Higonnet 80, 81). In "Northern visions of the war," as Elisabeth Young says, "the suitor was Northern and male; the wooed, Southern and female" (as opposed to Southern fictions that constructed the same historical momentum as rape plot as it became most aggressively visible on a national public scale in *Birth of a Nation*). For the "Northern" point of view, its

> victory signalled a happy marriage, with the marital union standing in for the newly forged re-union of the nation. The subsuming of the South into the "national union" neatly paralleled that of wife into her husband, as the head of both unions – marital and national – was male. (E. Young 310)

Brown irreverently discards these plots altogether. Indeed, as Kathleen Diffley has recently argued in reference to Civil War fiction, the nation in wartime appeared as a "house invaded," with the disruption of national stability intimately linked to the control of domestic space:

> [T]he operative technique was to realign a sexually coded language with the military opposition the war brought about. The resulting figures of a feminine South, a masculine North and the threat of violence in their relations shaped histories as early as 1866 (...). (Diffley 359)

In *CW*, the "house invaded," the controlling gendered metaphor of civil war fiction, is not a symbolic equation but the real issue of the text. The private white 1970s home is divided unto itself, split up by actors who do not follow the commanding script of a larger war but their own conflicting personal desires and ambitions. In both cases, in older Civil War fiction directly, in *CW* via the very title's connotations, home conflict signifies in a larger context for conflicts concerning the entire nation; the subtext of *CW*, however, is no longer disturbed national domesticity – a gendered **topos** – but actual gender **struggle** (occasioned by racialized conflicts) figuring for itself.

The very troping of the Civil War, however, a quintessentially American literary strategy Brown partakes in, seems to me to be allowed by a white subject position that may disregard, or displace racial conflict as both cause and effect of a war ostensibly fought over "the race question." By its title and its immediate evocation of an American literary obsession, i.e. civil war fiction, *CW* is bound to a certain white imperative immanent in white American historical consciousness, Northern and Southern: a nostalgia for a house uninvaded and undivided, a "Southern" fantasy meaning the white prewar plantation stability, a "Northern" fantasy speaking to the illusion of having solved the "race problem" with the war. Though the novel has shifted the focus from gender topos to gender struggle, it re-instates this imperative's hegemony by playing on the widespread American desire for harmonious homes, national and domestic, even if that collective hope is answered with resignation and a saddening sense of its ultimate futility.

Genre: melodrama and history

CW is driven by an antagonistic tension between the impact of its narrative realism, its mimetic truthfulness to the memories of Civil Rights Movement insiders and its ever more melodramatic plot complete with a flood and the white child almost drowning in it, biblical implications intended. As a reader, one remains constantly worried. Should one's main attention address an extremely contrived plot (which appears as if straight out of a manual of junk novel writing: how to put the most unlikely but still technically possible events together to create a conflict that may push towards closure)? Or should one focus on CW's recasting of the Civil Rights Movement, on its fine-tuned ear for the gendered conflict over possibly safe demarcations between the personal and the political, on its philosophical observations on the competition between social claims and private history, on its struggle over what and how to remember and why?

Ultimately, the melodramatic plot makes reconciliation (or, in those implied biblical terms, redemption) possible: Helen, mainly because of her ultimate innocence as a white **child**, can be integrated into the novel's white progressive family, can be reconstructed as a "new Southerner," one of a kind with Jessie and her children. However, the price to pay is to cut the ties to the past, both, of a morally discredited "old South" on Helen's part, and of radical resistance to it, on Jessie's part. Brown enables her white woman protagonist to thus save herself and the white child by letting her renounce, in her factual decisions, if not in her personal rhetorics of longing, her political involvement as ultimately sentimental. The plot indeed evacuates any white **politics** against racism from the novel, along with Teddy's demise, however ridiculously narcissistic political engagement has become figured in his desperate vanity. The narrative itself, however, in enacting Jessie's and Teddy's painful struggle, magically intensified by this melodramatic plot (and, maybe, only that way being made into a white American novel at all), does save the (black) memory of the Civil Rights Movement – as if its very duration, overwhelmed by endless repetitive verbal fights between Teddy and Jessie, wants to win out over the plot's future-mindedness.

Significantly, it is the white, uptight, Klan sympathizer teenager Helen (whose portrayal as a highly intelligent, perceptive child, by way of the access we have to her through her diary, strangely contradicts the melodramatic turn to have her join Klan action because of childish spite) who finally controls a plot set in motion by her dead parents' testament. She is granted the power to put Jessie **and** Teddy on the moral (and the textual) defensive: if the plot starts out with Jessie and Teddy in conflict about whether or not to leave (behind) their black neighborhood (in a crucial phase of their own/and American history) – a conflict that does not envisage a winner because of their rather equal weight and power in it – it is the children's arrival that causes the move to the new house (and a different life).

The new South makes its white children a responsibility for the Civil Rights Movement generation and thus effectively deters them from a preoccupation with integration (that is, with black people's situation, and with racism), referring them back to a social and private concentration on their immediate families, and on the gender war splitting those families. That older, larger, blackened history is being dismissed as having "outlived" its "usefulness" along with Teddy's skills, presumably outdated. But, ironically, the genre reserved for this historical model development is melodrama, a genre classically known as hysterical and, above all, unrealistic – in the sense of its plot machinations.

Is Helen's possible assimilation the sign of a future 'real' integration beyond political rhetoric, as the plot seems to imply, because it will then be anchored in inner-family, one-to-one emotional confrontation, transcendence and trust? Jessie's (white, female-headed redemptive household) a metaphor for American post Civil Rights Movement society and for what is left of the movement: white women, their families and their feminist concerns? Or does the text itself, energetically holding out against its melodramatic plot, safeguard history by way of its rather uncompromising forays into the problematics of white American historical investments, Southern or Northern, male or female, Jewish or Christian? By assembling a group of characters and making us engage all of their own particularly invested fictions of postwar American history, and by playing the struggle over memory out between them without delivering final textual authority, the moral issue of remembering is kept alive; memory is not passed on as a correct, but dead story.

"Just whose history is it?"

> In its broad outline the story of freedom summer is a familiar one: the orientation sessions in Oxford, Ohio, where the volunteers had to come to grips with their own prejudices; the murders of Chaney, Schwerner and Goodman, which cast a poll over the entire project; the intense activity in the forty-seven schools and numerous community centers. Statistics tell part of the story: a thousand arrests; thirty-five shooting incidents; thirty homes and other buildings bombed; thirty-five churches burned; eighty persons beaten; and, in addition to the Neshoba county lynchings, at least three other murders. Freedom summer had brought Mississippi to center stage, both in the nation and throughout the world. (Dittmer)

The novel's employment of 'black history' thus is ambiguous. The text does not decide whether its relation to it should be one of appropriation: occasioning a moral conflict? backgrounding the plot? or whether it wants to signify an integration of historical memory.

164

The most aggressive confrontations between the adult protagonists are fought out over the question of what Helen and O'Neill are supposed to learn with respect to Teddy's and Jessie's own and Southern history, and how they are to be taught. Jessie seemingly argues for tolerance, patience and empathic strategies of education that take into account the children's hurt and their very childishness in their judgements and behavior. Teddy, by contrast, pushes the small boy into a rather violent confrontation with his own legacy of movement activities, and remains throughout the text hostile towards Helen, who, for him, embodies his enemy South:

> "(W)hat could we do with her, she'll never let herself be happy here. She's set herself up as a kind of deepsworn enemy. She hasn't heard a thing we've said since she came -"
> "So you talk a little more, and patiently. Although kids don't learn from that, anyway, this is not a freedom school. And if you want her to learn tolerance, you could begin by showing a little more of it yourself. (...) She's a child and you're not a child, you're responsible for your thoughts and actions in a way she just isn't prepared to be." (..) Teddy's face was dark with anger. (...) "Do I have to be psychoanalyzed before I'm allowed to be disgusted by a strange girl at my table picking through the food like we're trying to poison her, and getting herself involved with some murderous ruffians who would dynamite us out of our skins if they thought they could get away with it?" (*CW* 412)

With all this narratively engaging conflict playing itself out between the two, it becomes seductive to read past the fact that both of them, in their respective approaches, instrumentalize black history for their own ends. Teddy's hijacking O'Neill to a protest action against a racist incident in Mourning Dove, and Jessie's taking the little boy completely unprepared to visit her old black friend Varona – both of these historical demonstrations function by way of appropriation. It is only Jessie's own hubris to pride herself of being the more adequate parent as well as the more appropriate guardian of movement history that marks a textual difference between the two adults. Whereas Jessie's enforced initiation rite for O'Neill (*CW* 212-221) is not highlighted as an occasion for further controversy, and whereas her egotistical motives to meet Varona, and to take O'Neill along, are not examined between the two adults, the Mourning Dove episode becomes one of the key levers in the text to achieve the couple's separation.

Brown has The *New York Times* feature an article on Mourning Dove's demonstration, which calls it "a sad exercise in yesterday's tactics, an exercise in nostalgia" – which in itself is not a wrong observation – and the narrative voice indirectly criticizes Northern glee of "that pseudoneutral tone which beguiles by innuendo and juxtaposition" (*CW* 287); however, Jessie's commentary to Teddy goes undisputed: "'It's bad for business,' Jessie agreed. 'But did you think he'd write a blurb just to cheer you on and recruit sympathy?'" (*CW* 288).

What the narrative power of Jessie's perspective tends to obscure is that for both of them these visits to the past have the same meaning: to find a consoling identification with black history that soothes their present day alienation. Despite their self-serving idealism, however, it becomes visible that their ostensible purpose to pull the children over onto the 'right' side of history and counterweigh their parents' reactionary mis-education effects results that will not be lost on Southern right wing political forces. Helen registers these effects with hostile acuity, thus bespeaking a power struggle over the question of who owns history that lies far beyond Jessie's and Teddy's petty competitive appropriations:

Before he went to sleep I came to O'Neill's bed and sat on the side and warned him his uncle Teddy is trying to brainwash him. (...) He goes "Maybe they'll shoot at us!" and his face gets all pink with excitement. "Teddy says there are these places where people actually got killed and stuff, and we can go and visit them, he says they ought to make them just like the Civil War monuments with markers and everything. So people will always remember. He told me I have to learn all this stuff like his own kids. It's history." Then he says, "One place there's this dam," – this is disgusting – "and they buried these three guys under it, first they whipped them and burned out their car and then they dragged them -" and I said "O'Neill, you better stop right now before I throw up." I told him he enjoys all those gross stories too much, if he's going to listen I don't think he supposed to be thinking oh goody, dead bodies and blood and chases and all. Anyway, what I am trying to do is get him to see it's like cowboys and Indians and suddenly does he realize he's riding with the Indians? Just whose history is it? (*CW* 280)

Jessie and Teddy both own rather sentimental versions of black history. Whereas Teddy, after his acquaintance with the attractive Northern editor of his prospective book about the movement, abandons idealism in favor of cynicism in his renouncement of 1960s activities as Washington's ploys, Jessie, feeling called upon to defend the values of an authentic movement against Teddy's "paranoia," abandons 'blackness' (in the form of lower class petty crime and lack of space) by moving into a new spacious house in a middle class white suburb. Actually, for both of them, their personal (white) mobility enables individual and fluidly changing responses to diverse figurations of racialized history.

Paradoxically, it is left to Helen's teenage neurotic displacement of her fears and her sexual anger at black people to provide a site for racialization in the new Carll's suburban home, with a vengeance. Her Klan activities still and again bid the question of "whose history is it?," which has not been solved to everybody's contentment, and which cannot be tamed by nostalgia, nor disowned by suburban affluence and journalistic maneuvers. Helen's viciousness, even if it is borne by a child's immaturity, contradicts Jessie's claim that "everyone's 'history,' even Southern obsessive, goes up in bulldozer dust" (*CW* 17). This relentless modernization – creating a New South, a more generically American capitalistic environment sup-

166

posedly devoid of history's legacies, a society where class distinctions may override racial difference – only provides unforeseen options for progressive white people to focus on their personal lives. As Tommy, Andrea's white husband, says:

> [t]he paradox about Teddy and his certainty he has that moving over here is the end of commitment and decency and all the rest of it is that he of all people isn't acknowledging that anything much has changed for the better around here. You'd think he might be impressed that the people on this street could care less who your friends are nowadays, when they would have frozen you out – or burned you out, even better – fifteen years ago. (*CW 310*)

The plot ultimately sanctions this historical regrouping; its melodramatic construction, however, throws its possibilities and limitations into sharp relief.

The black woman bearing the burden of history

Within the text, and speaking across the text to readers, it is the black women who make sense out of history, and who also have to bear the astute memory of black history. Their very presence and their activities remind us of the ultimately vain effort of a Civil War fought to bring about an "undivided nation," of the everpresent separation of the so-called civil society that the Civil Rights Movement finally tried to **overcome**, leaving both a legacy of successful results and a large number of unfulfilled promises and unsolved problems.

The only black male character[168] with a name is Teddy's ex-friend Skelly, who has ended up a religious fanatic; any kind of effective black male agency is altogether missing from the text, except for a passing, only half-ironical acknowledgement of the myth of black movement members avidly laying white women. By contrast, Andrea and Varona embody black history: its success and its stagnation, the desperation but also the black endurance in its wake. By way of this embodiment, they become authorized in Jessie's mind to be drawn upon as moral guideposts.

Jessie's relation to the movement's strategies and rhetoric is punctuated by disaffections; her close friend Andrea, however, "her sanity and certainty," will not be forsaken. Andrea is in the text only for her – she does not have any subplot of her own, or even a major function in the plot's denouement. Coming from an early black professor's fragile middle-class family, boldly outspoken, practical, reasonable, irreverently satirical and funny, compassionate, realistically free of sentimental memories, morally legitimized by being politically active in her lawyer's work as a late result of her Civil Rights Movement engagement, happily married to a

---

168 Except for celebrities, like Stokeley Carmichael.

white Civil Rights ex-hero, very quintessentially the 'Ebony' superwoman of white projections, Andrea bolsters Jessie's interests. By way of her critical, unsentimental, uncorrupted judgements, Jessie obtains narrative permission, as it were, to think and act in ways she herself doubtfully discredits because of her residual white progressive guilt. To enable the white protagonist's day-to-day life is Andrea's sole textual function. She is the one to support Jessie's plans to move out of Plywood Barracks. She is the one to give everybody, including the readers, a completely unimpressed no-nonsense reading of Teddy's limitations: according to her, Teddy is a white Mississippi boy, after all, who is "in love with his pessimism" (*CW* 310) and has "chosen an impossible campaign so that he could hang his flag in surrender" (*CW* 369). She is the one to – of all things – intervene successfully to integrate the redneck white child into this family of 'race traitors':

"Jessie," Andrea went on. "Listen, I want you to know I did this. I took that lil ole girl of yours out to lunch with me." (...) "Of course, she came. She's my house guest, she'd better have come. I took them in to Holmes in the mall, that pretty restaurant they have. Just like a couple of ladies. (...)" "Was she civil?" "Oh Jessie, your expectations. More like cowed than civil. I think the girl's more of a little scared grieving thing than some of the other forbidding kinds of horrors you and T.C. put out about her. All the racist gunk? What does she know? She was polite as you please and couldn't find her voice where she put it, and even tried to ask me some questions about my work, if you can believe it. (...)" "Could she meet your eyes?" "Oh shit, Jessie. Meet my eyes. That's the trouble with the two of you, you look at the whole world like it's all a page or two out of Henry James. The whole civilized universe does not have an obligation to meet your eyes or mine and get off on this simultaneous moral reverence of yours. Or gratitude either. (...) Now, what I'd really like to see is what would happen in a very laidback – unjudging – ordinary – situation, where she didn't get pushed to any conclusions about what's bad behavior. None of this committee agreement about how to – uh – belong – in the Carll household. Do you know what I'm saying?" (*CW* 336, 337)

Just as Andrea has foreseen it, Helen is impressed by her charm, intelligence and class, in the most literal sense, which hints at a shift of race to class loyalties indicative not only of Helen's "maturing" into an adult of the "new" South, but of a general social/political development. As Helen writes in her diary:

About Andrea. (...) I think for a Negro she isn't like anyone I ever knew, even though Mom always said there were plenty who could live in our neighborhood and be as good as anybody else, and some even had that kind of money. Lurene was sure of herself the same way but only in the kitchen or wherever, with a million opinions about what to use, Ajax or Comet and she gave the same kind of look if you did something wrong or said a dumb thing. (...) Andrea is just like any white woman only I think she is actually much smarter than most. (Like she is much neater and more precise than Jessie.) I shouldn't be surprised but I am that I can (almost) forget what color she is. It is probably that she is leading us around and we would not dream of sassing her or telling or what to do the way I could Lurene, nicely, Mom would always say, but firmly. I would never want Lingham

168

to know what I am thinking on this subject but I am seeing now that Daddy was really always talking about poor people, not just black people. I don't even know what some of the awful habits and contagious problems are anymore that he was protecting us from. Maybe Lingham being pretty poor herself she never got to meet any Negroes like Andrea who are actually lawyers and doctors and things. I am not sure. (*CW* 344)

Andrea, thus, not only offers an alternative script for Jessie's life, she becomes a black narrative agent to aid the inadvertent Southern modernization Brown depicts so ambivalently.

Varona, on the other hand, is Brown's version of black female endurance against the tide of forgetfulness and inhumane progress, the "touchstone":

She never saw Varona anymore, and missed her. She was one of the touchstones, the incorruptibles, of all the women she had known the dearest teacher. She made them all look callow. (...) She told [O'Neill] this was Andy's godmother they were going to see, told him she was black and large and grand and looked, maybe, like an African princess. (*CW* 213)

Varona signifies unconditional moral and practical black strength, with her "hair back behind a white band, well greased for company. That rich brown bobbing head seemed to Jessie never to age or change" (*CW* 214). Jessie feels a need to know whether Varona, in her activities as one of the first black mayors in the South, has "failed or succeeded" (*CW* 220). She is aware that her interest in Varona might be more to find a strong shoulder to lean her worried head on than to actually engage in Varona's problems:

Jessie gave her a smile so sad and undefended that Varona looked away; probably it was more of her visitor than she was willing to see just now at her kitchen table, this poor old white girl. Jessie was embarrassed. (*CW* 218)

Moreover, she even comes to qualify her own assumptions of Varona's never-ending resourcefulness and "irreverent energy" (*CW* 220) upon realizing Varona's "weariness": "How many layers down did that depression go, Jessie wondered" (*CW* 215), and the disgust and cynicism shining forth after a shared bottle of whiskey: "See, even my own people got me down for an uppity nigger. (...) Make me wish I kept my damn mouth shut all these years" (*CW* 215, 220). But Jessie's embarrassment does not keep Brown from enlisting Varona in her protagonist's struggle to distance herself from Teddy:

She could hear Varona say it: when you ready to kiss the man goodbye, girl, that's when you come and take this here thing [the new car inherited from white supremacist Roger] out of where it come from, ride it right on over him." (*CW* 236)

Ultimately, Varona's hurt melts into Jessie's and – fittingly – into one of the very few openly corny sentiments the character is allowed to express:

> In spite of everything, she'd always thought she rather starve under a Mississippi sunset, or under such a moon, than starve on 125th Street facing an airshaft. (...) And the moon shines hopefully on us so we can find each other in the dark as if we were food, she thought, to fill each other's mouths. But we will still be hungry in the morning. (*CW* 221)

This kind of kitsch that swallows up respect and intimacy in self-pity makes Jessie's relation to Varona appear as one-sided as her relation to Andrea. They both provide motherly orientation for Jessie, teaching her lessons in historical realism. It appears as if the novel's secret protagonists, the voices that Brown trusts most to speak with undisputed authority, are Andrea and Varona, which makes any distance between her character's parasitism and her own rather hard to measure.

Locations: how white is Jessie?

> To have no doctrine was to have no protection. (*CW*)

> Her father's fiction was that he still had some effect on the way the world moved; her mother's was that she had been excused and had none at all. (*CW*)

> Would there ever be a time when she was in the right place at the right time with the right assumptions? (*CW*)

Jessie is – above all – characterized by an explosive mix of loyalties: a Jewish New York upbringing, a communist father, a mother who renounced ideology because of anti-patriarchal anger, her own radical partisanship for the Civil Rights Movement, feminist consciousness-raising experience, a group of black friends, a white Southern ex-redneck movement hero for a husband, living in 1970s Jackson, Mississippi, with two of her own and two 'unreconstructed' white children. Thus, she must be read as an embodiment of the very boundary of American female whiteness, a heroine on the farthest edge of narrative refusal of comfortably identical, homogeneous white middle class womanhood – the figure readers have grown accustomed to in so much white women's literature.[169]

What is left to her of the Civil Rights Movement are memories of an involvement in extreme danger, a subjection to the most aggressive hostility that – perversely – offered an entry into a "black and white together" communion of pain. Judged in retrospect, this communal exhilaration enabled her to live through racist

---

169 See Lauret for a discussion of post-1960s feminist literature.

assaults on bodies and personalities psychically intact; she does not seem to be aware of it, but her memory clearly reveals the whiteness of her position as a woman for whom racism's "terror" was "short-lived and specific" (*CW* 118).

By contrast, the challenge to accommodate the two spoilt and racist children into her family, and to have to do it on her own, as an individual act, plunges her into a deepening depression. Children, however mis-educated, are not convenient enemies; and to face the task of raising these two so extremely white children as her own, that is, to teach them 'race treason,' throws Jessie back on her own resourcefulness:

> Why assume that lying on jail-cell cement was the hardest thing you would ever be asked to do? Terror was accessible. It was short lived and specific and shared, shared all around. A communion. There was no shame in being afraid to die or be maimed. (...) [E]ven as he reached for the hand that held her tin dinner dish and plunged her arm, to the quivering elbow, into boiling water. (...) And everyone in the cell had to do the same. There was a low moan, humiliation, anger, disgust, not pain. Still, still... Surviving together, they were shriven. They were exhilarated. That pain only became part of the history of their endurance; and it became one more thing to laugh about later, in self-congratulation. (*CW* 118)

Jessie misses the spirit of the (black) times, but on the other hand, her anger at Teddy's vain and self-endangering side shows in Mourning Dove seems also caused by the fact that this action will take him away from the safety of his white family (which will in turn take away safety from them): a return of a 'female' anxiety and a desire to keep her home together that used to be pushed to the backs of minds before, and repressed for the sake of blackness' attraction:

> What they were was famous (he was); brave (both of them, she intermittently); endlessly endangered. They had spent an enormous amount of time holding the hands of strangers and singing, or urging them to song. Most of the hands were black – Negro at the time – and horny hard, like crocodile skin, with work the likes of which Teddy and Jessie would never know, unless as an affectation. (...) Jessie remembered that confrontation with body – her own, light-headed, pared down dangerously – better than she remembered her confrontations with Teddy's though that may be because that long pleasure had gone on all these years. And she remembered the press of general affection, the sharp quick hugs of the men and the sweaty bosom-to-bosom embraces of the women, better too. (*CW* 19)

The only moment, thus, Teddy may level a sticking accusation against Jessie is when he turns the tables on her and calls her "the adventurer, or the opportunist":

> You got what you could use of this whole experience – doing the South, I guess – and that's it. And now you're bored. (*CW* 380)

Since readers know at this point how to put Teddy's anger at Jessie in perspective, we do not take his angered statement about Jessie's politics at face value; it does work, however, to make us aware of a possible sceptical distance vis-à-vis her ostensible white Northern goodwill. As such, his anger functions as a textual replay of a critical black attack white Jessie withstood from a black woman in the early days of Mississippi summer:

"I never wanted you-all," Edith Eddy told Jessie coolly, a large woman in overalls, whose bust was at the level of Jessie's chin. (...) "Some did, some didn't. You-all more trouble than you'll ever work out to be worth, if you don't mind my saying so. Or even if you do. (...)" "Just because you were born poor," Jessie said. "Who said born poor. You think we're all alike. Just black," she said. "I got everything to gain, everything to lose. You got nothin much to give, and that's the truth." (*CW* 40)

In passages like this one, Brown delicately manages to sound the contradictions and complications of the Civil Rights Movement as one of the very few interracially constituted moments in American cultural memory, and very carefully traces white options and limitations within that moment.

Jessie's astuteness and intelligence (and her 'training' by her CPUSA father) enables her to see American history for what it is – the disabling flipside of which is a guilt she can, to her dismay, neither disavow, nor transform into meaningful social or political action any longer:

Sometimes it angered Jessie that she and Teddy derived satisfaction from what they chose to forego: there was not meant to be compensation in renouncing, every religion said so. And they did it in half-measures, too: they gave up so very little in real fact. They were moving now, after all; they would live in a very fine house and badmouth it, lowrate it, oh, it was so self-righteous and no one gained an ounce from their squirming guilt. That was their Simone Weil streak, she would say to Teddy: Simone Weil who starved to death because there were workers and prisoners all around her who had nothing to eat. She who ate what they ate and when it ceased to be enough, took the sentence as doom, broke herself into passivity, denied herself choice just as the others were denied it. Well, Jessie loved and hated Simone Weil – like all saints, she was blessed and unforgivable, her death put not a morsel in a single human mouth; all it stanched was the hunger of her own voracious conscience, before it rattled and gasped out. And that, Jessie thought, solved no problem but the crisis of one woman's ego. And yet, and yet... she had forever been haunted by the act. She had always had to work at suppressing awe, which was a kind of envy, that someone had so followed through – she thought of a dancer's body in total extension – had so purely resolved a motion to its ultimate outcome, had obliterated the distance, white-skin privilege, class privilege, the luxury of self-consciousness. What she had refused was a hierarchy that valued one life over another, like a child who took every promise literally. The glare of her simplicity hurt Jessie's eyes. (*CW* 236)[170]

---

170 Two things are remarkable here: the fact that it is a European example of renouncing white skin privilege, bespeaking a dearth of American models? Second, the

The narrative way out of this white dilemma, though, for Brown, is to have Jessie seeking and receiving absolution on her doubt-ridden self by placing the burden of insight and action on black women who may signify the resolve Jessie lacks.

Brown's portrayal of her protagonist reveals a however strongly repressed desire to share in whiteness that overwhelms Jessie in the most unlikely place; the episode pushes Jessie's conflictedness to the limits of a painfully honest characterization. Meeting her dead sister-in-law's Southern Belle friends, she realizes her ambivalence about their complacency, their complicity even:

> Her assumptions about so many things were more dissimilar from these women's than they were similar. But it hurt to think that. She was a traitor to female solidarity. Well, how many ways could one divide oneself? The women who threw stones at small black children, were they women before they were racists, were they allies first, or deadly foes? Oh, to love mine enemy, she thought. To embrace these 'girls' as mine. (*CW* 227)

It is immediately obvious from these lines that the very possibility to **ask** those questions owes to the privilege of a white subject position; a position that Brown's novel painstakingly outlines.

Jessie's eventual upward mobility to move to a white suburb hides from view another scenario of whiteness: the house obtains its heavy metonymic burden by way of displacement of other choices. In fact, the responsibility Jessie has to take on is not that she wants to live in a decent house. What she does have to face (and what the melodramatic plot spares her to acknowledge) is: she wants to integrate the memory of the Civil Rights Movement in ways that facilitate a distance from its moral challenge – reaching from the violently charged Sixties over into the only superficially more benevolent 1970s – to respond to the social problems it left unresolved. The question of engagement for Jessie boils down by way of plot, to Helen and O'Neill, to the white children's faces of desperate fear of the new and other, to taking care of children in need of safety. The text gives away its evasiveness in an instance of letting Jessie fantasize of leaving the South for good and making her shamelessly resort to personal melodrama:

> Danger, danger everywhere and not a drop to drink: Helen had understood. The wild silver Mercedes bobbed and lurched behind their eyes. Even the Haves have it, the plummy parts of town brought low. It was a pretty unimpressive apocalypse, she thought, but if you wanted one badly enough. Because there was no absolute safety, Helen had rejected relative. That was so self-defeating Teddy should have sympathized. (...) The only absolutes were that she had four undefended people in her care. However inept they were, she and Teddy were not undefended. (*CW* 413)

---

closeness to Meridian's plagueing doubts, with the decisive difference that Walker's Meridian does not have the other race to absolve her from guilt.

The protagonist is caught between Brown's capacity to make black American memory vivid amongst her white characters, and her decision for a plot that suspends Jessie, as the bearer of readerly identification, in a (white) present so demanding there is no room for memory:

All she could hear was the intimate lick and suckle of the instant, which was deepening around her. She would walk in it a good deal longer before it became the past. (*CW* 419)

Afterthoughts

> Poetry can repair no loss but it defies the space which separates (...) by its continual labor of reassembling what has been scattered. (John Berger)

The point of this study was to pinpoint whiteness within a racialized discursivity of American history. What has become readable, I hope, is a significant correlation between authors' subject positions as white and their respective investments in historical memory; however much inflected by political or aesthetic loyalties, regional inheritance, and period affinities their whiteness appears. As I argued in my introduction, the textual momentum of whiteness of/in the texts is not – at least not to white readers – their most compelling, their most forceful feature, even if it might stand out familiarly enough to be taken for an inevitable property. A reading for whiteness thus necessarily runs the risk of bordering on the obvious, because it has to assign a particular meaning where, traditionally, white readers have naively identified with the unequivocally presumed universality of their own invisible skin color and its naturalized hegemonial privilege of signification. As has become obvious by now, whiteness only becomes productive as a category of **reading**. Accordingly, while implicitly criticizing a white readership for its selective suppressions my work actually strengthens the position of the (white) reader in that it focalizes his/her vision. It aims at displacing white readers' diffuse and unreflected acceptance of whiteness as textual property by foregrounding it as precisely a shared, and therefore hitherto unproblematized feature of the reader's and the text's consciousness. This rather partial de- and reconstruction of textual meanings, however, bears no closure; it has not been meant as a verdict on the selected texts but rather as an invitation to follow a different trace across the canonical and anti-canonical terrain of US-American women's writing. Thus, instead of a conclusion, I opted for afterthoughts on the implications of 'reading white' for the diverse cultural criticisms that have marked this terrain over the last decades: American Studies, Black Studies as well as Gender Studies and Feminism.

Heated controversies have been fought in the 15-year time lapse between Adrienne Rich's moral urgency to press for an acknowledgement on the part of white feminists to own their particular social, cultural and political location, and the textual sophistication of white analyses like Robyn Wiegman's *American Anatomies. Theorizing Race and Gender* (1995). Wiegman deliberately takes white feminisms to task for their complicity and self-gratifying agency in the historical production

175

of a competitive and highly racialized, even racist constellation of the discourses of Black liberation, and subsequently Black Studies on the one hand, and feminism, including Gender Studies, as white on the other. Echoing the early Black feminist insight that "all the blacks were men and all the women where white" Wiegman's study argues that any white interest in gender (liberation) that does not come to terms with white women's racialized history ultimately will neither be able to develop an appropriate theory of gender inclusive of all the social and cultural implications of race, particularly in the US-American context, nor will it convincingly address the question of necessary political alliances to press for the complex gendered and racial/anti-racist emancipation of the entire society. Wiegman's work thus supports my argument about the particular historical legacy white women need to grapple with in order to construct and evaluate their own cultural and literary canons from a perspective that surpasses white benevolence and liberal goodwill. Gunnar Myrdal's *American Dilemma* taken as a pre-Black Liberation and pre-Second-Wave-Feminism metaphor has finally experienced unforeseen echoes and reverberations in the studies of *American whiteness*, but with a twist. The interventions of Black feminism in the 1980s and 1990s have finally had lasting effect on the impossibility of an American white self-definition that by insisting on categorizing oppression either in terms of gender or in terms of race might indict white patriarchy but would let white women off the hook conveniently – ignoring black female agency altogether.

As my pointing backwards to *American Dilemma*[171] as one of the key texts of post-war American Studies and early Black Studies shows, the enwhitening shift in perspective extends to the field of American studies as well. Of late the discipline has undergone a profound self-correction of the additive multicultural premises it had been accumulating over the last two decades. Even though in some cases whiteness seems to have been only a shade added to the impressive palette of fashionable American colorfulness, Toni Morrison's call to shift the attention "from the server to the served" has resulted in a wealth of critical studies ranging from close readings of singular cultural phenomena and/or events to essays at a more general philosophical re-orientation.[172] The veritable explosion of an interest in whiteness in its diverse articulations, visible in the web, in email discussion lists and a sudden proliferation of articles in almost all of the prestigious critical jour-

---

171 To assess the long term impact of *An American Dilemma* would need a separate study which could be particularly rewarding from a black feminist perspective, comparable to the evaluations of the Moynihan report. I thank Werner Sollors for teasing this point out of my chapter on Lillian Smith, where *An American Dilemma* functions more as a subtext.

172 See in particular the recent anthologies by Hill, Daniels, Fine et.al.

nals[173] has surpassed, I take it, even Fisher-Fishkin's 1995 sweeping optimism. Within the two years since the writing of this text for submission as my Habilitation, the textual environment for a re-examination of white writing has changed dramatically enough to make my text appear already somewhat dated.

Even though I thus have to accept the inevitable contingency of my readings, my hope is to have contributed to the recent far-reaching shift in American Studies which at least in the German context may still be judged as a rather passively accepted transformation. The ethical investments in and implications of white privilege, white epistemology, historiography, even critical theory all have ended up under scrutiny in this transformation. At the point of convergence of American Studies and Gender Studies an investigation of whiteness has resulted in a profound de-naturalization of what America, American history, American cultural memory and such concepts as American national character, American identity, and the nexus of gender and race in America could possibly signify. A tracing of the literary legacies of a white historical consciousness steeped in amnesia, in ignorance of the Middle Passage – taken here as chronotopic metaphor – appears particularly pressing since a number of publications recently have celebrated black-and-white-intercultural interactions **as if** that relation could be constituted at will, devoid of its haunting genealogy.[174]

Indeed, one crucial charge in the realm of epistemological white exclusions has been the counter-writing of American history, the re-making of memory as I have demonstrated in my acknowledgement of *Beloved*'s implications. The end of the 20th century has seen a most rapid transition from print culture to virtual reality. That cultural paradigm shift has supported an extreme urgency to reconstruct memory to the effect of restoring modernity's victims to postmodern historical consciousness as if to dare a future forgetfulness looming before us for want of "eye" (as in first person) – witnesses. In the process of re-memory, as Morrison has called it, the grand masternarratives that used to frame modernity's historical recollections had to be refracted in order to make space for the seemingly insignificant particulars, for the small details – like the body count of a slave-ship or the relations between a white abolitionist woman and black radical suffragettes – lost in the sweeping panoramas of white progress. Thus, a reading of the lack or evasiveness of historical self-consciousness in white women's writing, an examination of their unquestioned participation in US-American mythologized memory has necessarily entailed a narrowing of my vision of/on the texts to trace those ellipses. The fault lines of whiteness as it were, could only be seen in bas-relief – an approach that

---

173 *The White Issue* of *Transition* is a particularly rewarding example of how encompassing the scrutiny has become of late.
174 see Lott 1997.

necessarily shows up the problematics of any signification of substance to be secured in identificatory labels, necessary as they might be in the processes of distribution and re-distribution of empowerment, entitlement, as well as in political, cultural and social circulation.

In forging a site for re-reading, in tracing the novels' white memory, I read against a textual resistance always pulling on me to take account of other complexities. It is rather a reckless exclusion not to spend closer attention, for example, on the reworking of the post-World War II period in Rosellen Brown's *Civil Wars* for the strategic reason that the momentum of whiteness stands out most poignantly in the novel in its relation to the Civil Rights Movement. It would need another study to focus on the interrelation, within that particular text, between the social amnesia flattened out over the history of communism in the United States, and the white amnesia deleting political traditions of African-Americans.

In the same vein, there are of course a series of questions which cut the other texts' racialized momentum: O'Connor's vexed relation to femininity in Southern history, Smith's post Second World War Americanness and the impact of lesbianism on her writing, Didion's contradiction between female protagonism and her antifeminism, Herbst's international affiliations and the meaning of German fascism for her work, Stein's Jewishness and its Americanization. I purposefully bracketed those considerations, did not read for the imaginary fullness and immediate presence of texts, but submitted them to a disciplinary practice of a singular paradigm approach, to produce new potential readings.

Whereas this practice has made visible levels of racialized signification that Americanists need to decipher, for future American Studies projects I would like to suggest – by way of re-opening my own brackets, as it were – studies of conflictedness, rather than narratives of cohesion, be it cohesion of nation, class, race or gender. Beyond the productivity of the singular paradigm, my study ultimately added to my objections against unification, against subsumption under homogenizing narratives; instead I hit on sites of splits, contradictions, and competitive discursivities within and among individual and social subjectivities.

In that sense, the binary opposition of my title already anticipates its demise. To me, the most promising projects will be those that situate themselves on the cuts: of why, how, where and when does race cut gender, or the reverse; does maleness cut race, does female race cut class, does male cut race and class cut nation – all combinations are possible. **Cut** here is understood in the sense of destruct: silence, or double: recompose. Our culturally available grand récits (white feminism among them) have left lacunae around those cuts that need to be traced and filled up. How to "re-assemble" without reverting to the reductive impact of those narratives, but also without projecting a newly parasitical, consumptive globalized gaze, disrespectful of the particularities of cuts, will raise the ante for our critical work.

Bibliography

Primary Sources

Brown, Rosellen. *Civil Wars.* New York: Knopf, 1984.

Didion, Joan. *Sentimental Journeys.* 1992. London: Flamingo, 1994.

–. *Slouching Towards Bethlehem.* 1968. London: Flamingo, 1993.

–. *The White Album.* 1979. New York: Pocket Books, 1980.

French, Marilyn. *The Woman's Room.* 1977. New York: Warner Books, 1994.

Herbst, Josephine. *The Executioner Waits.* 1934. New York: Warner, 1986.

–. *Pity Is Not Enough.* 1933. New York: Warner, 1986.

–. *Rope of Gold.* 1939. New York: Warner, 1986.

Morrison, Toni. *Beloved.* New York: Knopf, 1987.

O'Connor, Flannery. "The Artificial Nigger." *Collected Works.* 1953. Ed. Sally Fitzgerald. New York: Library of America, 1988. 210-231.

–. "A Late Encounter With the Enemy." *Collected Works.* 1953. Ed. Sally Fitzgerald. New York: Library of America, 1988. 252-262.

Smith, Lillian. *Killers of the Dream.* 1949. New York: Norton, 1978.

–. *Strange Fruit.* 1944. Athens: University of Georgia Press, 1985.

Stein, Gertrude. *The Autobiography of Alice B. Toklas.* 1933. London: Penguin, 1986.

–. "The Gradual Making of *The Making of Americans.*" *Selected Writings of Gertrude Stein.* Ed. Carl Van Vechten. New York: Vintage, 1972.

–. *The Making of Americans.* 1925. Preface and Ed. Bernhard Fay. New York: Harcourt, Brace & World, 1934.

Stowe, Harriet Beecher. *Uncle Tom's Cabin.* 1852. New York: Penguin, 1986.

Secondary Sources

Abel, Elisabeth. "Black Writing, White Reading: Race and the Politics of Feminist Interpretation." *Critical Inquiry* 19 (1993): 470-98.

Abel, Elisabeth, Barbara Christian, and Helene Moglen, eds. *Female Subjects in Black and White. Race, Psychoanalysis, Feminism,* Berkeley: University of California Press, 1997.

Allinson, Ewan. "It's a Black thing: Hearing how whites can't." *Cultural Studies* 8 (1994): 438-456.

Ammons, Elisabeth, ed. *Critical Essays on Harriet Beecher Stowe*. Boston: Hall, 1980.

Anzaldúa, Gloria. *Borderlands/La Frontera*. San Francisco: Spinsters/Aunt Lute, 1987.

Aptheker, Herbert. *The Correspondence of W.E.B. Du Bois. Vol. II. Selections, 1934-1944*. Amherst: University of Massachusetts Press, 1976.

Baldwin, James. "On Being 'White'... And Other Lies." *Essence* (April 1984): 90-92.

Bammer, Angelika, ed. *Displacements. Cultural Identities in Question*. Blooming-ton: Indiana University Press, 1994.

Barnett, Pamela A. "Figurations of Rape and the Supernatural in *Beloved*," *PMLA* 12.3 (May 1997) 370-380.

Barthes, Roland. *The Pleasure of the Text*. Trans. Richard Miller. New York: Hill and Wang, 1975.

Beal, Frances, "Double Jeopardy: To Be Black and Female," *Sisterhood is Power-ful*. Ed. Robin Morgan. New York: Vintage, 1970. 382-396.

Benedict, Ruth. *Race and Racism*. London: Routledge, 1943.

Benjamin, Walter. 1955. *Illuminations. Essays and Reflections*. Trans. Harry Zohn. Ed. Hannah Arendt. New York: Random, 1988.

Benston, Kimberly. *Speaking For You. The Vision of Ralph Ellison*. Washington: Howard University Press, 1987.

Bercovitch, Sacvan, ed. *Reconstructing American Literary History*. Cambridge: Harvard University Press, 1986.

Bernabe, Jean, Patrick Chamoiseau and Raphael Confiant. "In Praise of Creole-ness." *Callaloo* 13 (1990): 886-909.

Bernal, Martin. *Black Athena: The Afroasiatic Roots of Classical Civilization*. London: Free Association Books, 1987.

Bevilacqua, Winifred Farrant. *Josephine Herbst*. Boston: Twayne, 1985.

Bhabha, Homi. *Nation and Narration*. London: Routledge, 1990.

–. "Postcolonial Authority and Postmodern Guilt." Grossberg, Nelson, Treichler, eds. 56-66.

–. "Race, Time and the Revision of Modernity." *Oxford Literary Review*. 13.1-2 (1991): 193-219

Binder, Wolfgang, ed. *Slavery in the Americas*. Würzburg: Königshausen & Neu-mann, 1993.

Boulton, Alexander. "The American Paradox: Jeffersonian Equality and Racial Science." *American Quarterly* 47.3 (1995): 468-492.

Brady, Jennifer. "Points West, Then and Now: The Fiction of Joan Didion." E. Friedman 43-59.

Braidotti, Rosi. *Nomadic Subjects*. New York: Columbia University Press, 1994.

–. *Patterns of Dissonance*. New York: Routledge, 1991.

Bröck, Sabine. "Gertrude Stein's "Melanctha" in den Diskursen zur Natur der Frau." *Amerikastudien/American Studies* 37.3 (1992): 505-516.

–. "Beloved. A Trace of Body Writing." Fabre and Raynaud 133-139.

Bröck-Sallah, Sabine. "Women Writing: Plotting Against History" *Reconstructing American Literary and Historical Studies*. ed. Günter H. Lenz, Hartmut Keil and Sabine Bröck-Sallah, Frankfurt: Campus, 1990. 225-237.

Bronfen, Elisabeth. "Weiblichkeit und Repräsentation – aus der Perspektive von Ästhetik, Semiotik und Psychoanalyse." Bußmann and Hof 408-445.

Peter Brooks, *Reading for the Plot* (New York: Knopf, 1984).

Brooks Higginbotham, Evelyn. "African-American Women's History and the Metalanguage of Race." *Signs* 17.2 (1992): 91-114.

Brown, Matthew. "Funk music as genre: Black aesthetics, apocalyptic thinking and urban protest in post-1965 African-American pop." *Cultural Studies* 8 (1994): 484-508.

Brown, Gillian. *Domestic Individualism: Imagining Self in Nineteenth Century America*. Berkeley: University of California Press, 1990.

Bulkin, Elly, Minnie Bruce Pratt, and Barbara Smith. *Yours in Struggle: Three Feminist Perspectives on Anti-Semitism and Racism*. New York: Long Haul Press, 1984.

Bußmann, Hadumod and Renate Hof. *Genus. Zur Geschlechterdifferenz in den Kulturwissenschaften*. Stuttgart: Kröner, 1995.

Cade Bambara, Toni. "A Conversation." *Black Women Writers at Work*. Ed. Claudia Tate. New York: Continuum, 1983, 12-38.

Carby, Hazel. "Multi-Culture." *Screen* 34 (1980): 62-70.

Carr, C. "Dreams Deferred." *Village Voice Literary Supplement* (September 94): 20-22.

Carr, David. *Time, Narrative and History*. Bloomington: Indiana University Press, 1986.

Castronovo, Russ. "Radical Configurations of History in the Era of American Slavery." Moon and Davidson 169-194.

Chafe, William H. "The End of One Struggle, the Beginning of Another." Eagles 127-148.

Chernoff, John Miller. *African Rhythm and African Sensibility. Aesthetics and Social Action in African Musical Idioms*. Chicago: University of Chicago Press, 1981.

Chessman, Harriet Scott. *The Public Is Invited To Dance*. Stanford: Stanford University Press, 1989.

Childers, Mary, and Bell Hooks. "A Conversation about Race and Class." Hirsch and Fox Keller 60-82.

Chukwudi Eze, Emmanuel, ed. *Race and the Enlightenment. A Reader*. London: Blackwell Publishers, 1997.

Cliff, Michelle. *Free Enterprise*. 1993. London: Penguin, 1995.

–. ed. *The Winner Names the Age. A Collection of Writings by Lillian Smith*. New York: Norton, 1978.

Cohen, Ralph, ed. *The Future of Literary Theory*. London: Routledge, 1989.

Colatrella, Carol, and Joseph Alkana, *Cohesion and Dissent in America*. New York: SUNY Press, 1994.

Coles, Robert. *Flannery O'Connor's South*. Baton Rouge: Louisiana University Press, 1980.

Dabydeen, David. *Turner*. London: Cape Poetry, 1994.

Daniels, Jesse. *White Lies. Race, Class, Gender and Sexuality in White Supremacist Discourse. New York:* Routledge, 1998.

Darling, Marsha. "In the Realm of Responsibility: A Conversation with Toni Morrison." *The Women's Review of Books* 5.6 (1988): 3-5.

Davis, Angela. *Women, Race and Class*. New York: Random House, 1981.

Davis, Charles T., and Henry Louis Gates, Jr., eds. *The Slave's Narrative*. New York: Oxford University Press, 1985.

Davis, David Brion. *The Problem of Slavery in the Age of Revolution*. 1966. Ithaca: Cornell University Press, 1975.

Dayan, Joan. "Amorous Bondage: Poe, Ladies and Slaves." Moon and Davidson, 109-143.

De Koven, Marianne. *A Different Language: Gertrude Stein's Experimental Writing*. Madison: University of Wisconsin Press, 1983.

–. "Half In and Half Out of Doors: Gertrude Stein and Literary Tradition." Kellner 75-83.

De Lauretis, Teresa. "Eccentric Subjects: Feminist Theory and Historical Consciousness." *Feminist Studies* 16.1 (1990): 115-50.

–. *Technologies of Gender*. Bloomington: Indiana University Press, 1987.

Dent, Gina, ed. *Black Popular Culture*. Seattle: Bay Press, 1992.

Diffley, Kathleen. "The Roots of Tara. Making War Civil." *American Quarterly* 36 (1984): 359-372.

Dittmer, John. "The Politics of Mississippi Movement 1954-1964." Eagles 65-93.

Doane, Janice L. *Silence and Narrative. The Early Novels of Gertrude Stein*. London: Greenwood Press, 1986.

DuBois, Ellen Carol. *Feminism and Suffrage. The Emergence of an Independent Women's Movement in America, 1848-1869*. Ithaca: Cornell University Press, 1978.

182

Du Bois, W. E. Burghardt. *The Souls of Black Folk.* 1903. New York: Fawcett, 1961.

DuCille, Ann. "The Occult of True Black Womanhood: Critical Demeanor and Black Feminist Studies." *Signs* 19 (1994): 591-629.

–. "Postcolonialism and Afrocentricity: Discourse and Dat Course." Sollors and Diedrich 29-41.

DuPlessis, Rachel Blau. "Hoo, Hoo, Hoo: Some Episodes in the Construction of Modern Whiteness." *American Literature* 67.4 (1995): 667-699.

–. *The Pink Guitar. Writing as Feminist Practice.* London, New York: Routledge, 1990.

Dydo, Ulla. "Reading the Hand Writing: The Manuscripts of Gertrude Stein." Kellner 84-95.

Dyer, Richard. "White." *Screen* 29.3 (1988): 44-62.

Eagles, Charles, ed. *The Civil Rights Movement in America.* Jackson: University of Mississippi Press, 1986.

Eco, Umberto. "An Ars Oblivionalis? Forget It!" *PMLA* 103.1 (1988): 254-261.

Ellison, Ralph. *Invisible Man.* 1952. New York: Random House, 1995.

–. *Shadow and Act.* New York: Random House, 1964.

Ermarth, Elisabeth Deeds. "The Crisis of Realism in Postmodern Time." Levine 214-224.

Evans, Sara. *Born For Liberty. A History of Women in America.* New York, London: Macmillan, 1989.

–. *Personal Politics: The Roots of Women's Liberation in the Civil Rights Movement and the New Left.* New York: Vintage, 1980.

Fabre, Geneviève, and Claudine Raynaud, eds. *Beloved. She's Mine. Essais sur Beloved de Toni Morrison.* Paris: Cetanla, 1993.

Feeley, Kathleen. *Flannery O'Connor: Voice of the Peacock.* New Brunswick: Rutgers University Press, 1972.

Felman, Shoshona. "Camus, *The Plague*, or A Monument to Witnessing." Felman and Laub 93-119.

Felman, Shoshona, and Dori Laub. *Testimony. Crises Of Witnessing In Literature, Psychoanalysis and History.* New York: Routledge, 1992.

Ferguson, Moira. *Colonialism and Gender Relations. From Mary Wollstonecraft to Jamaica Kincaid.* New York: Columbia University Press, 1993.

–. *Subject to Others: British Women Writers and Colonial Slavery, 1670-1834.* London: Routledge, 1992.

Fiedler, Leslie. *Love and Death in the American Novel.* New York: Stein and Day, 1966.

–. *The Inadvertent Epic. From Uncle Tom's Cabin to Roots.* New York: Simon and Schuster, 1979.

Fine, Michelle, Linda C. Powell, Louis Weis and L. Mun Wong, eds. *Off White. Readings on Race, Power and Society*. New York: Routledge, 1998.

Fisher, Philip, ed. *The New American Studies*. Berkeley: University of California Press, 1991.

Fisher Fishkin, Shelley. "Interrogating Whiteness, Complicating Blackness: Remapping American Culture." *American Quarterly*. 47.3 (1995): 429-66.

Flax, Jane. "Postmodernism and Gender Relations in Feminist Theory." Nicholson 39-62.

–. "Re-Membering the Selves: Is the Repressed Gendered?" *Michigan Quarterly Review* 23.1 (1987): 93-110.

Foley, Barbara. *Radical Representations. Politics and Form in U.S. Proletarian Fiction, 1929-1941*. Durham: Duke University Press, 1993.

Fout, John C., and Maura Shaw Tantillo, eds. *American Sexual Politics. Sex, Gender and Race since the Civil War*. Chicago: University of Chicago Press, 1993.

Frank, Manfred. *Was ist Neostrukturalismus?* 1983. Frankfurt am Main: Suhrkamp, 1984.

Frankenberg, Ruth. *White Women. Race Matters: The Social Construction of Whiteness*. Minneapolis: University of Minnesota Press, 1993.

Freeman, Barbara Claire. *The Feminine Sublime. Gender and Excess in Women's Fiction*. Berkeley: University of California Press, 1995.

Fredrickson, George. *The Black Image in the White Mind: The Debate on Afro-American Character and Destiny, 1817-1914*. New York: Harper & Row, 1971.

Friedlander, Saul. "Introduction." Friedlander 1-22.

–. ed. *Probing the Limits of Representation. Nazism and the Final Solution*. Cambridge: Harvard University Press, 1992.

Friedman, Ellen. "The Didion Sensibility: An Analysis." Friedman 81-90.

–. ed. *Joan Didion. Essays and Conversations*. Princeton: Ontario Review Press, 1984.

Friedman, Susan Stanford. "Beyond White and Other: Relationality and Narratives of Race in Feminist Discourse." *Signs* 21. 1 (1995): 1-49.

Frye, Marilyn. *Willful Virgin. Essays in Feminism*. Freedom, Ca.: The Crossing Press, 1992.

Fuss, Diana. *Essentially Speaking. Feminism, Nature and Difference*. New York: Routledge, 1989.

Gallop, Jane. *Around 1981: Academic Feminist Literary Theory*. New York: Routledge, 1992

Gates, Henry Louis Jr. "Beyond the Culture Wars: Identities in Dialogue." *Profession* (1993): 6-11.

–. ed. *Black Literature and Literary Theory*. New York, London: Methuen, 1984.

184

–. "Writing 'Race' and the Difference It Makes." *Critical Inquiry* 12.1 (1985): 1-20.

Gates, Henry Louis Jr., and Kwame Anthony Appiah, eds. *Toni Morrison. Critical Perspectives Past and Present*. New York: Amistad, 1993.

–. *The White Issue. Transition* 73 7.1 (1998).

Giddings, Paula. *When and Where I Enter: The Impact of Black Women on Race and Sex in America*. New York: Bantam, 1984.

Gikandi, Simon. *Writing in Limbo. Modernism and Caribbean Literature*. Ithaca: Cornell University Press, 1992.

Gilroy, Paul. *The Black Atlantic. Modernity and Double Consciousness*. Cambridge: Harvard University Press, 1993.

Girgus, Sam. *The American Self: Myth, Ideology and Popular Culture*. Albuquerque: University of New Mexico Press, 1981.

Giroux, Henry, and Peter McLaren, eds. *Between Borders. Pedagogy and the Politics of Cultural Studies*. New York: Routledge, 1994.

Glissant, Edouard. *Caribbean Discourse*. Trans. Michael Dash. 1981. Charlottesville: University of Virginia Press, 1989.

Goldberg, David Theo, ed. *Anatomy of Racism*. Minneapolis: University of Minnesota Press, 1990.

Goldfield, Michael. "The Color of Politics in the United States: White Supremacy as the Main Explanation for the Peculiarities of American Politics from Colonial Times to the Present." *The Bounds of Race. Perspectives on Hegemony and Resistance*. Ed. Dominick LaCapra. Ithaca: Cornell University Press, 1991. 104-133.

Gossett, Thomas F. *Race: The History of an Idea in America*. New York: Methuen, 1963.

Grossberg, Lawrence, Cary Nelson, and Paula Treichler, eds. *Cultural Studies*. New York: Routledge, 1992.

Grimké, Angelina. *Appeal to the Christian Women of the South*. 1836. New York: Arno, 1969.

Halbwachs, Maurice. *Das kollektive Gedächtnis*. 1967. Frankfurt am Main: Fischer, 1991.

Hall, Jacquelyn Dowd. *Revolt Against Chivalry: Jessie Daniel Ames and the Women's Campaign against Lynching*. New York: Columbia University Press, 1979.

Hall, Stuart. "Cultural Identity and Diaspora." *Identity: Community, Cultural Difference*. Ed. Jonathan Rutherford. London: Lawrence and Wishart, 1990. 220-247.

Haraway, Donna. "A Manifesto for Cyborgs: Science, Technology, and Socialist Feminism in the 1980s." Nicholson 190-233.

185

Harris, Trudier. *Exorcising Blackness: Historical and Literary Lynching and Burning Rituals*. Bloomington: Indiana University Press, 1984.

Hawkesworth, Mary E. "Knowers, Knowing, Known: Feminist Theory and Claims of Truth." *Signs* 14.3 (1989) 533-557.

Henderson, Katherine U. "*Run River*: Edenic Vision and Wasteland Nightmare." E. Friedman 91-104.

Henderson, Mae. *Borders, Boundaries, Frames. Essays in Cultural Criticism and Cultural Studies*. New York: Routledge, 1995.

–. "Toni Morrison's *Beloved*: Re-membering the Body as Historical Text." Spillers 1991, 62-86.

Higonnet, Margaret. "Civil Wars and Sexual Territories." *Arms and the Woman: War, Gender and Literary Representation*. Ed. Helen M. Cooper, Adrienne Auslander Munich, and Susan Merrill Squier. Chapel Hill: University of North Carolina Press, 1989. 80-102.

Hill, Mike, ed. *Whiteness. A Critical Reader*. New York: New York University Press, 1997.

Hine, Darlene Clark, Wilma King, and Linda Reed, eds. *We Specialize in the Wholly Impossible. A Reader in Black Women's History*. New York: Carlson, 1995.

Hirsch, Marianne, and Evelyn Fox Keller, eds. *Conflicts in Feminism*. New York: Routledge, 1990.

Hobson, Fred. Foreword. *Strange Fruit*. By Lillian Smith. Athens: University of Georgia Press, 1985. vii -xviii.

Hoch, Paul. *White Hero, Black Beast: Racism, Sexism and the Mask of Masculinity*, London: Routledge, 1979.

Hodes, Martha. "The Sexualization of Reconstruction Politics: White Women and Black Men in the South after the Civil War," Fout and Shaw Tantillo 59-74.

Hof, Renate. "Die Entwicklung der Gender Studies". Bußmann and Hof 2-33.

Hoffmann, Gerhard, ed. *Der zeitgenössische amerikanische Roman*. München: Fink, 1988.

Holloway, Joseph, ed. *Africanisms in American Culture*. Bloomington: Indiana University Press, 1990.

Hollowell, John. "Against Interpretation: Narrative Strategy in *A Book of Common Prayer*." E. Friedman 164-176.

Homans, Margaret. "'Women of Color' Writers and Feminist Theory." *New Literary History* 25.1 (1994): 73-94.

Hong Kingston, Maxine. "Eccentric Memories: A Conversation with Maxine Hong Kingston." *Michigan Quarterly Review* 26.1. (1987): 177-187.

Hooks, Bell. *Ain't I a Woman? Black Women and Feminism*. Boston: South End Press, 1989.

–. *Black Looks. Race and Representation.* London: Turnaround, 1992.

–. *Feminist Theory: From Margin to Center.* Boston: South End Press, 1984.

–. *Yearning.* Boston: South End Press, 1990.

Hornung, Alfred. "The Making of Americans: Mary Rowlandson, Benjamin Franklin, Gertrude Stein, Maxine Hong Kingston." Lenz and Milich 96-117.

Huggins, Nathan. *Harlem Renaissance.* New York: Oxford University Press, 1971.

Hutcheon, Linda. *A Poetics of Postmodernism. History, Theory, Fiction.* New York: Routledge, 1988.

–. ed. *Special Topic. Colonialism and the Postcolonial Condition.* PMLA 110.1 (1995).

–. "Introduction. Complexities Abounding." Hutcheon 1995, 7-16.

Huyssen, Andreas. "Mapping the Postmodern." Nicholson 234-280.

Inikori, Joseph, and Stanley Engerman, eds. *The Atlantic Slave Trade.* Durham: Duke University Press, 1992.

Jameson, Elisabeth. "Toward A Multicultural History of Women in the Western United States." *Signs* 13 (1988): 761-791.

Jameson, Fredric. *The Ideologies of Theory. Essays 1971-1986.* Vol.2. Minneapolis: University of Minnesota Press, 1988.

Jordan, Winthrop. *The White Man's Burden. Historical Origins of Racism in the United States.* New York: Oxford University Press, 1974.

–. *White Over Black. American Attitudes Toward the Negro, 1550-1812.* Chapel Hill: University of North Carolina Press, 1968.

Kaplan, Amy and Donald Pease, eds. *Cultures of United States Imperialism.* Durham: Duke University Press, 1993.

Kaplan, Carla. "Reading Feminist Readings: Recuperative Reading and the Silent Heroine of Feminist Criticism." *Listening To Silences.* Ed. Elaine Hedges and Shelley Fisher Fishkin. New York: Oxford University Press, 1994. 168-194.

Kaplan, Sidney. *American Studies in Black and White. Selected Essays 1949-1989.* Ed. Allan Austin. Amherst: University of Massachusetts Press, 1991.

Kayser, Wolfgang. *The Grotesque in Art and Literature.* Bloomington: Indiana University Press, 1963.

Kellner, Bruce, ed. *A Gertrude Stein Companion. Content with the Example.* New York: Greenwood Press, 1988.

Kelly, Joan. *Women, History and Theory.* Chicago: University of Chicago Press, 1984.

Kiley, Frederick. "Beyond Words: Narrative Art in Joan Didion's *Salvador.*" E. Friedman 181-188.

Koenen, Anne. "Toni Morrison's *Beloved* and the Ghost of Slavery." Fabre and Raynaud 53-66.

Koselleck, Reinhart. *Vergangene Zukunft.* 1979. Frankfurt: Suhrkamp, 1995.

187

Kovel, Joel, *White Racism: A Psychohistory*. New York: Pantheon, 1970.

Kunow, Rüdiger, "Beginning/ Ending/ Rewriting History: Historiographical Scenarios in the Multiculturalism Debate." Lenz and Milich 77-95.

Kuppler, Elisabeth. "Weiblichkeitsmythen zwischen *gender, race* und *class*: *True Womanhood* im Spiegel der Geschichtsschreibung." Bußmann and Hof 262-291.

Kutzinksi, Vera. *Against the American Grain*. Baltimore: Johns Hopkins University Press, 1987.

LaCapra, Dominick. *The Bounds of Race. Perspectives on Hegemony and Resistance*. Ithaca: Cornell University Press, 1991.

Langer, Elinor. *Josephine Herbst. The Story She Could Never Tell*. 1983. New York: Warner Books, 1985.

Laub, Dori. "Bearing Witness or the Vicissitudes of Listening." Felman and Laub 57-74.

Lauret, Maria. *Liberating Literature. Feminist Fiction in America*. London: Routledge, 1994.

Lauter, Paul. "American Proletarianism." *The Columbia History of The American Novel*. Ed. Emory Elliott et al. New York: Columbia University Press, 1991. 331-356.

Le Goff, Jaques. *History and Memory*. New York: Columbia University Press, 1992.

Lenz, Günter H. "The Radical Imagination: Revisionary Modes of Radical Cultural Cultural Criticism in Thirties America." *Looking Inward Looking Outward: from the 1930s to the 1940s*. Ed. Steve Ickringill. Amsterdam: Free University Press, 1990. 94-126.

Lenz, Günter H., Hartmut Keil and Sabine Bröck-Sallah, eds. *Reconstructing American Literary and Historical Studies*. Frankfurt: Campus; New York: St. Martin's Press, 1990.

Lenz, Günter H., and Klaus Milich, eds. *American Studies in Germany. European Contexts and Intercultural Relations*. Frankfurt: Campus; New York: St. Martin's Press, 1995.

Levine, George, ed. *Realism and Representation. Essays on the Problem of Realism in Relation to Science, Literature and Culture*. Madison: University of Wisconsin Press, 1993.

Lewis, David Levering. "The Origins and Causes of the Civil Rights Movement." Eagles 3-17.

Lipsitz, George. "Swing Low, Sweet Cadillac: White Supremacy, Antiblack Racism, and the New Historicism." *American Literary History* 7.4 (1995): 701-725.

Lott, Eric. "White Like Me: Racial Cross-Dressing and the Construction of American Whiteness." Kaplan and Pease 474-498.

–. "The New Cosmopolitanism". *Transition* 72 (1997): 108-136.

Loris, Michelle Carbone. *Innocence, Loss and Recovery in the Art of Joan Didion.* New York: Lang, 1989.

Marcus, Jane. "Bonding and Bondage: Nancy Cunard and the Making of the *Negro* Anthology." Henderson 1995, 33-63.

Mayr, Christian. *Geschichtsverständnis und Textstruktur im sozialkritischen Roman der 30er Jahre.* Heidelberg: n.p., 1985.

McClintock, Anne. "The Angel of Progress: Pitfalls of the Term 'Postcolonialism'." *Social Text* 31/32 (1992): 84-98.

McDowell, Deborah E. *The Changing Same. Black Women's Literature, Criticism and Theory.* Bloomington: Indiana University Press, 1995.

McKay, Nellie. "An Interview with Toni Morrison," Gates and Appiah 396-411.

Meese, Elisabeth, and Alice Parker, eds. *The Difference Within: Feminism and Critical Theory.* Philadelphia: John Benjamins, 1989.

Möckel-Rieke, Hannah. "Introduction: Media and Cultural Memory." Möckel-Rieke, Hannah and Randi Gunzenhäuser, eds. *Media and Cultural Memory. Amerikastudien/American Studies* 43.1 (1998): 5-19.

Mohanty, Chandra Talpade, Ann Russo, and Lourdes Torres, eds. *Third World Women and the Politics of Feminism.* Bloomington: Indiana University Press, 1991.

Moi, Toril. *Sexual/Textual Politics: Feminist Literary Theory.* New York: Methuen, 1985.

Moon, Michael and Cathy Davidson, eds. *Subjects & Citizens. Nation, Race and Gender. From Oroonoko to Anita Hill.* Durham: Duke University Press, 1995.

Morgan, Edmund. *American Slavery. American Freedom. The Ordeal of Colonial Virginia.* New York: Norton, 1975.

–. "Slavery and Freedom: The American Paradox." *Journal of American History* 59 (1972): 5-29

Morrison, Toni. "The Pain of Being Black." *Time* (22 May 1989): 120.

–. *Playing in the Dark: Whiteness and the Literary Imagination.* Cambridge, Mass.: Harvard University Press, 1992.

–. "Unspeakable Things Unspoken: The Afro-American Presence in American Literature," *Michigan Quarterly Review* 28, 1 (Winter 1989) 1-34.

–. "The Site of Memory." *Inventing the Truth: The Art and Craft of Memoir.* Ed. William Zinsser. Boston: Houghton-Mifflin, 1987. 103-123.

Mullen, Harryette. "Optic White: Blackness and the Production of Whiteness." *diacritics* 24. 2-3 (1994): 71-89.

Muller, Gilbert. *Nightmares and Visions. Flannery O'Connor and the Catholic Grotesque*. Athens: University of Georgia Press, 1972.

Müller-Hartmann, Andreas. "'The Nigger in the Woodpile': The Southern Literary Discourse of Race." *Amerikastudien/American Studies* 39.4 (1994): 537-550.

Murray, Albert. *The Omni-Americans. New Perspectives on Black Experience and American Culture*. 1970. New York: Vintage, 1983.

Myrdal, Gunnar. *An American Dilemma: The Negro Problem and Modern Democracy*. New York: Harper and Row, 1944.

Nadel, Alan. "Postwar America and the Story of *Democracy*." Pease 95-120.

Nelson, Dana. *The Word in Black and White: Reading "Race" in American Literature*. New York: Oxford University Press, 1992.

Newton, Judith, and Deborah Rosenfelt. *Feminist Criticism and Social Change. Sex, Class and Race in Literature and Culture*. New York: Methuen, 1985.

Nicholson, Linda, ed. *Feminism/Postmodernism*. New York: Routledge, 1990.

North, Michael. *The Dialect of Modernism. Race, Language and Twentieth Century Literature*. New York, Oxford: Oxford University Press, 1994.

O'Connor, Flannery. *Collected Works*. Ed. Sally Fitzgerald. New York: The Library of America, 1988.

–. *The Habit of Being*. Ed. Sally Fitzgerald. New York: Farrar, Straus and Giroux, 1979.

–. *Mystery and Manners*. Ed. Sally and Robert Fitzgerald. 1961. New York: Farrar, Straus and Giroux, 1983.

–. "The Regional Writer." O'Connor 1988, 843-852.

Olney, James. "I Was Born: Slave Narratives, Their Status as Autobiography and as Literature." Davis and Gates 148-174.

Omi, Michael and Howard Winant. *Racial Formation in the United States: From the 1960s to the 1980s*. London: Routledge, 1986.

Oppenheimer, Priscilla. "A Biographical Dictionary." Kellner 242,3.

Ostendorf, Berndt. "Cultural Studies: Post-Political Theory in a Post-Fordist Public Sphere." *Amerikastudien/American Studies* 40.4 (1995): 709-724.

Patterson, Orlando. *Slavery and Social Death: A Comparative Study*. Cambridge, Mass.: Harvard University Press, 1982.

Pease, Donald, ed. *National Identities and Post-Americanist Narratives*. Durham: Duke University Press, 1994.

Peterson, Carla. "The Remaking of Americans: Gertrude Stein's 'Melanctha' and African-American Musical Traditions." Wonham *Criticism*, 140-157.

Peterson, Nancy. "History, Postmodernism and Louise Erdrich's *Tracks*." *PMLA* 109.5 (1994): 982-993.

Pieterse, Jan Niederven. *White on Black. Images of Africa and Blacks in Western Popular Culture*. New Haven: Yale University Press, 1992.

190

Pratt, Mary Louise. "Arts of the Contact Zone." *Profession* 91 (1991): 33-40.

Rabinowitz, Paula. *Labor and Desire. Women's Revolutionary Fiction in Depression America.* Chapel Hill: University of North Carolina Press, 1991.

Radhakrishnan, Radha. "The Changing Subject and the Politics of Theory." *differences* 2 (1990): 126-52.

–. "Postcoloniality and the Boundaries of Identity." *Callaloo* 16.3 (1993): 750-71.

Rath, Sura P. "Introduction." Rath and Neff Shaw 1-11.

Rath, Sura P., and Mary Neff Shaw, eds. *Flannery O'Connor. New Perpectives.* Athens: University of Georgia Press, 1996.

Reising, Russell. *The Unusable Past: Theory and the Study of American Literature.* New York: Methuen, 1986.

Remmler, Karen. "Sheltering Battered Bodies in Language: Imprisonment Once More?" Bammer 216-232.

Rich, Adrienne. *Blood, Bread and Poetry: Selected Prose, 1979-1985.* New York: Norton, 1986.

–. *On Lies, Secrets and Silence: Selected Prose, 1966-1978.* New York: Norton, 1979.

Roberts, Diane. *The Myth of Aunt Jemima. Representations of Race and Region.* London: Routledge, 1994.

Ricoeur, Paul. *The Reality of the Historical Past.* Milwaukee: Marquette University Press, 1984.

Roediger, David R. "*Guineas, Wiggers* and the Dramas of Racialized Culture." *American Literary History* 7.4 (1995): 655-668.

–. *Towards the Abolition of Whiteness. Essays on Race, Politics and Working Class History.* London: Verso, 1994.

–. *The Wages of Whiteness. Race and the Making of the American Working Class.* London: Verso, 1991.

Rogin, Michael. "Blackface, White Noise: The Jewish Jazz Singer Finds His Voice." *Critical Inquiry* 18 (1992): 417-53.

Ross, Andrew. *No Respect: Intellectuals and Popular Culture.* New York: Routledge, 1989.

–. ed. *Universal Abandon. The Politics of Postmodernism.* Minneapolis: University of Minnesota Press, 1988.

Ruddick, Lisa. *Reading Gertrude Stein. Body, Text, Gnosis.* New York: Cornell University Press, 1990.

Ruskin, John. *Modern Painters.* Ed. David Barrie. London: Deutsch Verlag, 1989.

Saldivar Hull, Sonia. "Wrestling Your Ally." *Women's Writing in Exile.* Ed. Mary Lynn Broe and Angela Ingram. Chapel Hill: University of North Carolina Press, 1989. 182-198.

Sánchez-Eppler, Karen. "Bodily Bonds: The Intersecting Rhetorics of Feminism and Abolition." 1988. Fisher 228-259.

–. *Touching Liberty. Abolition, Feminism and the Politics of the Body*. Berkeley: University of California Press, 1993.

Sandoval, Chela. "U.S. Third World Feminism: The Theory and Method of Oppositional Consciousness in the Postmodern World." *Genders* 10 (Spring 1991): 1-24.

Scarry, Elaine. *The Body in Pain. The Making and Unmaking of The World*. New York: Oxford University Press, 1985.

Scheich, Elvira. *Vermittelte Weiblichkeit. Feministische Wissenschafts- und Gesellschaftstheorie*. Hamburg: Hamburger Edition, 1996.

Scherpe, Klaus. "Dramatisierung und Entdramatisierung des Untergangs – zum aesthetischen Bewußtsein von Moderne und Postmoderne." *Postmoderne. Zeichen des kulturellen Wandels*. Ed. Andreas Huyssen und Klaus Scherpe. Hamburg: Argument Verlag, 1986. 270-301.

Schiller, Georg. "Organizing Energies: Reference and Experience in the Work of Gertrude Stein." *Amerikastudien/American Studies* 39.4 (1994): 511-524.

Schmitz, Neil. "Gertrude Stein as Post-Modernist." *Journal of Modern Literature* 3 (1974): 1203-18.

Scott, Ann Firor. *The Southern Lady. From Pedestal to Politics. 1830-1930*. Chicago: University of Chicago Press, 1970.

Scott, Bonnie Kime, ed. *The Gender of Modernism*. Bloomington: Indiana University Press, 1990.

Segrest, Mab. *Memoir of a Race Traitor*. Boston: South End Press, 1994.

–. *My Mama's Dead Squirrel: Lesbian Essays on Southern Culture*. New York: Firebrand, 1985.

Sharrad, Paul. "The Art of Memory and the Liberation of History: Wilson Harris's Witnessing of Time." *Callaloo* 18.1. (1995) 94-108.

Shaw, Mary Neff. "'The Artificial Nigger: A Dialogical Narrative." Rath and Shaw 139-151.

Shohat, Ella and Robert Stam. *Unthinking Eurocentrism*. London: Routledge, 1994.

Siebers, Tobin. "Ethics ad Nauseam." *American Literary History* 6.4 (1994) 757-778.

Sitkoff, Harvard. *The Struggle For Black Equality*. New York: Hill and Wang, 1981.

Smith, Lillian. "Autobiography as Dialogue Between King and Corpse." 1962. Cliff 1978, 187-198.

–. "Humans in Bondage." 1944. Cliff 1978, 32-55.

Smith, Paul. *Discerning the Subject*. Minneapolis: University of Minnesota Press, 1988.

Smith, Sidonie. *Subjectivity, Identity and the Body. Women's Autobiographical Practices in the Twentieth Century*. Bloomington: Indiana University Press, 1993.

Smith, Valerie. "'Circling the Subject': History and Narrative in *Beloved*." Gates and Appiah 342-355.

Snead, James. "Repetition as a Figure of Black Culture." Gates 1984, 59-104.

Sollors, Werner, and Maria Diedrich, eds. *The Black Columbiad*. Cambridge: Harvard University Press, 1994.

Sosna, Morton. *In Search of the Silent South. Southern Liberals and the Race Issue*. New York: Columbia University Press, 1977.

Spillers, Hortense. "Changing the Letter: The Yokes, The Jokes of Discourse, or Mrs. Stowe, Mr. Reed." *Slavery and the Literary Imagination. Selected Papers from the English Institute 1987*. Ed. Deborah McDowell and Arnold Rampersad. Baltimore: Johns Hopkins University Press, 1989. 25-61.

–. ed. *Comparative American Identities. Race, Sex and Nationality in the Modern Text*. New York: Routledge, 1991.

–. "Mama's Baby, Papa's Maybe: An American Grammar Book," *diacritics* (Summer 1987): 65-81.

–. "Notes on an alternative model – neither/nor." Meese and Parker 165-187.

Spivak, Gayatri Chakravorty. "The Rani of Sirmur." *Europe and Its Others*. Vol. 1. Ed. Francis Barker et al. Colchester: University of Essex, 1985. 128-151.

Stacey, Judith. "Scents, Scholars and Stigma: The Revisionist Campaign for Family Values." *Social Text* 40 (1994): 51-71.

Stallybrass, Peter and Allon White. *The Politics and Poetics of Transgression*. Ithaca: Cornell University Press, 1986.

Steiner, Wendy. *Exact Resemblance to Exact Resemblance: The Literary Portraiture of Gertrude Stein*. New Haven: Yale University Press, 1978.

Steven, Gregory, and Roger Sanjek, eds. *Race*. New Brunswick: Rutgers University Press, 1994.

Stimpson, Catherine. *Where the Meanings Are*. New York: Methuen, 1988.

Stowe, David. "Uncolored People. The Rise of Whiteness Studies." *Lingua Franca* (September/October 1996): 68-77.

Sundquist, Eric. *New Essays on Uncle Tom's Cabin*. Cambridge: Cambridge University Press, 1986.

Tompkins, Jane. *Sensational Designs: The Cultural Work of American Fiction*. New York: Oxford University Press, 1985.

Torgovnick, Marianna. *Gone Primitive. Savage Intellects, Modern Lives*. Chicago: The University of Chicago Press, 1990.

Trinh T., Minh-Ha. *Woman, Native, Other. Writing Postcoloniality and Feminism.* Bloomington: Indiana University Press, 1989.

Wald, Priscilla. "A God Who Is Later A Terror: (En)countering the National Plot in Stein's *The Making of Americans.*" *Prospects* 16 (1991): 323-65.

Walker, Alice. "Advancing Luna – and Ida B. Wells." *You Can't Keep A Good Woman Down.* New York: Harcourt Brace Jovanovich, 1981.

–. *In Search of Our Mothers' Gardens.* New York: Harcourt Brace Jovanovich, 1983.

–. *Meridian.* New York: Harcourt Brace Jovanovich, 1977.

Walker, Jayne. *The Making of a Modernist: Gertrude Stein.* Amherst: University of Massachusetts Press, 1984.

Wall, Cheryl A., ed. *Changing Our Own Words. Essays on Criticism, Theory, and Writing by Black Women.* New Brunswick: Rutgers University Press, 1989.

Ware, Vron. *Beyond the Pale: White Women, Racism and History.* London: Verso, 1990.

West, Cornel. "The New Cultural Politics of Difference." *October* 53 (1990): 93-109

–. "Postmodernism and Black America." *Z Magazine* 6 (1988): 19-43.

White, Hayden. *The Content of the Form.* Baltimore: Johns Hopkins University Press, 1987.

–. "'Figuring the nature of the times deceased': Literary Theory and Historical Writing." Cohen 19-44.

–. "Historical Emplotment and the Problem of Truth." Friedlander 37-53.

Wiegman, Robyn. "The Anatomy of Lynching." Fout and Shaw Tantillo 223-246.

–. "Toward a Political Economy of Race and Gender." *Turning the Century:" Feminist Theory in the 1990s.* Ed. Glynis Carr. Lewisburg: Bucknell University Press, 1992. 47-67.

–. *American Anatomies. Theorizing Race and Gender.* Durham, London: Duke University Press, 1995.

Wilcox, Leonard. "Narrative Technique and the Theme of Historical Continuity in the Novels of Joan Didion." E. Friedman 68-80.

Wilson, Rob. "Techno-Euphoria and the Discourse of the American Sublime." Pease 205-229.

Wonham, Henry B., ed. *Criticism and the Color Line. Desegregating American Literary Studies.* New Brunswick: Rutgers University Press, 1996.

–. "Introduction." Wonham 1-15.

Wynter, Sylvia. "The Ceremony Must Be Found: After Humanism." *boundary 2* 12/13 (1984): 19-65.

–. "Sambos and Minstrels." *Social Text* 1 (Winter 1979): 149-156.

Yaeger, Patricia. "Flannery O'Connor and the Aesthetics of Torture." Rath and Shaw 183-206.

Yellin, Jean Fagan. *Women & Sisters. The Antislavery Feminists in American Culture*. New Haven: Yale University Press, 1989.

–. "Written by Herself: Harriet Jacobs's Slave Narrative," *American Literature* 53 (November 1981): 479-486.

Young, Elisabeth. "Warring Fictions: Iola Leroy and the Color of Gender." Moon and Davidson 293-318.

Young, Robert. *Colonial Desire. Hybridity in Theory, Culture and Race*. London: Routledge, 1995.

–. *White Mythologies. Writing History and the West*. London: Routledge, 1990.

Bremer Beiträge zur Literatur- und Ideengeschichte

Herausgegeben von Thomas Metscher und Wolfgang Beutin.
Mitbegründet von Dieter Herms

Band 1 Horst Rößler: Literatur und Arbeiterbewegung. Studien zur Literaturkritik und frühen Prosa des Chartismus. 1985.

Band 2 Priscilla Metscher: Republicanism and Socialism in Ireland. A Study in the Relationship of Politics and Ideology from the United Irishmen to James Connolly. 1986.

Band 3 Hagal Mengel: Sam Thompson and Modern Drama in Ulster. 1986.

Band 4 Gudrun Kauhl: Joseph Conrad: *The Secret Agent*. Text und zeitgeschichtlicher Kontext. 1986.

Band 5 Ingrid Kerkhoff: Poetiken und lyrischer Diskurs im Kontext gesellschaftlicher Dynamik. USA: »*The Sixties* «. 1989.

Band 6 Jennifer Farrell: "Keats - The Progress of the Odes. Unity and Utopia." 1989.

Band 7 Eckhardt Rüdebusch: Irland im Zeitalter der Revolution, Politik und Publizistik der United Irishmen 1791 - 98. 1989.

Band 8 Rudolf Fritsch: Absurd oder grotesk. Über literarische Darstellung von Entfremdung bei Beckett und Heller. 1990.

Band 9 Dieter Herms (ed.): Upton Sinclair. Literature and Social Reform. 1990.

Band 10 Karin Brenner: Theorie der Literaturgeschichte und Ästhetik bei Georg Lukács. 1990.

Band 11 Thomas Sorge: Gespielte Geschichte. Die ausgestellte Fiktion in Morus' Utopia und in Shakespeares englischen Historienspielen. 1992.

Band 12 Wolfgang Beutin / Klaus Lüders (Hrsg.): Freiheit durch Aufklärung: Johann Heinrich Voß (1751-1826). Materialien einer Tagung der Stiftung Mecklenburg (Ratzeburg) und des Verbandes Deutscher Schriftsteller (Landesbezirk Nord) in Lauenburg/Elbe am 23.-25. April 1993. 1995.

Band 13 Wolfgang Beutin / Thomas Bütow (Hrsg.): Gottfried August Bürger (1747-1794). Beiträge der Tagung zu seinem 200. Todestag vom 7. bis 9. Juni 1994 in Bad Segeberg. 1994.

Band 14 Günter Hartung: Außenseiter der Aufklärung. Internationales Kolloquium Halle a. d. Saale 26.-28. Juni 1992. 1995.

Band 15 Raimund Kemper: *Il était un petit navire* ... Zur Archäologie der *Narrenschiff*-Phantasien Michel Foucaults. 1996.

Band 16 Armin Bernhard: Der Bildungsprozeß in einer Epoche der Ambivalenz. Studien zur Bildungsgeschichte in der *Ästhetik des Widerstands*. 1996.

Band 17 Alfred Raucheisen: Orient und Abendland. Ethisch-moralische Aspekte in Wolframs Epen *Parzival* und *Willehalm*. 1997.

Band 18 Susanne Dähn: Rede als Text. Rhetorik und Stilistik in Luthers Sakramentssermonen von 1519. 1997.

Band 19 Wolfgang Beutin: ANIMA. Untersuchungen zur Frauenmystik des Mittelalters. Teil 1: Probleme der Mystikforschung – Mystikforschung als Problem. 1997.

Band 20 Wolfgang Beutin / Wilfried Hoppe (Hrsg.): Franz Mehring (1846-1919). Beiträge der Tagung vom 8. bis 9. November 1996 in Hamburg anläßlich seines 150. Geburtstags. 1997.

Band 21 Wolfgang Beutin / Thomas Bütow (Hrsg.): Europäische Mystik vom Hochmittelalter zum Barock. Eine Schlüsselepoche in der europäischen Mentalitäts-, Spiritualitäts- und Individuationsentwicklung. Beiträge der Tagungen 1996 und 1997 der Evangelischen Akademie Nordelbien in Bad Segeberg. 1998.

Band 22 Cecile Sandten: Broken Mirrors. Interkulturalität am Beispiel der indischen Lyrikerin Sujata Bhatt. 1998.

Band 23 Wolfgang Beutin: ANIMA. Untersuchungen zur Frauenmystik des Mittelalters. Teil 2: Ideengeschichte, Theologie und Ästhetik. 1998.

Band 24 Horst Höhne: Percy Bysshe Shelley, Leben und Werk. 1998.

Band 25 Sabine Bröck: White Amnesia – Black Memory? American Women's Writing and History. 1999.

Hermann Fink / Liane Fijas (Eds.)

America and Her Influence upon the Language and Culture of Post-socialist Countries

Frankfurt/M., Berlin, Bern, New York, Paris, Wien, 1998. VIII, 93 pp.
Freiberger Beiträge zum Einfluß der angloamerikanischen Sprache und
Kultur auf Europa.
Herausgegeben von Hermann Fink und Liane Fijas. Bd. 5
ISBN 3-631-33193-2 · pb. DM 45.–*
US-ISBN 0-8204-3577-5

After numerous predominantly quantitative and linguistic systems oriented
investigations of the Anglo-American influence upon the German and other
West European languages, this volume seeks to throw a little light onto the
respective conditions of so-called post-socialist societies. By means of
authentic opinions and experiences of some linguists living in these
countries, it aims less at the quantitative impact of the Americanism there
than at its possible economic, social, political, and cultural implications.

Contents: Socio- and psycholinguistic as well as cultural analysis of the
impact of the United States upon countries of the former East European
Socialism

Frankfurt/M · Berlin · Bern · New York · Paris · Wien
Distribution: Verlag Peter Lang AG
Jupiterstr. 15, CH-3000 Bern 15
Fax (004131) 9402131
*incl. value-added tax
Prices are subject to change without notice.

Peter Lang · Europäischer Verlag der Wissenschaften